Images of America
Richmond Cemeteries

ON THE COVER: The foster parents of Edgar Allan Poe, John and Frances Allan, took young Edgar into their family after his mother died from illness. The Allans are buried next to each other in Richmond's Shockoe Hill Cemetery. Pictured here are their snow-covered graves. (Courtesy of the Edgar Allan Poe Museum.)

IMAGES of America

RICHMOND CEMETERIES

Christine Stoddard and Misty Thomas
Foreword by Dr. Ryan K. Smith

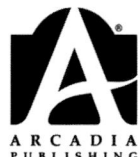

Copyright © 2014 by Christine Stoddard and Misty Thomas
ISBN 978-1-4671-2204-7

Published by Arcadia Publishing
Charleston, South Carolina

Printed in the United States of America

Library of Congress Control Number: 2013957042

For all general information, please contact Arcadia Publishing:
Telephone 843-853-2070
Fax 843-853-0044
E-mail sales@arcadiapublishing.com
For customer service and orders:
Toll-Free 1-888-313-2665

Visit us on the Internet at www.arcadiapublishing.com

For my parents, my beloved David, and The Quail Bell Crew.—CS
For my mother and my beautiful sister, Christy.—MT

Contents

Foreword		6
Acknowledgments		7
Introduction		8
1.	Hollywood Cemetery	11
2.	Evergreen and Oakwood Cemeteries	45
3.	Churches and Graveyards	55
4.	The Civil War and National Cemeteries	81
5.	Shockoe Hill and Hebrew Cemeteries	97
6.	The Burial Ground for Negroes	123
Bibliography		127

Foreword

Cemeteries and old burial grounds are oddly wonderful spots. While many people see nothing inviting about a cemetery sign, those in the know see them as nearly irresistible invitations to explore. Once inside, visitors find a certain sadness, but they discover much more. There is art, history, personality, faith, and horticulture, intertwined in striking ways. Larger themes lurk as well, such as war, freedom, and money. And there are always stories.

This is especially true for Richmond, Virginia, a place that can be difficult for outsiders to crack. But a stroll through one of the region's burial grounds brings the human aspects of Richmond's history into focus. For example, James McClurg's stone in St. John's churchyard tells of how one Revolutionary War surgeon relocated to the new state capital after the conflict. Across town, in Shockoe Hill Cemetery, Jane Stanard's stone highlights a mother's care for her neighborhood's children, which, for her, included young Edgar Allan Poe. At Hebrew Cemetery, Joseph and Louisa Millhiser's stone in the midst of their community tells of their successes in life and love. And one sculptured angel at Hollywood Cemetery points to the fame Varina "Winnie" Davis developed in her own right alongside that of her Confederate father. At Evergreen Cemetery, Maggie Walker's plot still holds sway, helping to draw renewed efforts to bolster her people's place in a city they helped build. The need for such efforts are apparent well beyond Evergreen, as seen in the streetlights still atop the onetime parking lot where Gabriel, Solomon, and other enslaved men and women who fought for their freedom rest. Even so, the simple marker for Amos Monroe at Richmond National Cemetery, standing alongside those of his other black and white Spanish-American War comrades, suggests other sacrifices and possibilities.

Christine Stoddard and Misty Thomas know all of this. Even more, they have found their own way to convey a selection of Richmond stories, opening up valuable windows onto the city's people and past. Their book invites us in, like a roadside sign, and illuminates some of the most colorful events, art, and characters this region has to offer. In the end, the authors return us to the present, newcomers and old-timers alike, to find a renewed sense of commonwealth, plus reason for hope. All from wandering within.

—Dr. Ryan K. Smith
Virginia Commonwealth University
Department of History
Richmond, Virginia

Acknowledgments

The authors are honored and thrilled to have the chance to bring a few stories of Richmond, Virginia's many cemeteries to the general public. This book would not have been possible without the support of Celina Williams and Ray Bonis of VCU James Cabell Library Special Collections; Chris Semtner of the Edgar Allan Poe Museum; John Shucks of Friends of Evergreen Cemetery; Dale Neighbors, Sonya Coleman, and Mark Fagerburg of the Library of Virginia; Ethan Bullard of the Maggie L. Walker National Historic Site; Jim Glass of Mount Calvary Cemetery; Edie Jeter of the Diocese of Richmond; Jeffrey Burden of the Friends of Shockoe Hill Cemetery; Scott and Sandi Bergman of Haunts of Richmond; Lisa Antonelli Bacon of *Virginia Living*; and Kristen Rebelo of *Quail Bell Magazine*. The authors are also indebted to the book's foreword writer, Dr. Ryan K. Smith, archival assistant Helen Stoddard, and Arcadia acquisitions editor Julia Simpson.

INTRODUCTION

As the former capital of the Confederacy and modern capital of the Old Dominion, Richmond, Virginia, lays claim to several historically significant cemeteries—ones not only of regional but also of national interest. While most of the grander cemeteries were established in the mid- to late 1800s, scores of smaller ones, particularly Native American and slave burial grounds, have existed for centuries. Because it is believed to be the longest continuously occupied European settlement in the Mid-Atlantic, Virginia remains a place of hidden history, and it often struggles to strike a balance between innovation and preservation.

American Indians are thought to have occupied what is now known as Virginia for at least 12,000 years prior to the arrival of European settlers. The Powhatan Paramount Chiefdom comprised 30 different Algonquian tribes, or about 15,000 people, around the founding of Jamestown settlement. Little is known about their burial customs, with Capt. John Smith's accounts being the most detailed of those recorded and preserved, to historians' knowledge. Smith reports that chiefs' bodies, for example, were disemboweled, dried, decorated with jewelry, stuffed with copper beads, and then covered in skins and rolled in mats before being buried.

Many of Richmond's historic cemeteries are not only famous for their location and beauty but also their stories of presidents, governors, writers, and actors. The city's most beautiful cemetery, Hollywood, perhaps has more stories to tell than any other. Overlooking the James River, Hollywood is one of Richmond's most popular tourist destinations in part because of its urban legends. Hearing about "the black dog" and the Richmond Vampire, visitors explore the grounds to share in the wonder and mystery.

Jewish cemeteries have always maintained cultural and religious traditions in regards to burials, often sparking controversy with the local Gentile community. Founded in 1817 by the members of Kahal Kadosh Beth Shalome, Richmond's Hebrew Cemetery is located at Hospital and Fourth Streets. The congregation petitioned the city for a new burial ground after noting how crowded its narrow Franklin Street Burying Ground, which was established in 1791, had become. The congregation was granted one acre in 1816. Today, the Hebrew Cemetery is the "oldest active Jewish cemetery in continuous use in the South," according to the National Park Service and US Department of the Interior.

Richmond has a wide variety of Christian graveyards, each carrying its own treasures and burdens. St. John's Church, built in 1741 in the heart of Church Hill, is one of the best-known of these graveyards. During this time, plots in church graveyards were reserved for members of Richmond's affluent families. Most of today's Richmonders, however, known St. John's less for its affluent families of yesteryear than they do its place in American history: In 1775, Patrick Henry gave his "Give Me Liberty or Give Me Death" speech there.

The stories continue belowground. Many of the Catholic churches in Richmond contain crypts that house remains of bishops and parishioners. Catholic graveyards, meanwhile, were some of the first established in Richmond. There are three main graveyards that are kept up by the Richmond diocese—St. Joseph, Holy Cross, and Mount Calvary. St. Joseph was established in the mid-1850s and saw its first burial in 1858. Holy Cross was a graveyard that was initially restricted to German Catholics, whose growing population the diocese needed to accommodate. It was not until 1942 that this restriction was abolished. Mount Calvary was purchased in 1885 by John Keane, the fifth bishop of Richmond. Several priests and bishops are buried at Mount Calvary.

During the Civil War, soldiers were often buried where it was most convenient. Soldiers did not wear dog tags at the time, and there was no other system in place to identify them. Thus, many soldiers who lost their lives were never identified. Unsurprisingly, local cemeteries were not equipped for the more than 600,000 men who fell during the war, either. Many battles occurred in farm fields, and burials tended to be hurried affairs, meaning the graves were shallow. It was not unusual for the soldiers' remains, therefore, to become exposed in a short matter of time. Rain, wind, and other elements often brought limbs or even entire bodies to the surface. After the war, efforts to properly bury these bodies were made.

In 1867, the federal government opened Richmond National Cemetery on Williamsburg Road in Richmond's East End as one of several cemeteries established to accommodate the thousands who died in the Civil War. Nearly 6,000 Union dead initially buried at battlefields, POW camps, and local cemeteries throughout the area were reinterred at Richmond National Cemetery. Even today, most of the graves remain anonymous. A keeper's lodge was built at the cemetery in 1870. Veterans from the Spanish-American War, World War I, World War II, the Korean War, the Vietnam War, and Middle Eastern conflicts are also buried there, which is under the care of the National Cemetery Administration within the US Department of Veterans Affairs. The cemetery is closed to new interments.

Unsurprisingly in the former capital of the Confederacy, one of the long-standing controversies regarding the city's cemeteries is a matter of black and white. European American cemeteries are often lauded for being well maintained, while the African American cemeteries tend to feature overgrowth and broken tombstones. During the time of slavery, black cemeteries were dug in unfavorable locations. Many of the records for African Americans' deaths and burials fail to mention individuals' names and simply call the lots "slave burial grounds." The cemeteries often lacked landscaping, and the graves were placed randomly. These cemeteries have been disregarded, and the upkeep of tombstones and grounds has fallen on community volunteers and family members of those buried there.

Since the closing of the so-called Burial Ground for Negroes in 1810, it had, in many ways, faded from public memory—until recently. About 200 years later, in the early 2000s, Virginia Commonwealth University (VCU) paved the site and turned it into a parking lot, citing limited campus parking for students and staff. In 2008, it became widely known that the spot was the site of a burial ground after a group survey matching modern urban structures with historical maps was conducted.

On April 15, 2011, Michael Paul Williams published an editorial in the *Richmond Times-Dispatch* entitled "VCU Must Remove Asphalt from Lot." In it, he criticizes VCU's decision to pave the lot:

> If VCU finds itself in a parking bind, whose fault is that? The desecration in its midst was exposed nearly three years ago amid university plans to repave its newly purchased lot. Despite protests, the university plowed stubbornly ahead with the repaving in August 2009. A school that has shown great vision in reinventing itself was shortsighted and insensitive on this issue. Potential parking inconvenience pales in comparison with historical insult and ancestral violation.
>
> Now, as this former Confederate capital commemorates the Civil War and the end of slavery, the spectacle of asphalt over the remains of free and enslaved Africans offers a brutal contrast to the Confederate soldiers memorialized on towering steeds on Monument Avenue. Is this what we want the tourists to see?

The latest development project to potentially threaten the Burial Ground for Negroes is a baseball stadium that was proposed by Mayor Dwight Jones in 2013. The stadium and related infrastructure improvements would cost the city $80 million, with a promised $187.6 million in tax revenue over the next two decades. As of January 2014, more than 2,100 people have signed a petition opposing the stadium due to its proximity to the burial ground. In November 2013, Reuters ran an international article with the headline "U.S. mayor plans ballpark near site of slave cemetery, market." The total cost of the development project would be $200 million, including a $300 million memorial at the site of or near the burial ground.

Though the burial ground's precise location is unknown, due to erosion and multiple construction projects that have taken place in the area over the years, it is believed to be at or near the intersection of Sixteenth and Broad Streets and Interstate 95. Dr. Ryan K. Smith's academic website, Richmond's Historic Cemeteries: A VCU Project, describes the burial ground's location: "This was poor quality land, and it was the site of the city gallows where convicts were publicly hung. Any memorials or markers left by survivors have disintegrated with time, or they are covered by many feet of later fill and construction, culminating in an asphalt parking lot, only recently removed."

Especially with the pending Shockoe baseball stadium project, the future of Richmond's cemeteries, graveyards, and burial grounds is uncertain. In December 2013, Norwegian architecture student Martin McSherry presented a skyscraper cemetery design to the Oslo Conference for Nordic Cemeteries and Graveyards as a possible solution to the country's decreasing space for burials. Might Richmond follow suit? Or, with cremation on the rise, perhaps bodies will one day no longer be buried. According to the National Funeral Directors Association, in 2007, cremation was the answer to 34.89 percent of "final dispositions" in the United States.

Yet, no matter how the residents of Richmond decide to honor the dead and dispose of bodies in the future, the question of how to preserve historic cemeteries remains. This book strives to serve as a pictorial overview of Richmond's many diverse cemeteries as they look today and have looked since the invention of photography.

One

Hollywood Cemetery

The resting place of two US presidents, the only president of the Confederate States of America, and many other notable figures in Richmond and the Old Dominion's history, Hollywood Cemetery is the city's best-known burial ground. So named because of the prevalence of holly trees there, Hollywood remains the city's most popular cemetery and the unofficial national cemetery of the Confederate States of America. Deep in the heart of it, America's 10th president, John Tyler, is laid to rest, along with Jefferson Davis, Lewis Ginter, popular Richmond mayor William Mayo, and aristocrat John Randolph. This is the resting ground of many historic figures in American history. Among them are nine generations of Valentines. They donated their family home to the City of Richmond to serve as a history museum. The family had a love of art and music, and it made quite the impact on Richmond and Hollywood Cemetery as well. It is a place of grand mausoleums, elaborate tombstones, well-manicured lawns, and James River views. With its proximity to Oregon Hill, Belle Isle, and the James River, Hollywood lures Civil War buffs. It also attracts students at Virginia Commonwealth University for art and history projects as well as gallivanting. Hollywood remains an active cemetery to this day, evidencing just how Richmond continues to tie its past to its present.

The following pages touch upon the cemetery's early development, notable features, and a few of the figures buried there.

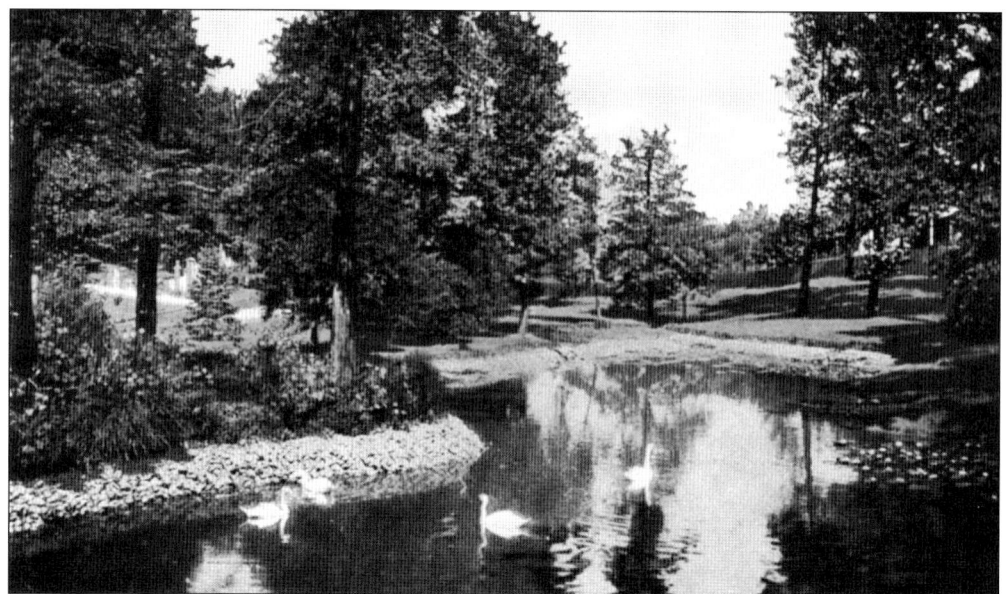

This postcard shows a reflection pond no longer in existence at Hollywood Cemetery. Today, a grove of cypress trees covers the area—a rare sight in Virginia, as cypress trees do not commonly grow in the Old Dominion. Initially 35 acres, Hollywood Cemetery, now the resting place of many Richmond citizens, surpasses its original size by more than 100 acres. (Courtesy of VCU James Branch Cabell Library Special Collections.)

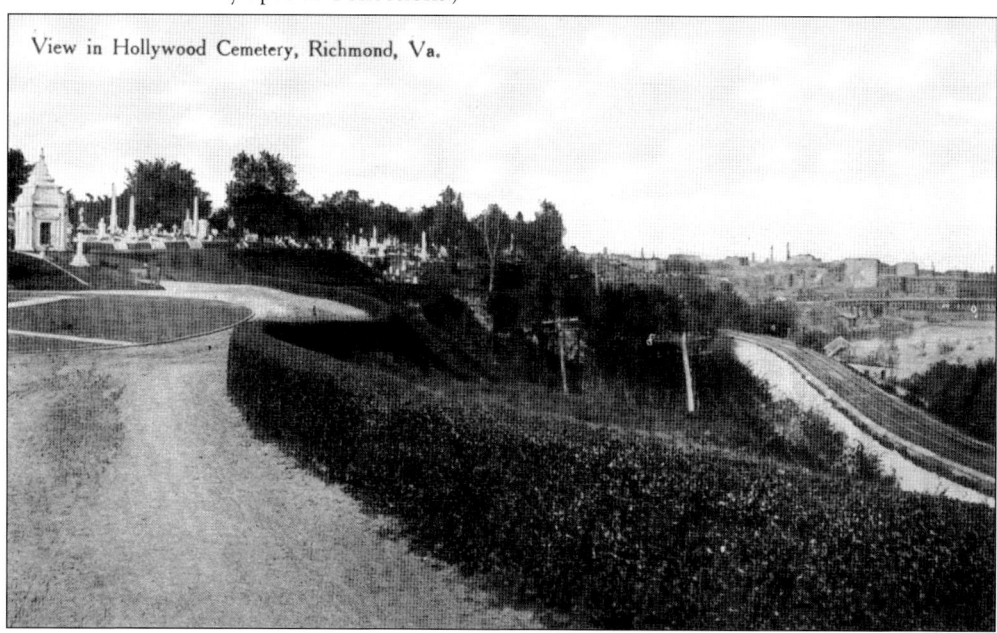

This postcard, printed by Southern Bargain House, is no. 57 in the Beautiful and Historical Richmond, Va. series. As no publishing or copyright year appears on the card, its date remains unknown. Like the other Hollywood Cemetery postcards included in this chapter, this postcard can be found in the collection "Rarely Seen Richmond: Early twentieth century Richmond as seen through vintage postcards" at VCU library. On the left, note the mausoleum of Maj. Lewis Ginter. (Courtesy of VCU James Branch Cabell Library Special Collections.)

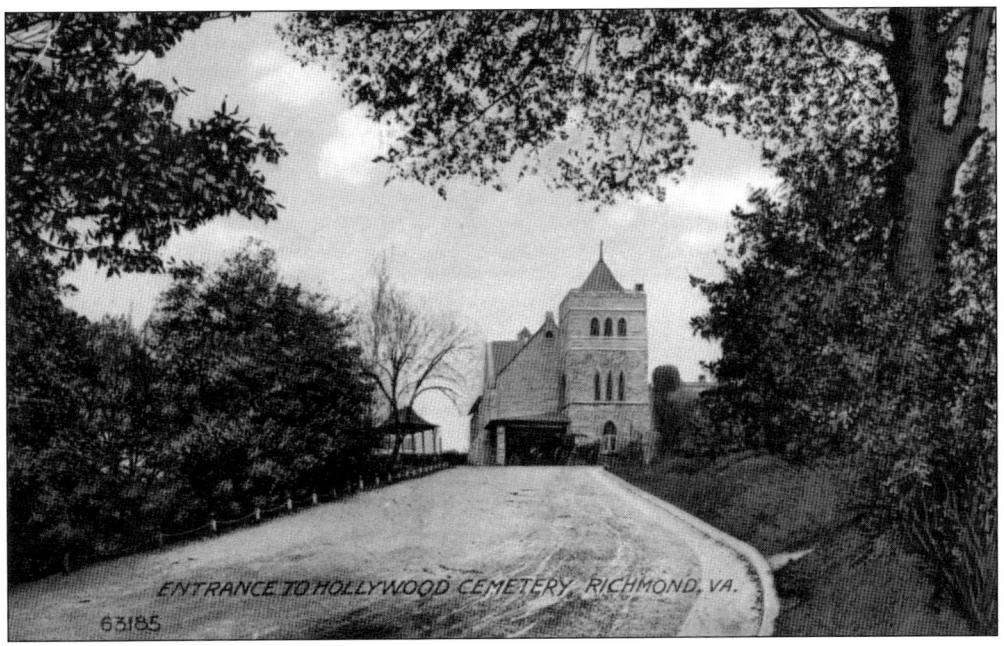

The dramatic stone entrance to Hollywood Cemetery lies at the intersection of Cherry and Albemarle Streets, hinting at the sights to be had within the property's confines. Originally built in 1876 to mimic a ruined medieval tower, the stone structure was later altered to accommodate the company office, receiving vaults, and a chapel. The entrance remains one of the best examples of the Gothic Revival style in American memorial art and was at last completed in 1897. (Both, courtesy of VCU James Branch Cabell Library Special Collections.)

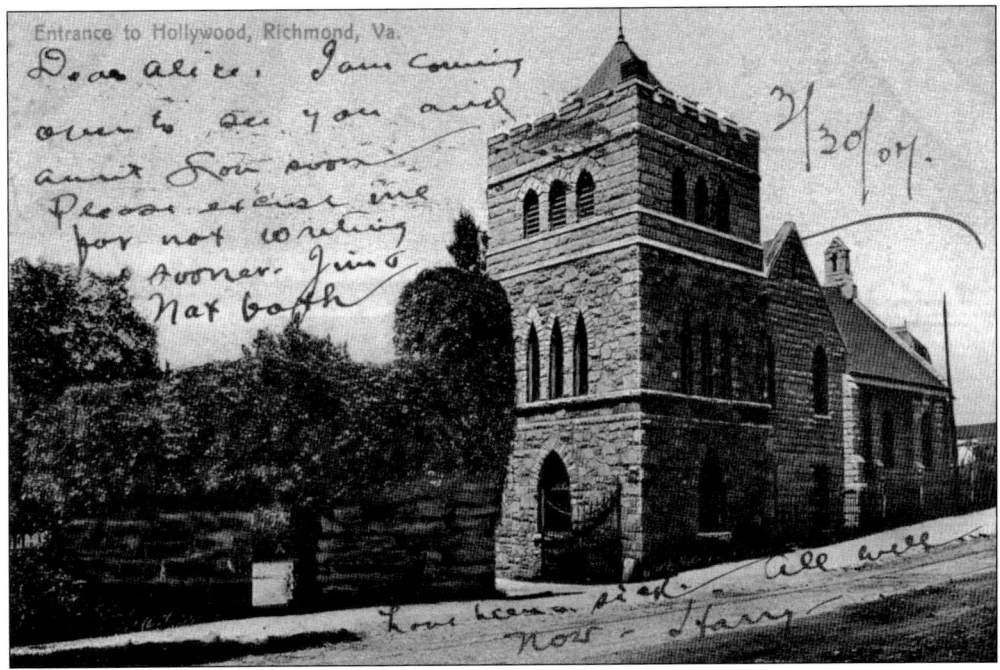

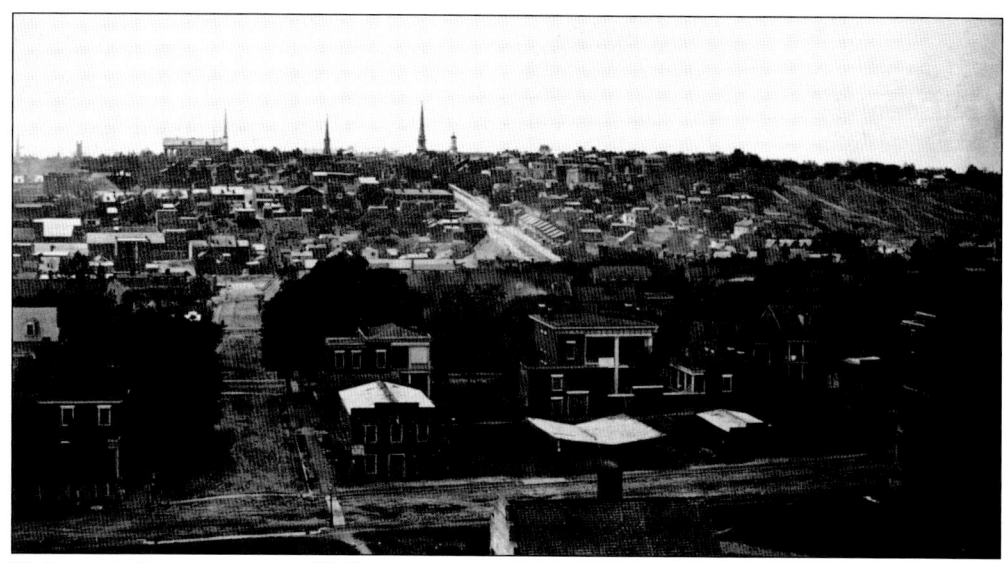

Hollywood Cemetery lies in William Byrd III's former estate, the Belvidere, in a section then known as "Harvie's Woods." The location is now referred to as the Oregon Hill neighborhood. The neighborhood's name sprang from the 19th-century joke that its residents had moved so far from Richmond's central hub that they might as well live in Oregon. This photograph of Richmond was taken from Oregon Hill in April 1865. (Courtesy of the Library of Congress.)

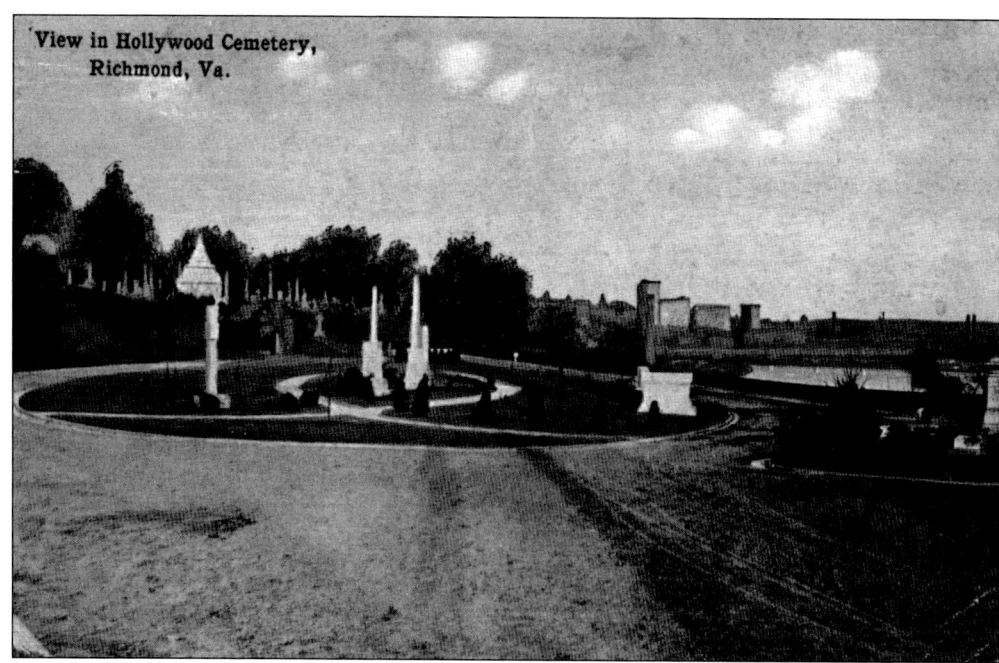

Postmarked in 1922, this postcard shows Hollywood Cemetery's "unsurpassed" view of the James River. An excerpt from the text on the back reads: "The landscape embraces every variety—forest and placid stream; hills crowned with woods, or with steeples; shaded valleys, and blazing furnaces; bridges on which railway trains are moving sixty feet in the air; and almost at your feet, the graceful curve of a broad canal." (Courtesy of VCU James Branch Cabell Library Special Collections.)

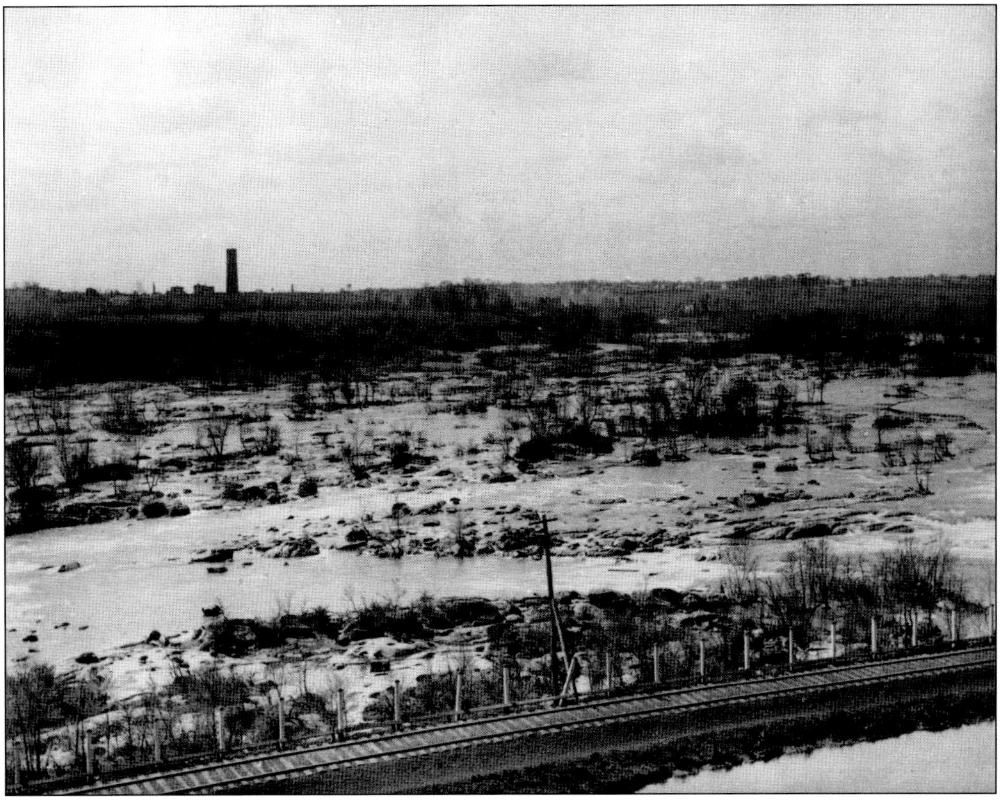

Hollywood Cemetery overlooks the James River, which bisects the city of Richmond into Northside and Southside. The grounds' location allows for views of whitewater, nearby islands, large rocks known to the American Indians as "shockoe," and, as seen in the foreground of this photograph, the railroad tracks. Hollywood Cemetery is visible from Belle Isle and other spots along Southside. (Courtesy of the Library of Congress.)

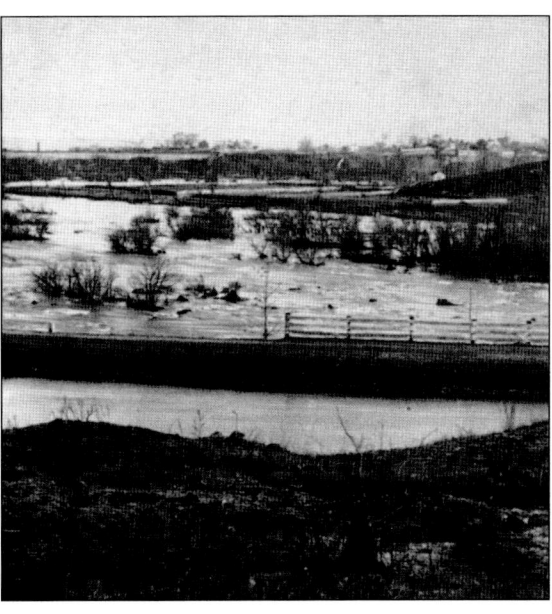

When William Byrd III faced the prospect of financial ruin, he divided his estate into several 100-acre plots for lottery. The Harvie family purchased several of these lots, including what is now Hollywood Cemetery. For years, Harvie's Woods was a popular location for Richmonders to go for strolls, host picnics, and hunt. Its towpath also allowed for easy access to the Kanawha Canal, built in 1800. (Courtesy of the Library of Congress.)

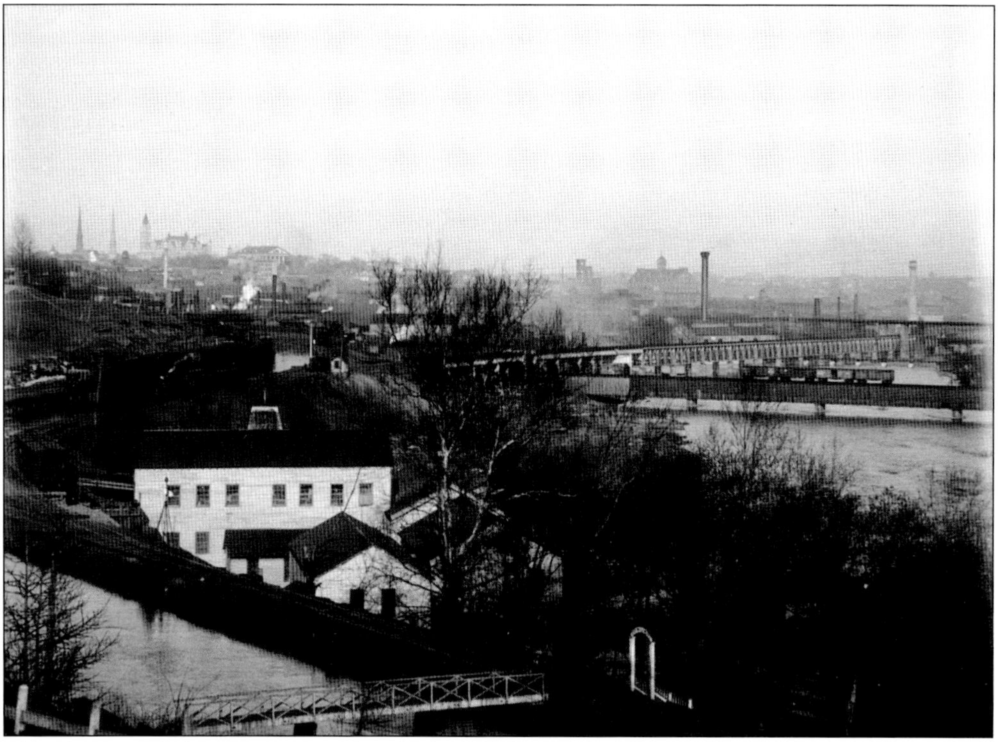

This photograph shows a section of Hollywood Cemetery by the train tracks on a bluff overlooking the James River. During the Civil War, five rail lines ran through Richmond, one of the reasons the Confederate States of America chose Richmond as its second capital city. The Confederacy had initially been briefly headquartered in Montgomery, Alabama, a city soon deemed too small, hot, and humid for Confederate operations. (Courtesy of the Library of Congress.)

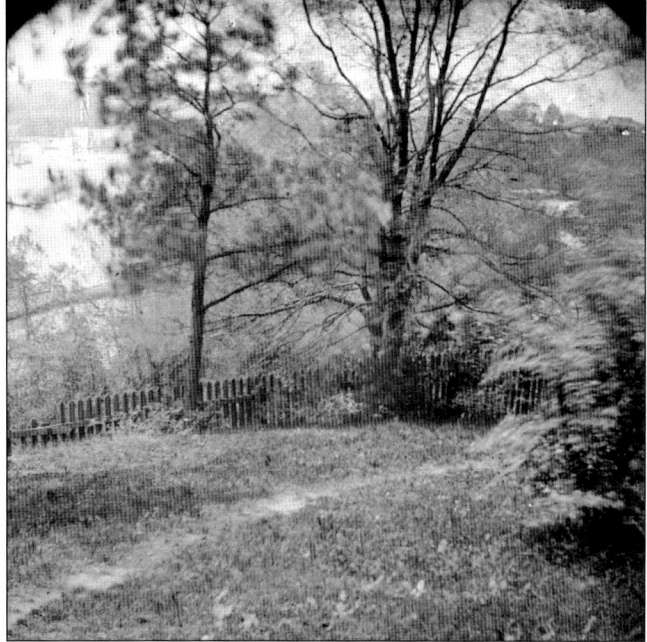

After their 1847 visit to Mount Auburn Cemetery in Cambridge, Massachusetts, William Henry Haxall and Joshua Jefferson Fry endeavored to make Hollywood one of the first grand garden cemeteries of the South. Investments from local business leaders allowed the cemetery to open in 1849. With its storied grave design, landscaping, and Confederate landmarks, Hollywood holds historical significance. More Confederate generals, for example, rest in Hollywood than in any other cemetery in the United States. (Courtesy of the Library of Congress.)

Pres. James Monroe's cast iron tomb is one of the most elaborate in Hollywood Cemetery. Designed by Albert Lybrock, the Gothic Revival structure resembles a birdcage encasing a simple, granite sarcophagus. Though Monroe was initially buried in New York City (where he died) in 1831, his body was relocated to Richmond in 1858. In 1971, the tomb was designated a National Historic Landmark. (Courtesy of VCU James Branch Cabell Library Special Collections.)

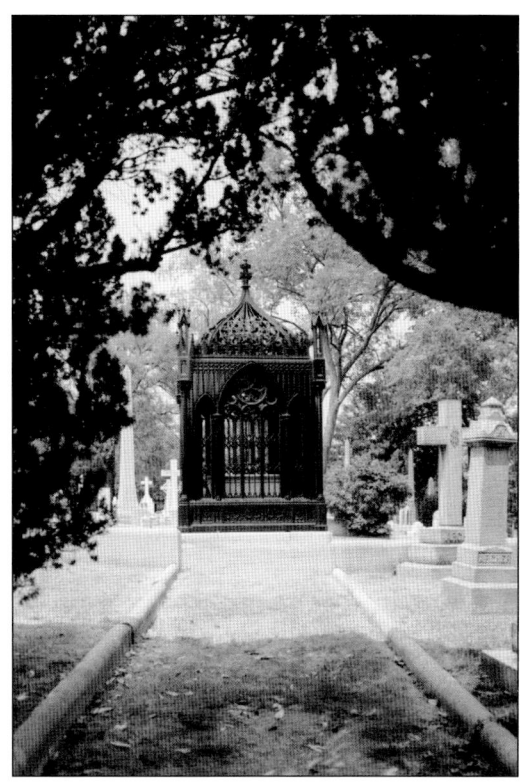

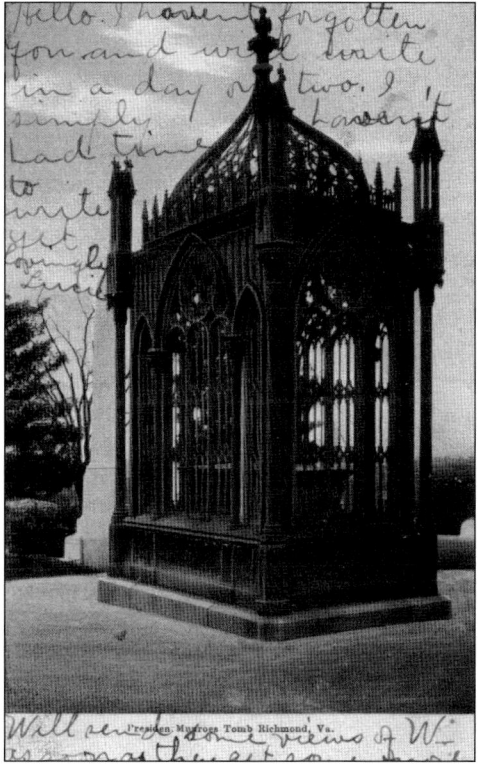

A century after Monroe's birth, Virginia petitioned for the former president's remains to be reburied in Hollywood Cemetery. The 7th Regiment of the New York National Guard accompanied Monroe's body on the steamboat *Jamestown*. A reburial ceremony presided over by Gov. Henry A. Wise of Virginia took place that same day, July 5, 1858. However, because Hollywood Cemetery's records were burned in 1865, little else is known about the event. (Courtesy of VCU James Branch Cabell Library Special Collections.)

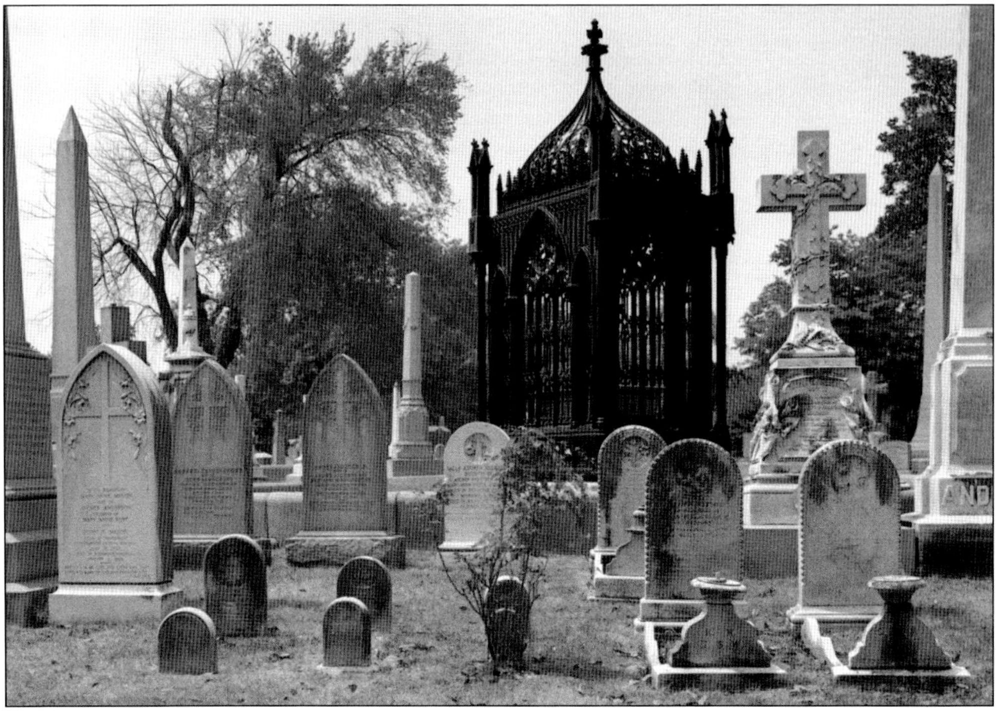

Alsatian architect Albert Lybrock ordered the cast iron used in Monroe's elaborate tomb from the Philadelphia firm Wood and Perot. Each facade on the structure features a lancet arch meant to resemble a cathedral window, with a series of arches and traceries. The highly decorative tomb pays homage to the last American president of the so-called Virginia Dynasty, a phrase that conveys the origins of four of the first five presidents. (Courtesy of VCU James Branch Cabell Library Special Collections.)

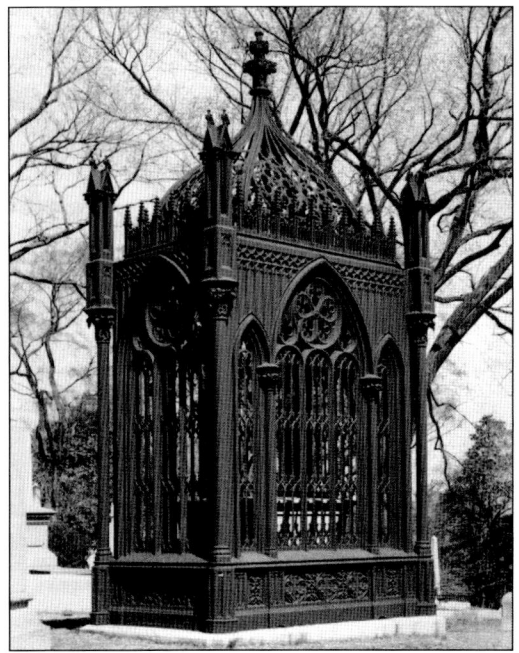

James Monroe was the third former American president to die on Independence Day, a poignant fact that symbolizes his contributions to early American history. Among other accomplishments, Monroe was elected to the Virginia House of Delegates, as well as to the Fourth, Fifth, and Sixth Continental Congresses. Monroe fought in the Revolutionary War. His tomb lies at President's Circle, where John Tyler and Jefferson Davis are also buried. (Courtesy of VCU James Branch Cabell Library Special Collections.)

John Tyler's funeral took place at St. Paul's Episcopal Church in Richmond, with his remains escorted by Jefferson Davis to his gravesite in Hollywood Cemetery. Tyler's second wife, Julia Gardiner, is buried beside him in the President's Circle. Congress dedicated the monument marker at his gravesite in 1915. These postcards depict the grave (right) and monument (below), facing south and north, respectively. (Both, courtesy of VCU James Branch Cabell Library Special Collections.)

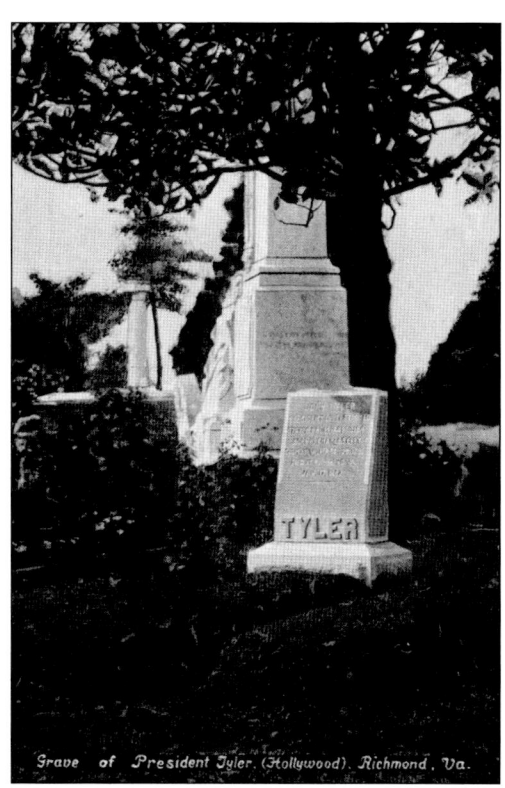

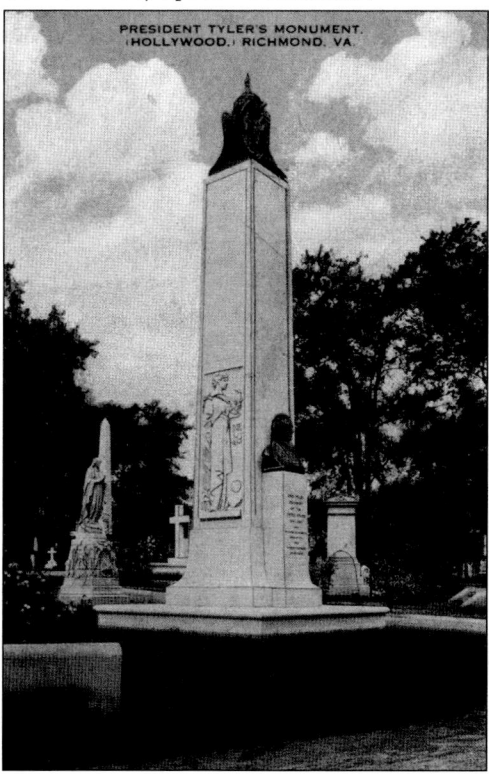

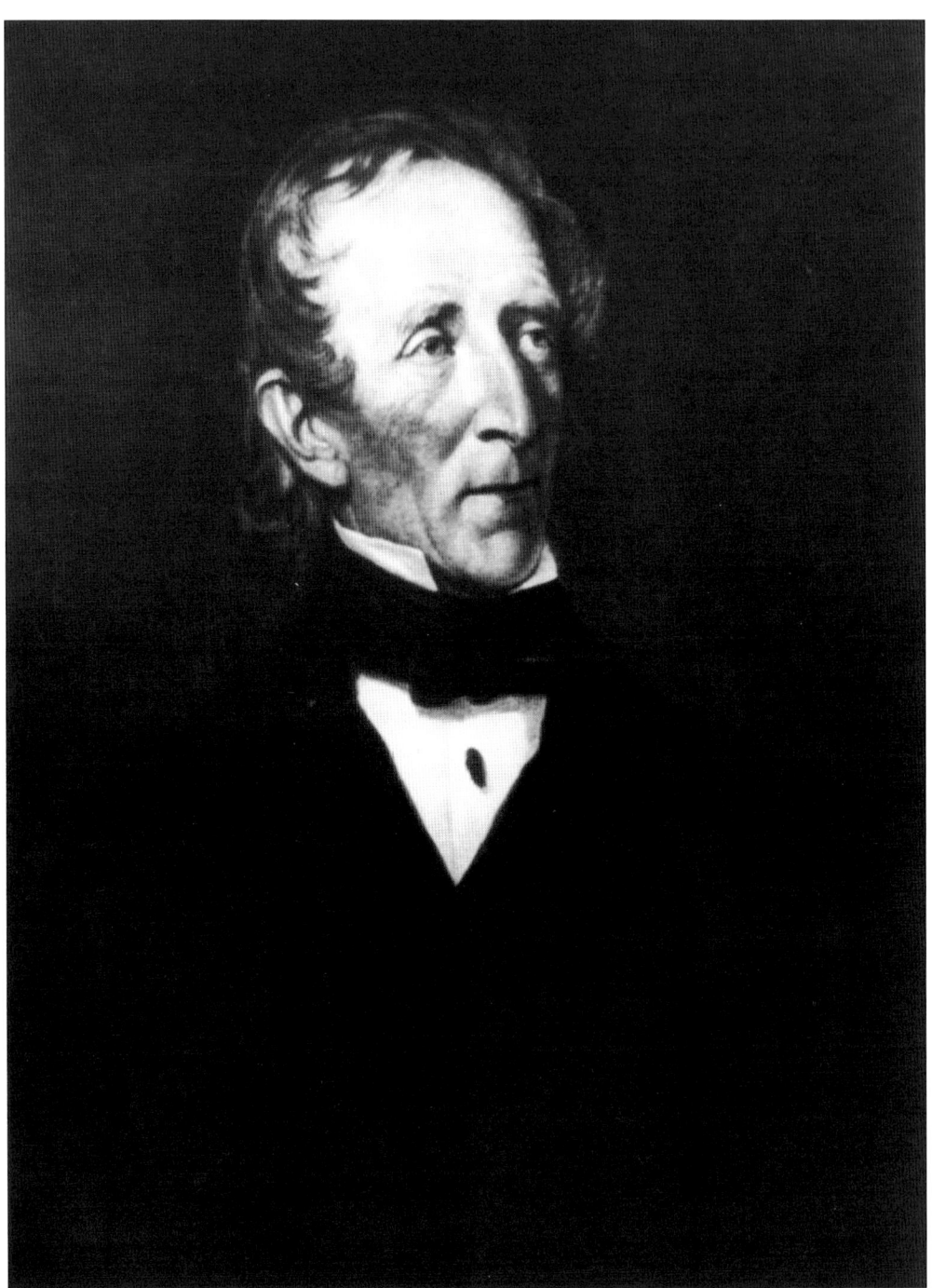

A native of Virginia, Pres. John Tyler suffered from poor health his whole life and died shortly after exiting the White House. Though he endured dizziness, vomiting, and dysentery before his death, Tyler is believed to have died from a stroke. Because of his allegiance to the Confederacy, Tyler's was the only presidential death not recognized in Washington, DC. In 1862, he had a grand burial at Hollywood Cemetery. (Courtesy of the Library of Congress.)

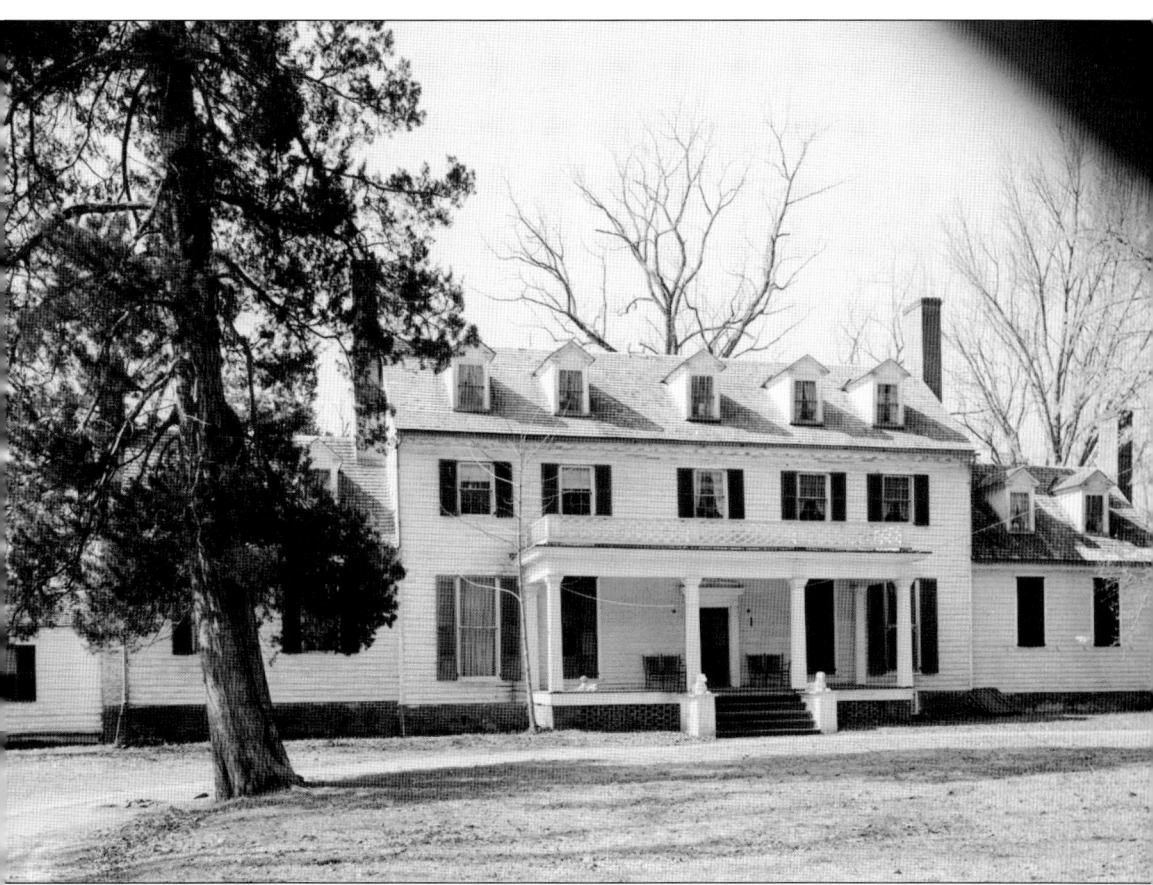

Sherwood Forest was John Tyler's family estate and the place where he had hoped to die after leaving the White House. Instead, he died at the Estate Hotel. Though Tyler is not buried at the Charles City property, several of his pets are, including his favorite horse, General. Pets—even the war horses of Confederate heroes—may not be buried at Hollywood Cemetery. (Courtesy of the Library of Congress.)

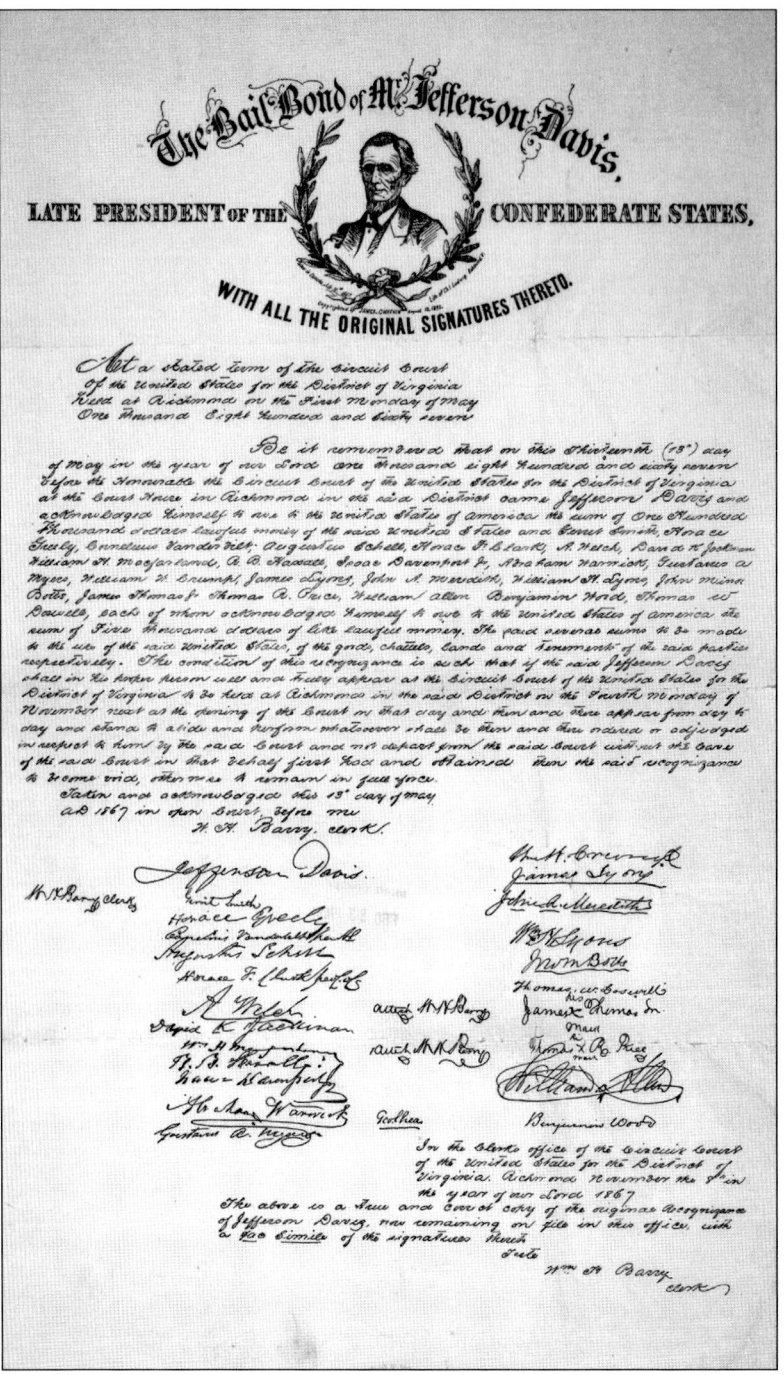

Union cavalrymen arrested Jefferson Davis near Irwinville, Georgia, on May 10, 1865, as a suspect in Lincoln's assassination. He was later charged with treason and imprisoned at Fort Monroe in Virginia for two years. Davis was released on $100,000 bail with the bond seen here. On Christmas Day 1868, Pres. Andrew Johnson's Fourth Amnesty Proclamation absolved Davis of any guilt for participating in the Civil War. (Courtesy of VCU James Branch Cabell Library Special Collections.)

After the Civil War, Jefferson Davis remained a controversial figure for the rest of his life. He spent most of his retirement at Beauvoir, an estate near Biloxi, Mississippi. During that time, he wrote his memoir, *The Rise and Fall of Confederate Government*, which was published as two volumes in 1881. He would eventually be laid to rest with many of his Confederate contemporaries at Hollywood Cemetery. (Courtesy of the Library of Congress.)

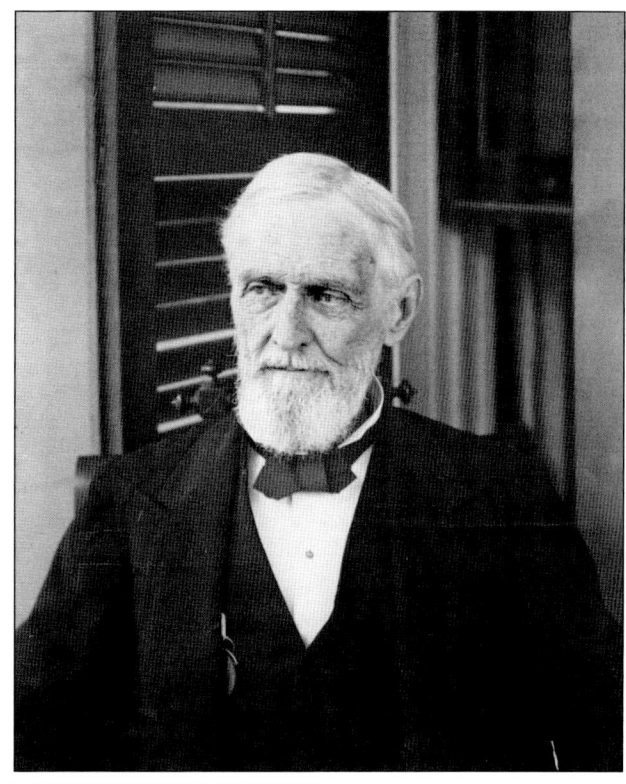

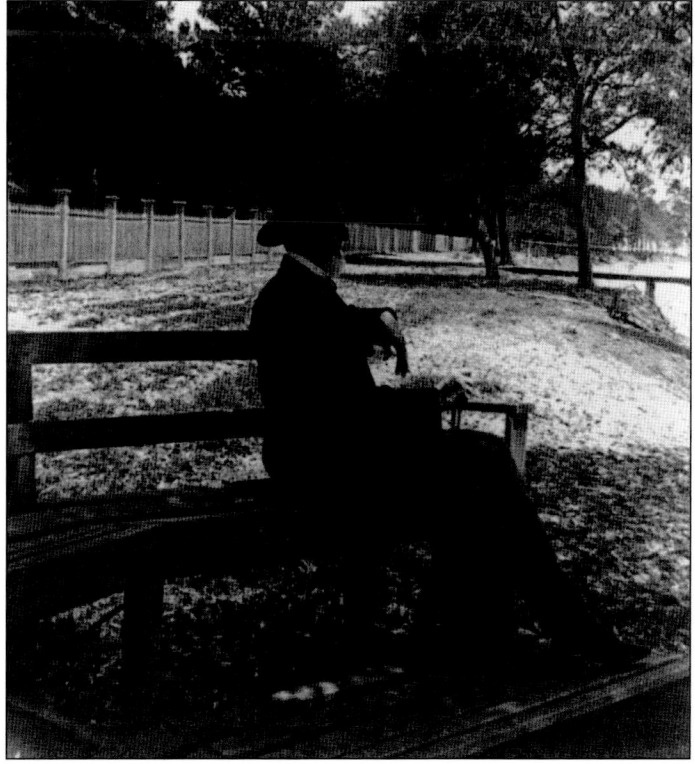

Just three months into his first marriage, Jefferson Davis nearly died of malaria after moving to his sister's estate, Locust Grove, in Louisiana. While the disease claimed his wife's life, Davis spent the next several years grieving, living as a recluse for some time before refocusing his efforts to build his plantation and enter politics. He is said to have died from acute bronchitis complicated by malaria from a single mosquito bite. (Courtesy of the Library of Congress.)

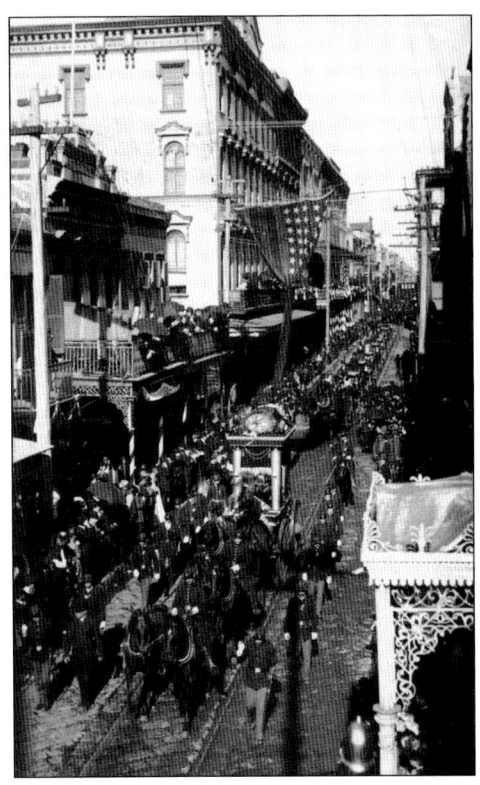

Jefferson Davis, president of the Confederacy, was originally interred in his hometown of New Orleans before his remains were relocated to Hollywood Cemetery in 1893. This photograph depicts his funeral procession on December 6, 1889, an event witnessed by more than 80,000 people. At the end of the procession, Davis's body was laid at New Orleans City Hall for public display through December 11. (Courtesy of the Library of Congress.)

The second wife of Jefferson Davis, Varina Banks Howell Davis, was buried in Hollywood Cemetery in 1906. She wrote Davis's memoir after the Civil War and also wrote for the *New York World*. She grew up in a very small town in Mississippi. Varina Davis had a total of six children with the former Confederate States of America president; four of them died at very young ages. This 1884 or 1885 photograph shows the Davis family in Beauvoir, Mississippi. (Courtesy of the VCU James Branch Cabell Library Special Collections.)

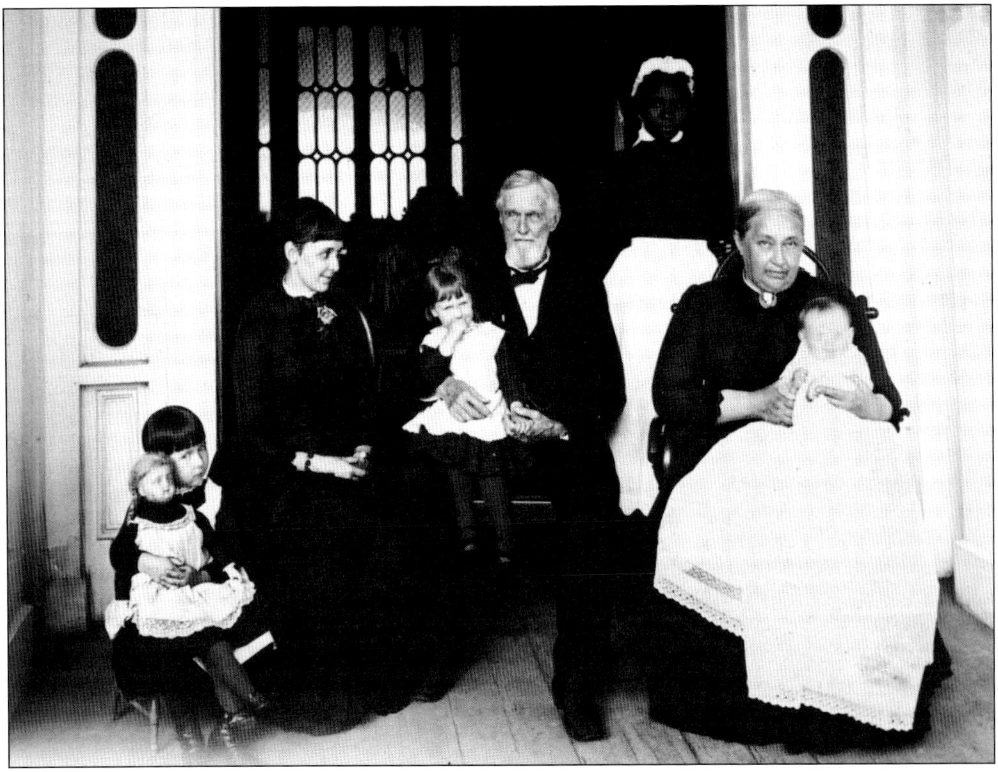

Known as "The Daughter of the Confederacy," Varina Anne "Winnie" Davis was the second daughter and sixth child of Jefferson Davis and Varina Howell Davis. Following her father's death, Winnie made her living as a writer, first as a correspondent for the *New York World* and later for magazines such as *Ladies' Home Journal*. She was also the author of two novels, *The Veiled Doctor* and *A Romance of Summer Seas*. She died at age 34. (Courtesy of the VCU James Branch Cabell Library Special Collections.)

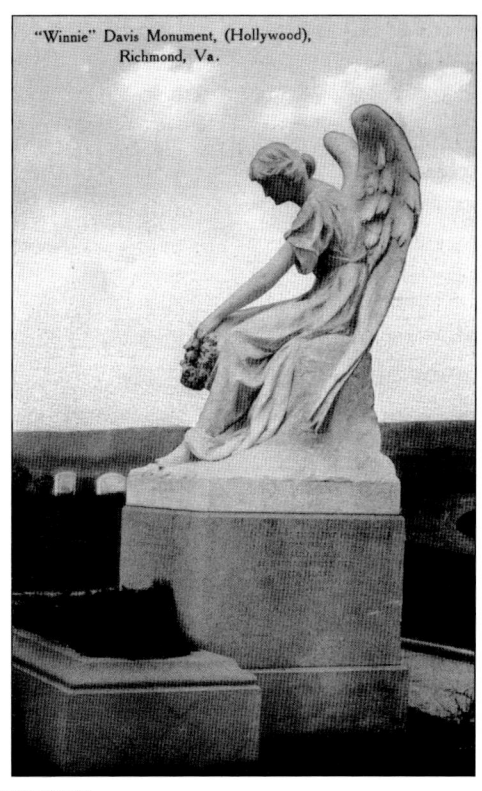

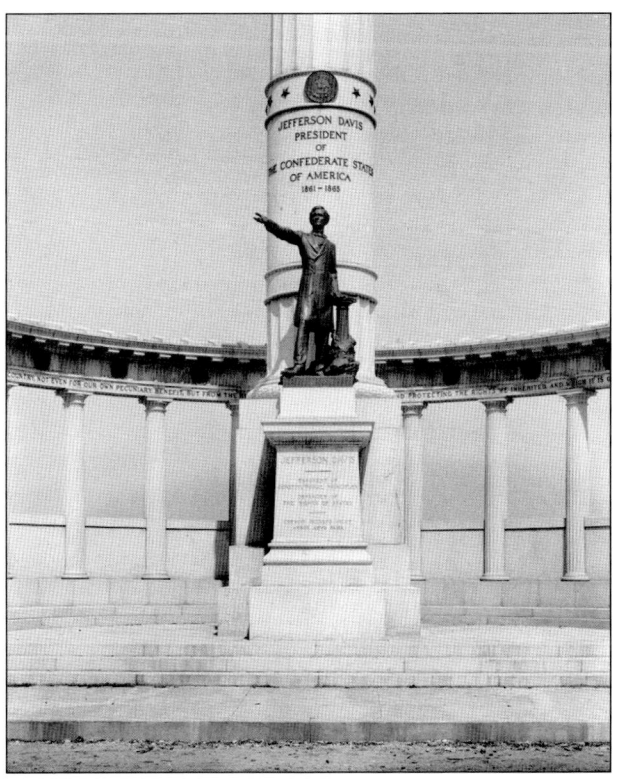

In addition to his tomb at Hollywood, Jefferson Davis has a marker in his honor on the city's Monument Avenue. The monument was unveiled in 1907. Designed by architect William C. Noland and sculptor Edward V. Valentine, the structure lies at the intersections of Monument and Davis Avenues. It represents the eleven states that seceded from the Union and the two that sent delegates to the Confederate Congress. (Courtesy of the Library of Congress.)

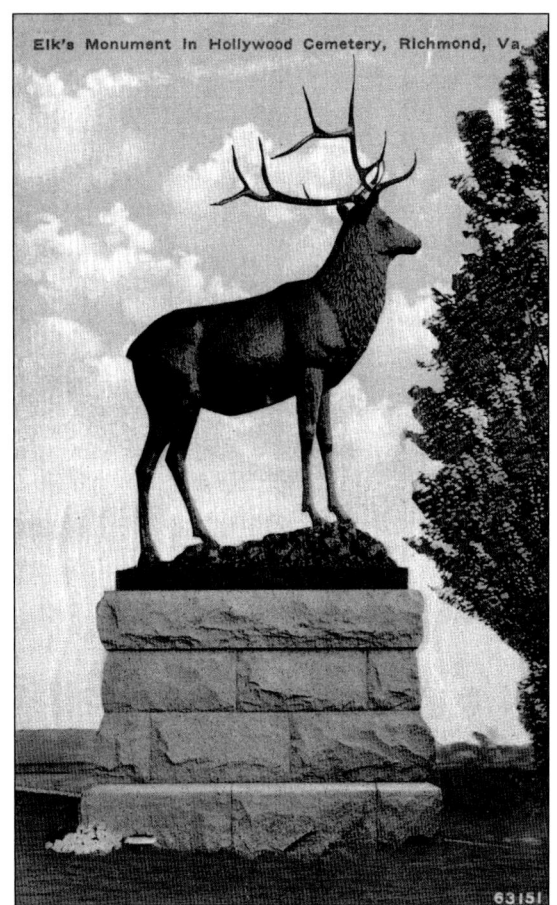

The Elks Rest is one of the most beautiful sites in Hollywood Cemetery. Owned and maintained by the Richmond Lodge of the Benevolent and Protective Order of Elks, the elk overlooks the cemetery's Davis Section. Gen. Fitzhugh Lee, also buried in this section of Hollywood Cemetery, brought more attention and allure to the cemetery and, in particular, this section. These postcards depict the elk facing the river, but from different angles. (Both, courtesy of VCU James Branch Cabell Library Special Collections.)

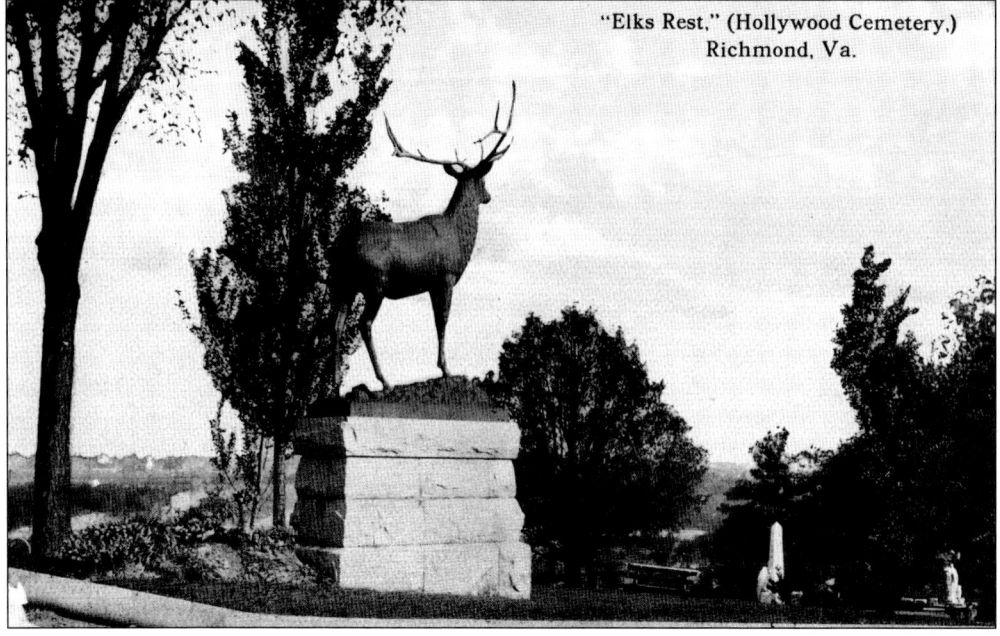

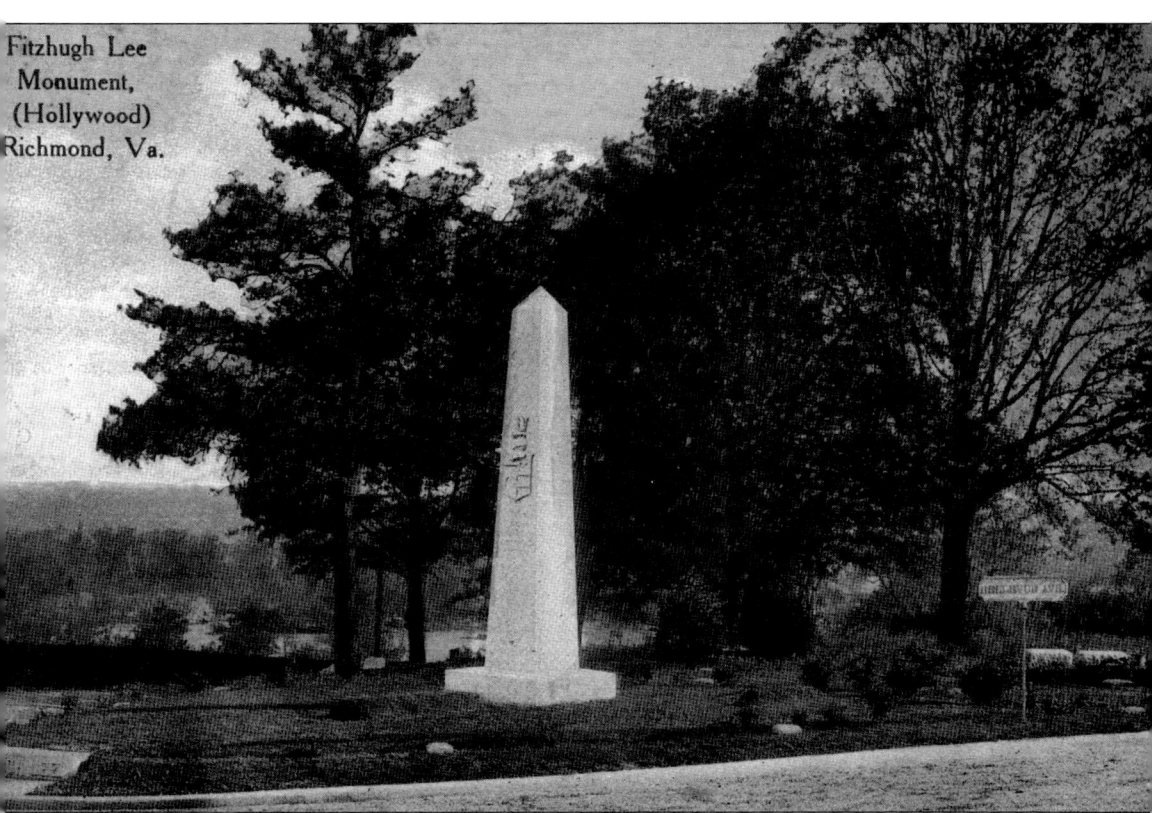

This postcard, no. 37 from the "Beautiful and Historical Richmond, Va. Series," depicts the Fitzhugh Lee Monument in Hollywood Cemetery. Lee retired as a brigadier general in 1901 after a career commanding Cavalry Corps of the Army of Northern Virginia during the Civil War. He later became governor of Virginia. Lee died in 1905. (Courtesy of VCU James Branch Cabell Library Special Collections.)

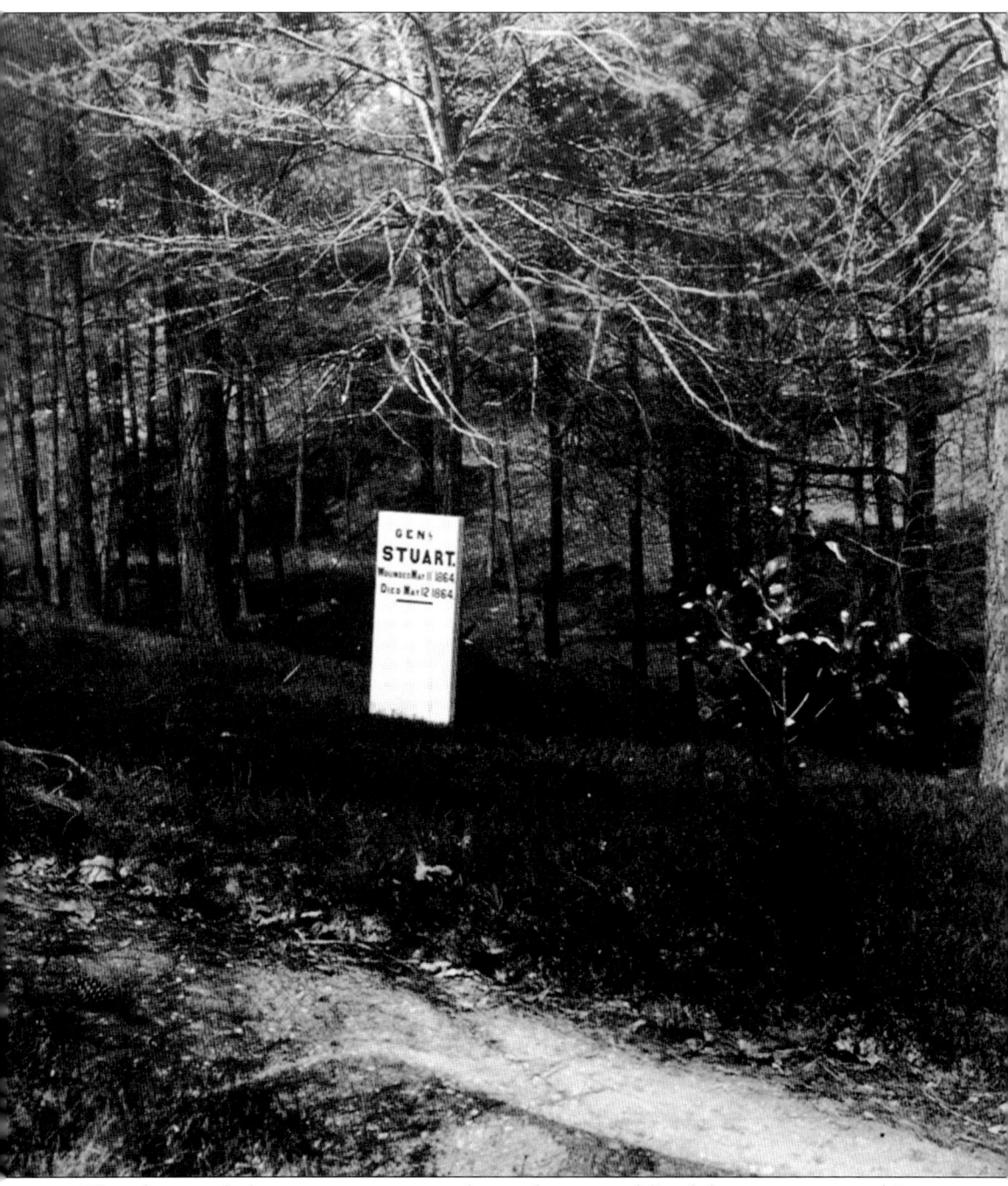

This photograph depicts a temporary marker at the grave of Confederate army general James Ewell Brown "J.E.B." Stuart. The grave was awaiting the more elaborate granite tombstone to come. Because of Stuart's presence in the cemetery, as well as that of numerous other "Rebels," Hollywood is sometimes referred to as the Confederate National Cemetery. (Courtesy of the Library of Congress.)

J.E.B. Stuart rests at Hollywood Cemetery with 24 other Confederate officers, including the Pegram brothers. After what some perceived to be his vanity-induced failure at the Battle of Gettysburg, Stuart became a symbol of the Lost Cause—the idea that the Confederacy's cause was a noble one. (Courtesy of the Library of Congress.)

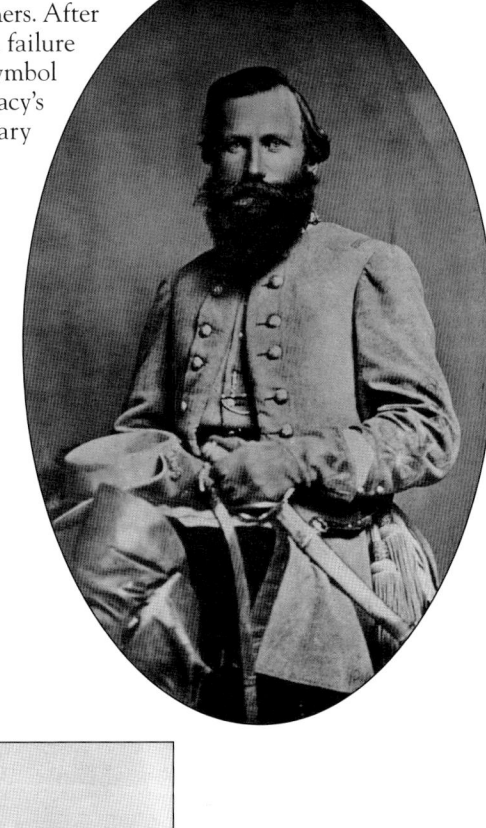

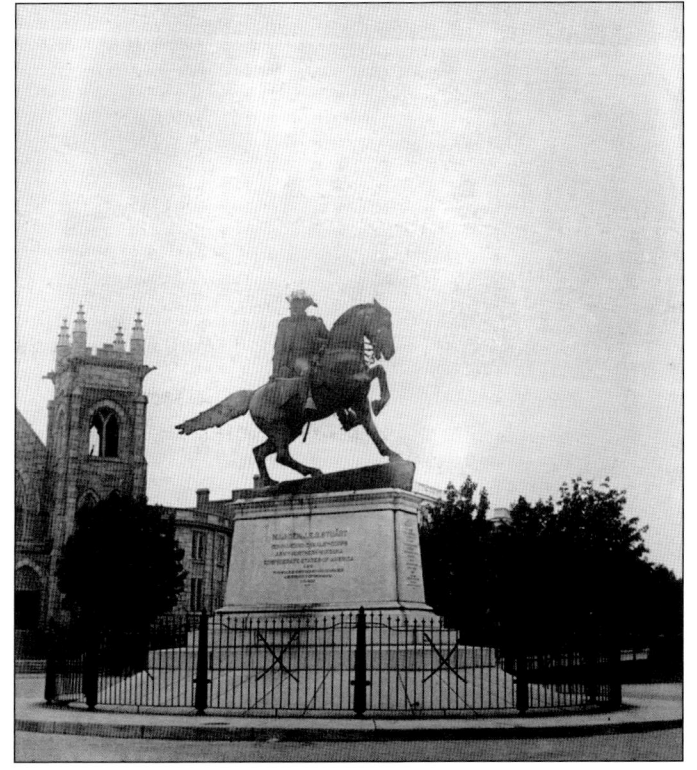

In addition to his tomb in Hollywood Cemetery, J.E.B. Stuart claims a monument in his honor on Richmond's Monument Avenue. The statue lies at the intersection of Monument Avenue and Lombardy Street in the city's Fan District. Sculpted by artist Fred Moynihan, the monument was dedicated on May 30, 1907. (Courtesy of the Library of Congress.)

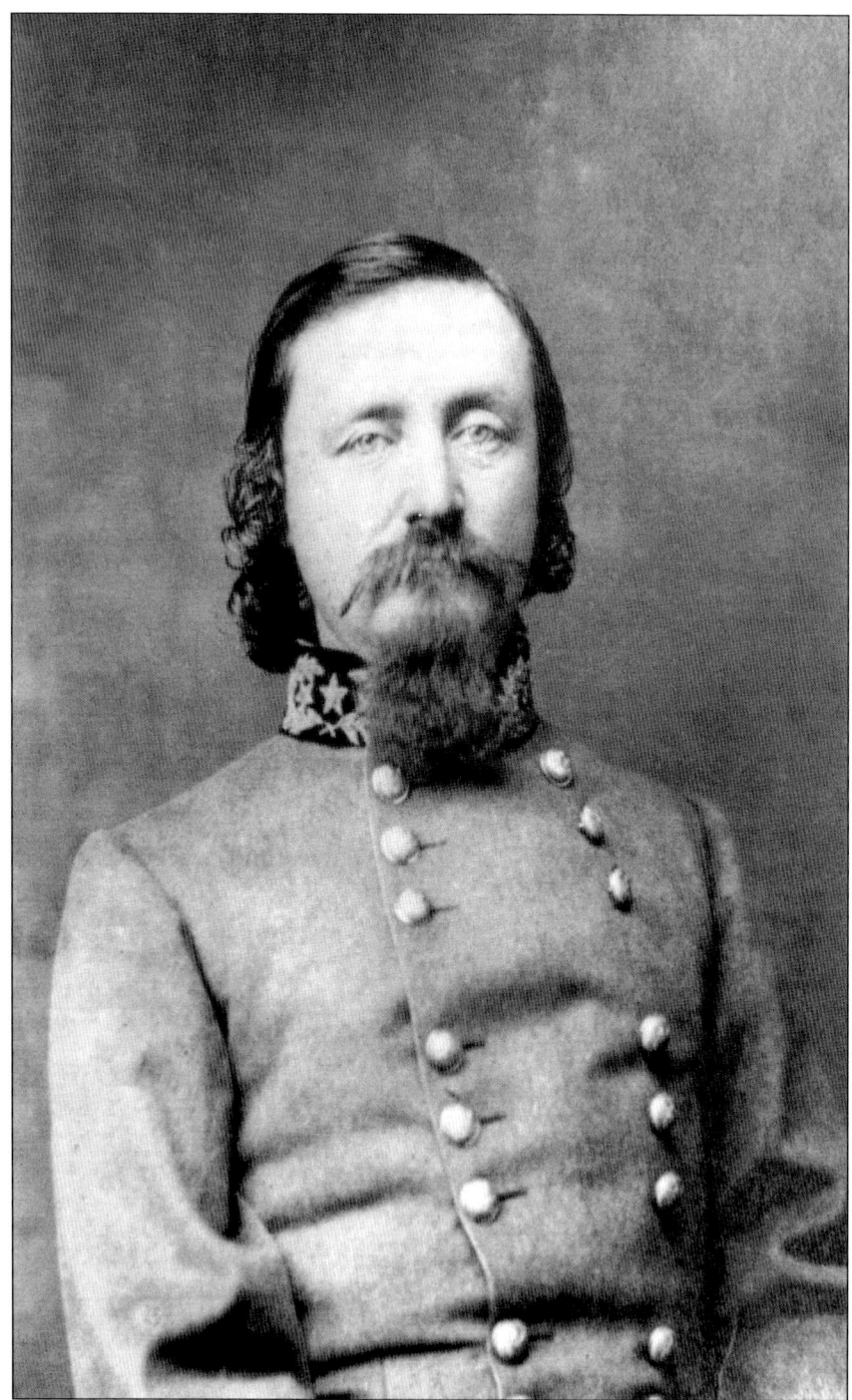

Famous for Pickett's charge at the Battle of Gettysburg, Maj. Gen. George Pickett was a native Richmonder, career US Army officer, and Confederate general. Pickett died of a liver abscess on July 30, 1875, in Norfolk, Virginia. Though first interred at Norfolk's Cedar Grove Cemetery, Pickett's remains were reburied in Hollywood Cemetery on October 24, 1875. (Courtesy of the Library of Congress.)

On October 5, 1888, a memorial for George Pickett was erected over his grave in Hollywood Cemetery. The exact location of Pickett's remains is not known, as the memorial was not erected directly over his burial site. No records indicating the exact location seem to exist, assuming they were ever created in the first place. (Courtesy of the Library of Congress.)

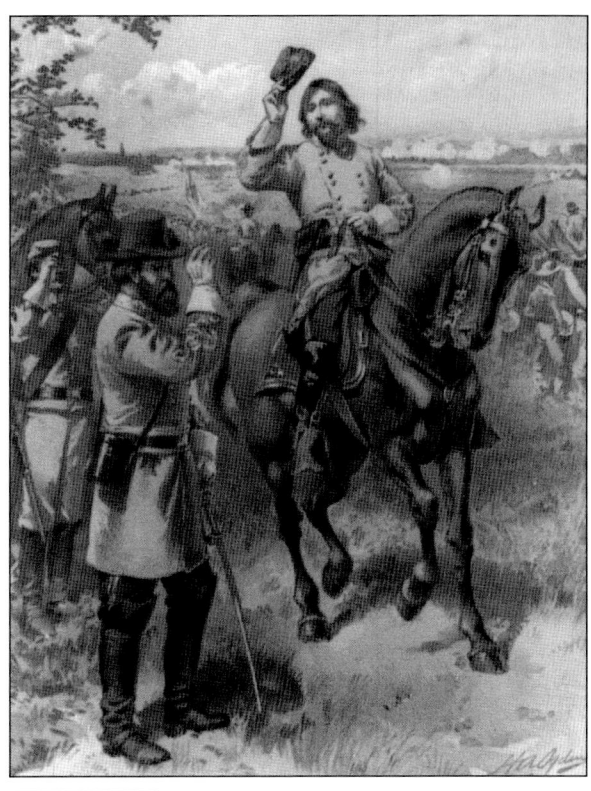

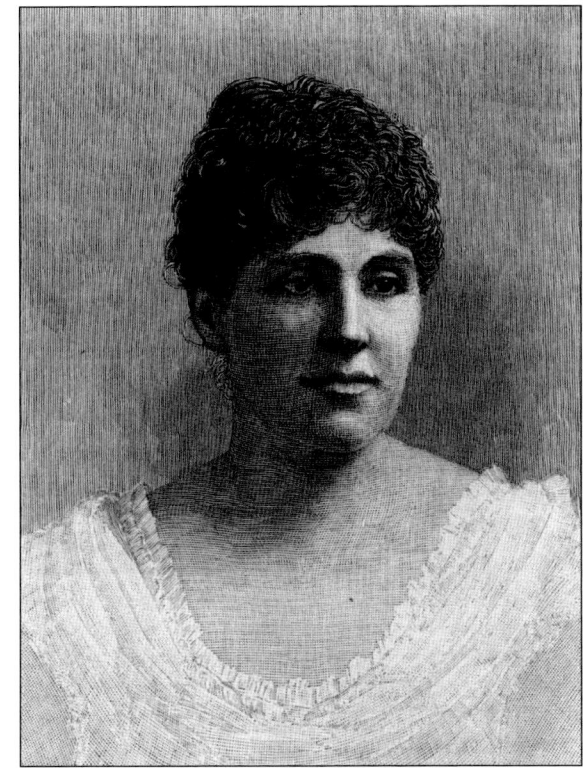

When George Pickett's third wife, LaSalle Corbell Pickett, died in 1931, she was not permitted to be buried alongside her husband. At that time, Hollywood did not allow women to be buried in the Confederate section of the cemetery. Instead, she was buried at Arlington National Cemetery's Abbey Mausoleum. In 1998, her remains were relocated to Hollywood and she was reinterred in front of her husband's grave. (Courtesy of the Library of Congress.)

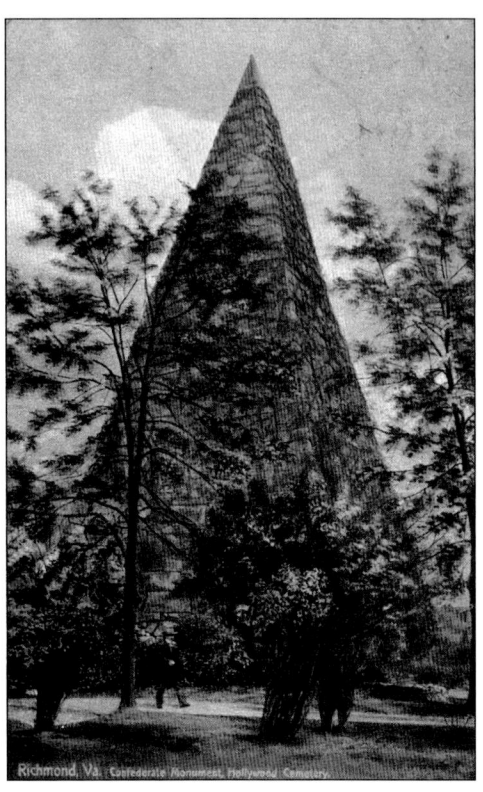

This 1907 postcard captures Hollywood's Monument to Confederate Dead. Postcards without a dividing line on the back—like this one—were published between 1901 and 1907 in the United States. Civil engineer Capt. Charles Dimmock designed the granite monument in 1869 as a $26,000 commission from the Daughters of the Confederacy. (Courtesy of VCU James Branch Cabell Library Special Collections.)

Completed three years after its commission by the Daughters of the Confederacy in 1866, the Confederate Pyramid honors the 18,000 Confederate men who died at the Battle of Gettysburg. These soldiers were removed from the battlefield and reinterred at Hollywood Cemetery. The Hollywood Cemetery Registry of Confederate Dead lists 10,500 of the soldiers' names. (Courtesy of the Library of Congress.)

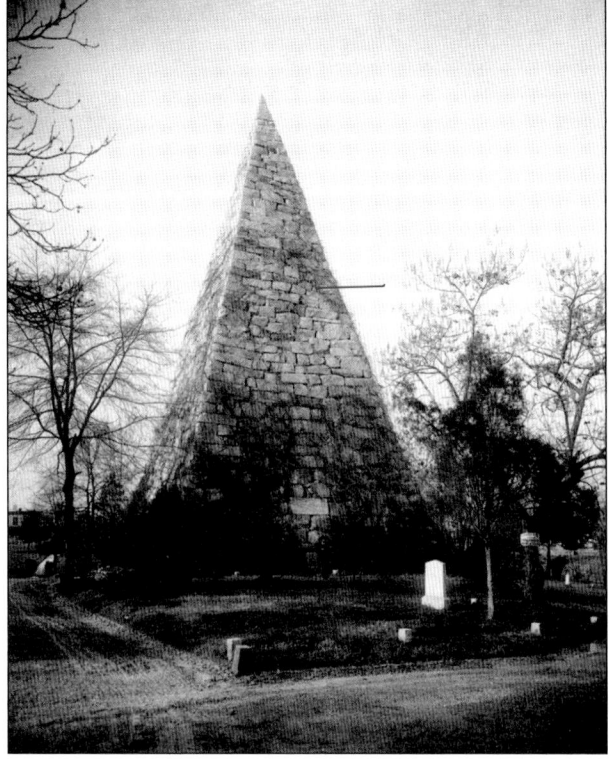

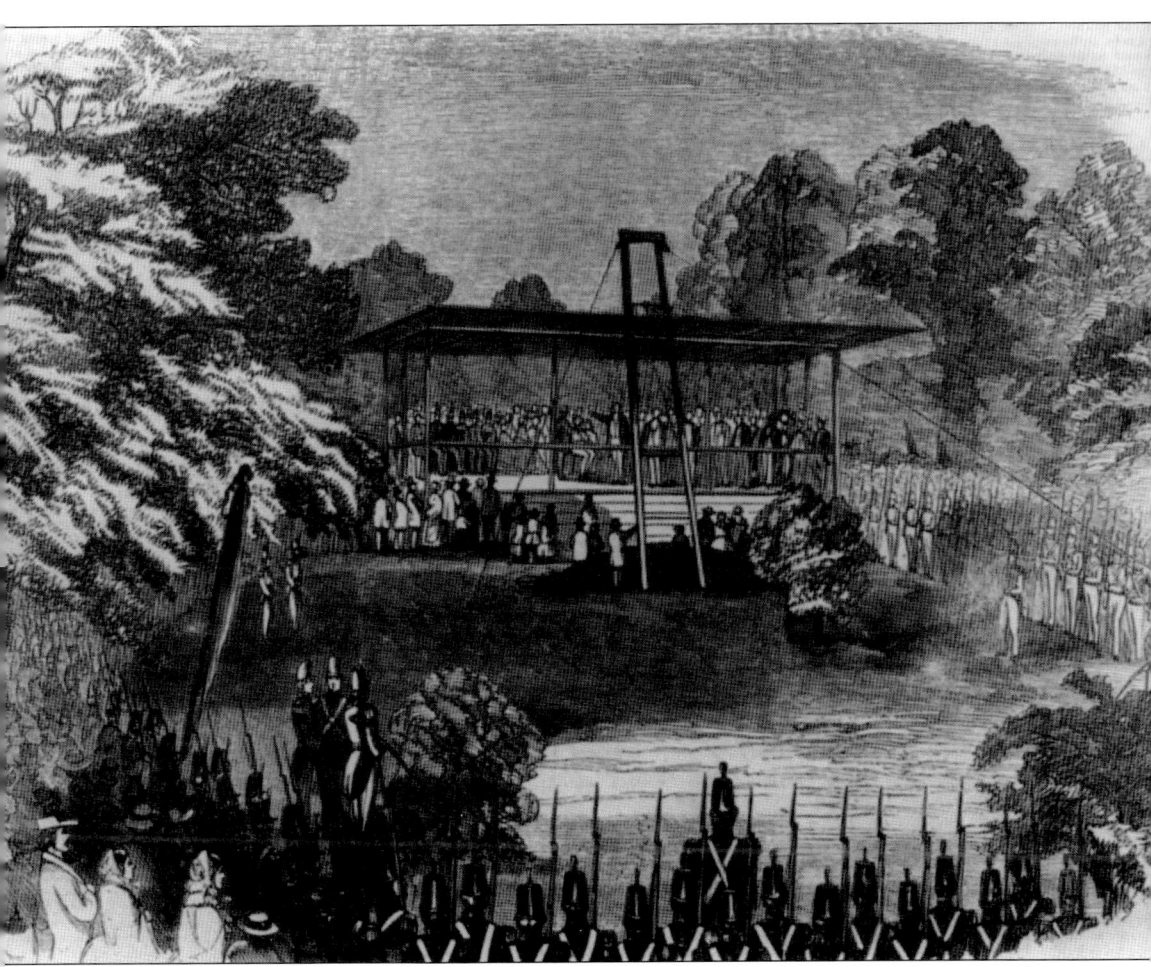

Pres. Abraham Lincoln dedicated the Gettysburg National Cemetery to Union dead on November 19, 1863. At that time, Confederate dead were buried quickly, because they were regarded as traitors on American land. In an effort to bury the soldiers in a respectful manner, the Hollywood Memorial Association raised funds to relocate the dead to Richmond. On June 15, 1872, the bodies arrived in a steamship docked at Rocketts Landing. (Courtesy of the Library of Congress.)

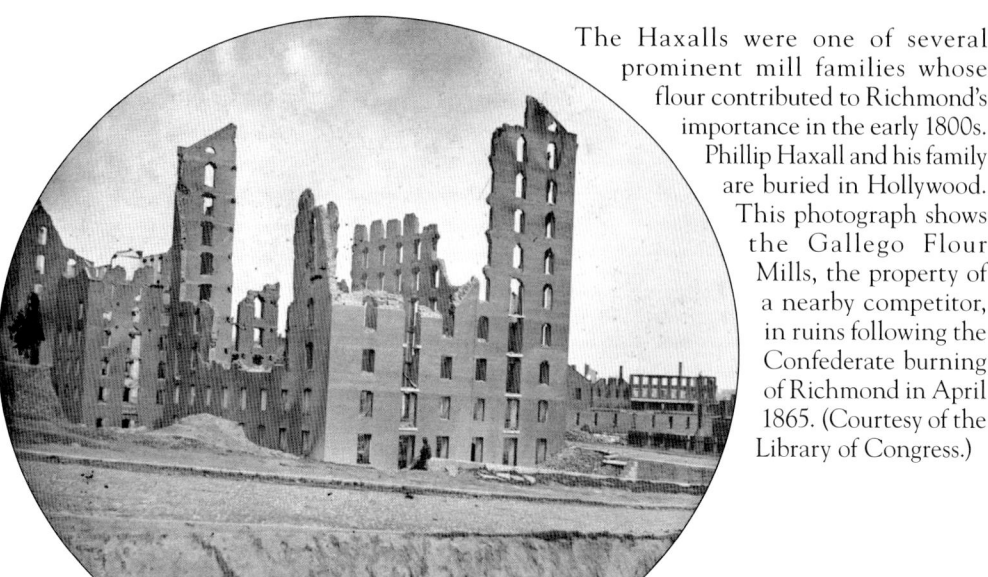

The Haxalls were one of several prominent mill families whose flour contributed to Richmond's importance in the early 1800s. Phillip Haxall and his family are buried in Hollywood. This photograph shows the Gallego Flour Mills, the property of a nearby competitor, in ruins following the Confederate burning of Richmond in April 1865. (Courtesy of the Library of Congress.)

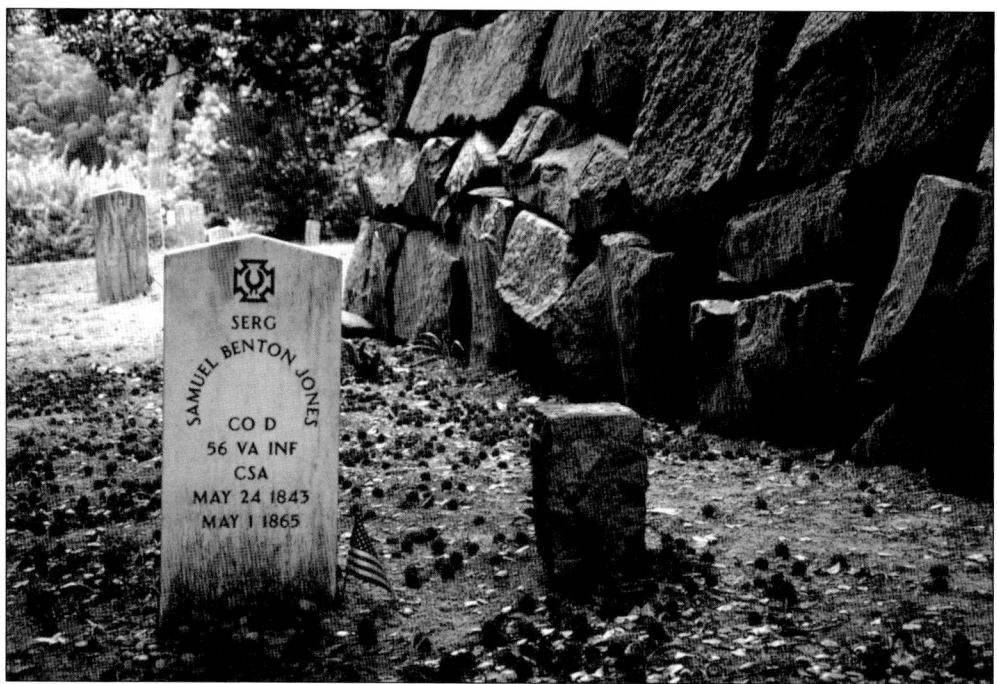

Sgt. Samuel Benton Jones died at age 21 after serving in the Confederate army. His grave in Hollywood Cemetery is seen here in 2011. About two percent of the US adult male population died during the Civil War—an estimated 620,000 men. Some 18,000 Confederate dead are said to rest at Hollywood. (Courtesy of the Library of Congress.)

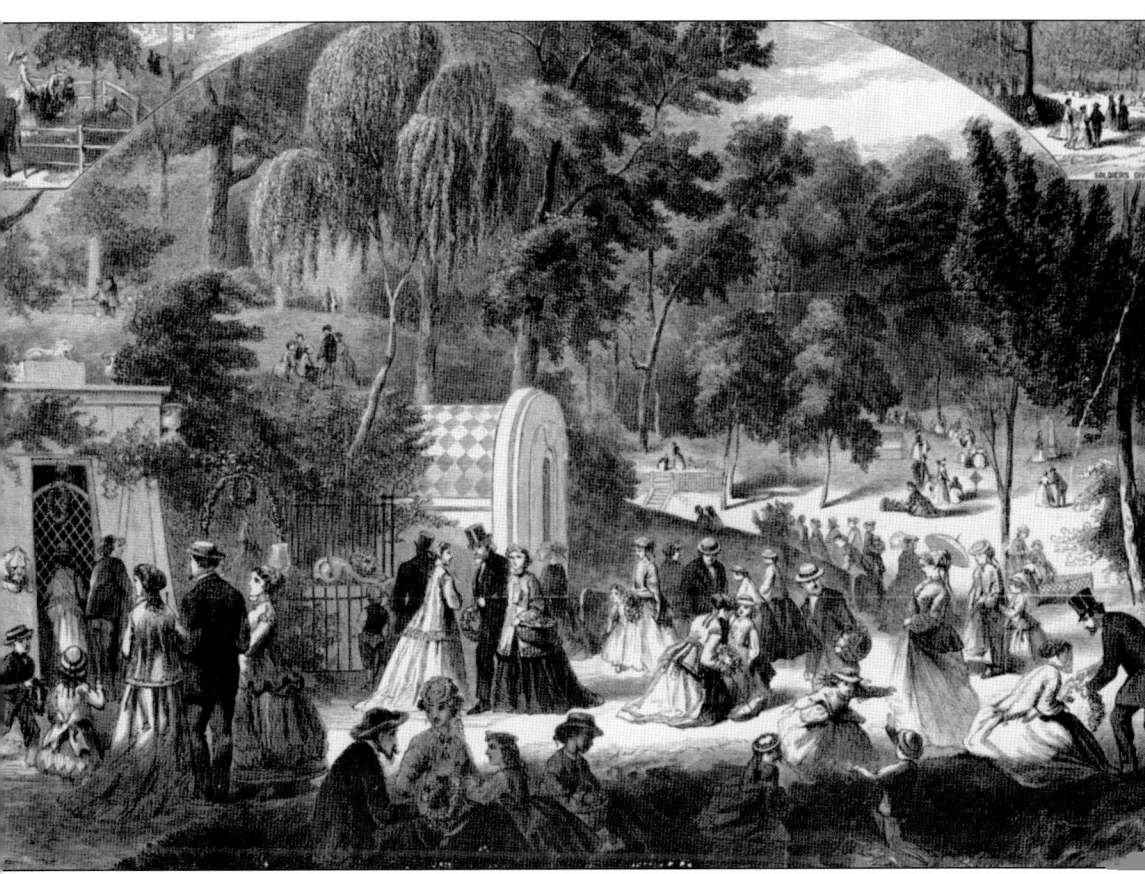

For years following the Civil War, Hollywood functioned as a popular and beautiful site for those interested in visiting and honoring the Confederate dead. Shortly after the War Between the States ended, a group of Southern women decorated the graves of Confederate soldiers, starting a tradition that eventually became the nationally recognized Memorial Day. (Courtesy of the Library of Congress.)

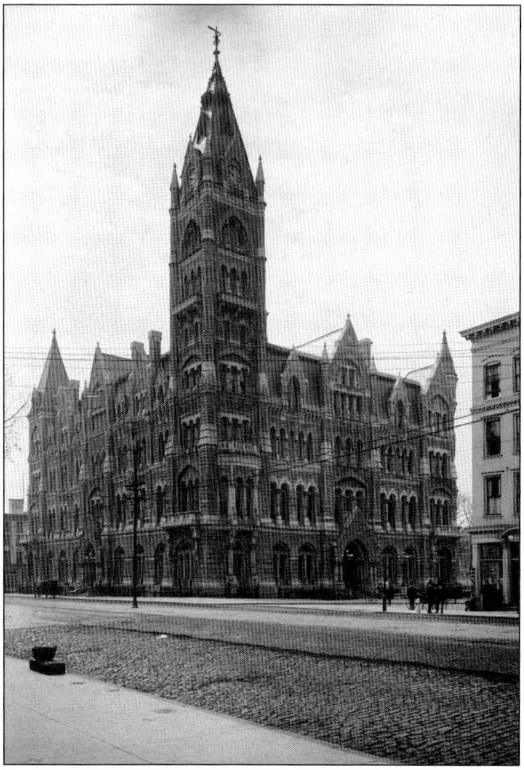

George Ainslie is among many City of Richmond employees buried in Hollywood. Ainslie served as the city's mayor from 1912 to 1924. He is perhaps best known for doubling the size of Richmond and planning the public works necessary to support the city's expansion. Pictured here is what is now referred to as Old City Hall, which served Richmond's city government from 1894 to the 1970s. (Courtesy of the Library of Congress.)

Several Virginia state politicians rest in Hollywood Cemetery. An incomplete list includes John Young Mason, Claude Augustus Swanson, John Williams Walker Fearn, John Randolph of Roanoke, Henry Alexander Wise, William Smith, Edmund Waddill Jr., Alexander Wilbourne Weddell, and James Alexander Seddon. Pictured here is the Virginia state capitol, which was designed by Thomas Jefferson. (Courtesy of the Library of Congress.)

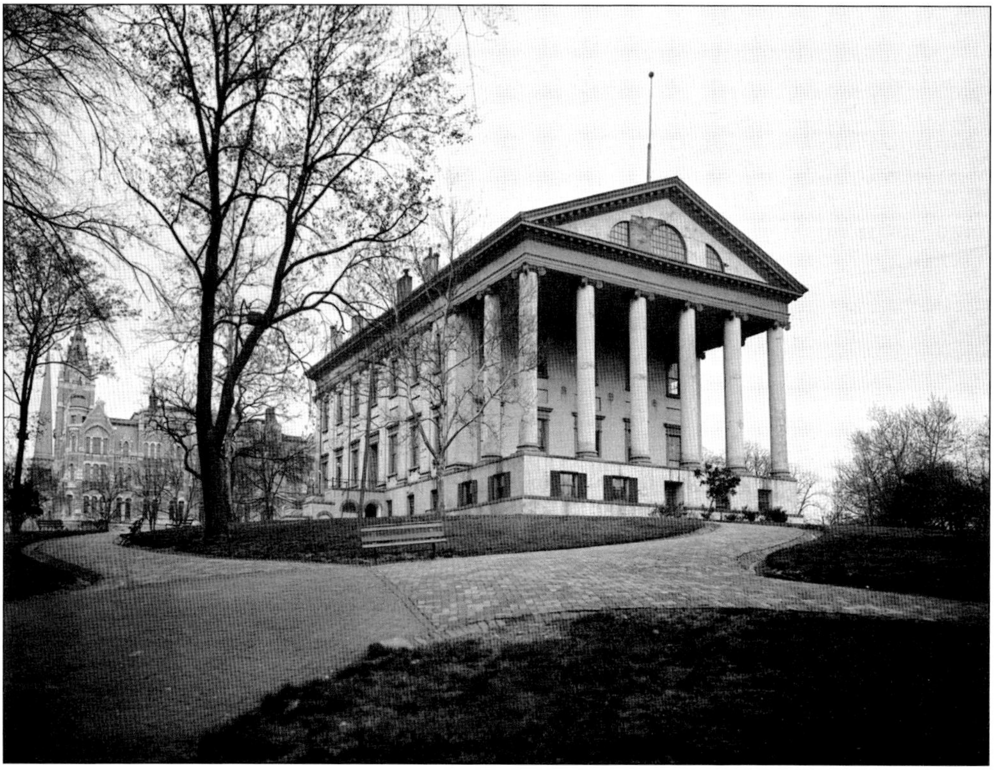

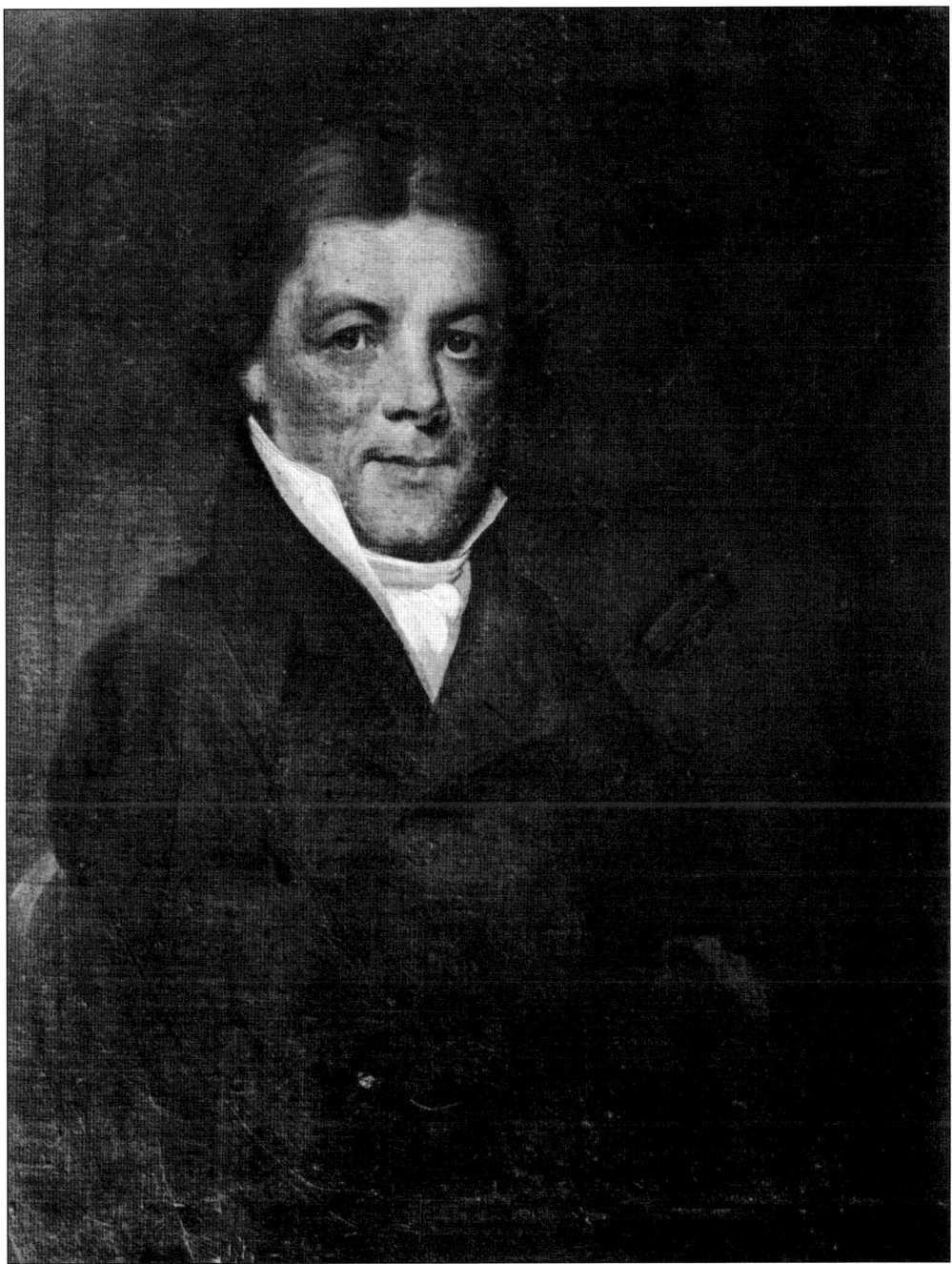

Despite his appellation, planter and politician John Randolph "of Roanoke" is buried in Hollywood. Known as a gifted orator, Randolph was a congressman from Virginia who also served in the House of Representatives on various occasions from 1799 to 1833 and in the Senate from 1825 to 1827. In 1830, Randolph served as minister to Russia. (Courtesy of the Library of Congress.)

AN ADDRESS TO THE PEOPLE OF THE FREE STATES

BY THE

PRESIDENT OF THE SOUTHERN CONFEDERACY.

RICHMOND, January 5, 1863.

Citizens of the non-slave-holding States of America, swayed by peaceable motives, I have used all my influence, often thereby endangering my position as the President of the Southern Confederacy, to have the unhappy conflict now existing between my people and yourselves, governed by those well established international rules, which heretofore have softened the asperities which necessarily are the concomitants of a state of belligerency, but all my efforts in the premises have heretofore been unavailing. Now, therefore, I am compelled e *necessitati rei* to employ a measure, which most willingly I would have omitted to do, regarding, as I always must, State Rights, as the very organism of politically associated society.

For nearly two years my people have been defending their inherent rights—their political, social and religious rights against the speculators of New England and their allies in the States heretofore regarded as conservative. The people of the Southern Confederacy have—making sacrifices such as the modern world has never witnessed—patiently, but determinedly, stood between their home interests and the well paid, well fed and well clad mercenaries of the Abolitionists, and I need not say that they have nobly vindicated the good name of American citizens. Heretofore, the warfare has been conducted by white men—peers, scions of the same stock; but the programme has been changed, and your rulers despairing of a triumph by the employment of white men, have degraded you and themselves, by inviting the co-operation of the black race. Thus, while they deprecate the intervention of white men—the French and the English—in behalf of the Southern Confederacy, they, these Abolitionists, do not hesitate to invoke the intervention of the African race in favor of the North.

The time has, therefore, come when a becoming respect for the good opinion of the civilized world impels me to set forth the following facts:—

First. Abraham Lincoln, the President of the Non-Slaveholding States, has issued his proclamation, declaring the slaves within the limits of the Southern Confederacy to be free.

Second. Abraham Lincoln has declared that the slaves so emancipated may be used in the Army and Navy, now under his control, by which he means to employ, against the Free People of the South, insurrectionary measures, the inevitable tendency of which will be to inaugurate a Servile War, and thereby prove destructive, in a great measure, to slave property.

Now, therefore, as a compensatory measure, I do hereby issue the following Address to the People of the Non-Slaveholding States:—

On and after February 22, 1863, all free negroes within the limits of the Southern Confederacy shall be placed on the slave status, and be deemed to be chattels, they and their issue forever.

All negroes who shall be taken in any of the States in which slavery does not now exist, in the progress of our arms, shall be adjudged, immediately after such capture, to occupy the slave status, and in all States which shall be vanquished by our arms, all free negroes shall, *ipso facto*, be reduced to the condition of helotism, so that the respective normal conditions of the white and black races may be ultimately placed on a permanent basis, so as to prevent the public peace from being thereafter endangered.

Therefore, while I would not ignore the conservative policy of the Slave States, namely, that a Federal Government cannot, without violating the fundamental principles of a Constitution, interfere with the internal policy of several States; since, however, Abraham Lincoln has seen fit to ignore the Constitution he has solemnly sworn to support, it ought not to be considered polemically or politically improper in me to vindicate the position which has been, at an early day of this Southern republic, assumed by the Confederacy, namely, that slavery is the corner-stone of a Western Republic. It is not necessary for me to elaborate this proposition. I may merely refer, in passing, to the prominent fact, that the South is emphatically a producing section of North America; this is equally true of the West and Northwest, the people of which have been mainly dependent on the South for the consumption of their products. The other States, in which slavery does not exist, have occupied a middle position, as to the South, West and Northwest. The States of New England, from which all complicated difficulties have arisen, owe their greatness and power to the free suffrages of all other sections of North America; and yet, as is now evident, they have, from the adoption of the Federal Constitution, waged a persistent warfare against the interests of all the other States of the old Union. The great centre of their opposition has been Slavery, while the annual statistics of their respective State Governments abundantly prove that they entertain within all their boundaries fewer negroes than any single State which does not tolerate slavery.

In view of these facts, and conscientiously believing that the proper condition of the negro is slavery, or a complete subjection to the white man,—and entertaining the belief that the day is not distant when the old Union will be restored with slavery nationally declared to be the proper condition of all of African descent,—and in view of the future harmony and progress of all the States of America, I have been induced to issue this address, so that there may be no misunderstanding in the future.

JEFFERSON DAVIS.

Richmond Enquirer Print.

Another notable Richmond figure buried in Hollywood Cemetery is Thomas Ritchie, founder of the *Richmond Enquirer*. In 1804, Ritchie established the newspaper that Thomas Jefferson would come to describe as the premiere newspaper in America. Ritchie bequeathed the newspaper to his son, Thomas, whose claim to fame was killing antislavery editor John Hampton Pleasants in a duel. This page from the *Richmond Enquirer* features an 1863 address from Jefferson Davis. (Courtesy of the Library of Congress.)

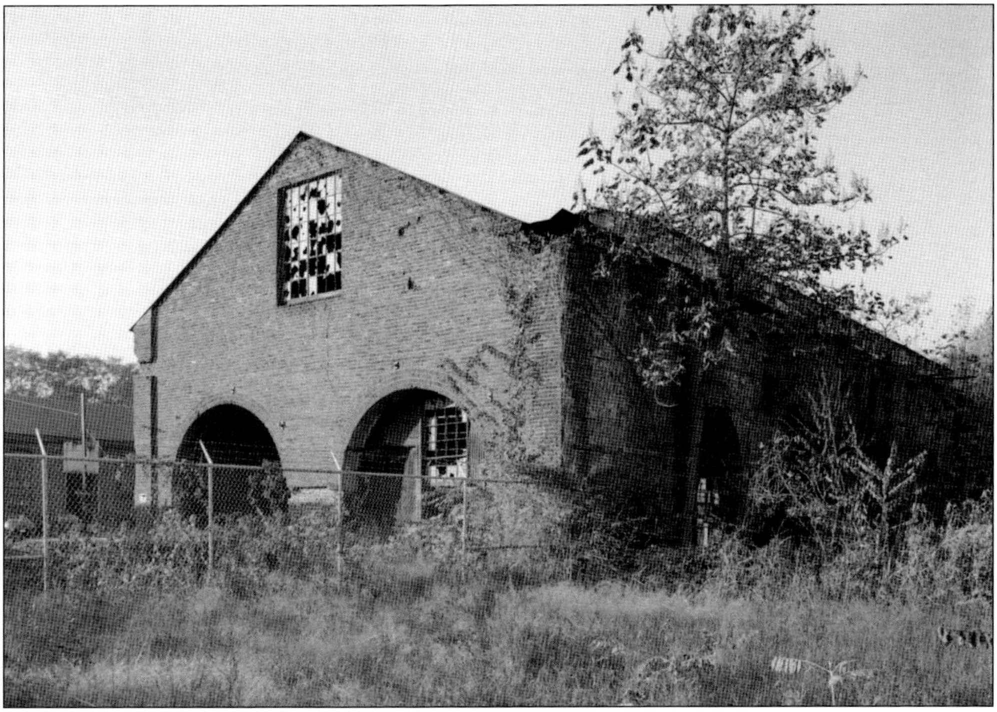

Joseph Reid Anderson, the egalitarian engineer, built the Shenandoah Valley Turnpike in 1840 and, more famously, turned Richmond's Tredegar Iron Works, pictured in part here, into a leading producer of iron goods, including rails, wheels, and boilers. He also championed equal pay for black workers. Nonetheless, he disliked Northern competition and supported secession. Anderson is buried in Hollywood, not far from the tomb of James Monroe. (Courtesy of the Library of Congress.)

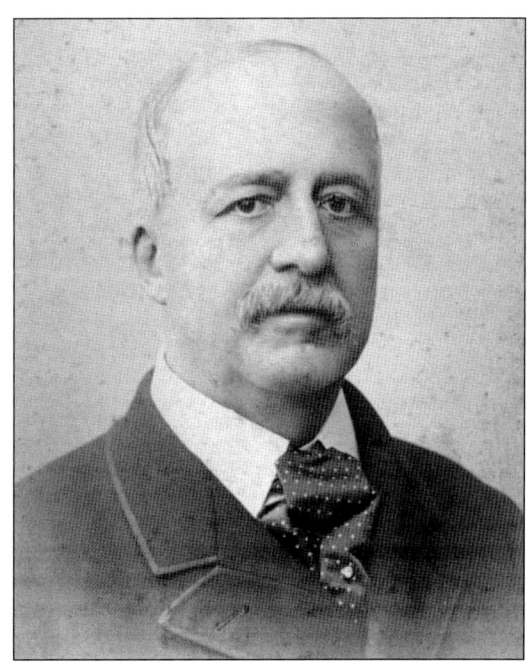

Confederate army major, businessman, and philanthropist Lewis Ginter moved to Richmond from New York in 1842. Using the fortune he had earned in the tobacco industry, he developed the city's Ginter Park neighborhood, where he helped relocate the Union Presbyterian Seminary from Farmville, Virginia. He died in 1897 and was laid to rest in Hollywood Cemetery. (Courtesy of VCU James Branch Cabell Library Special Collections.)

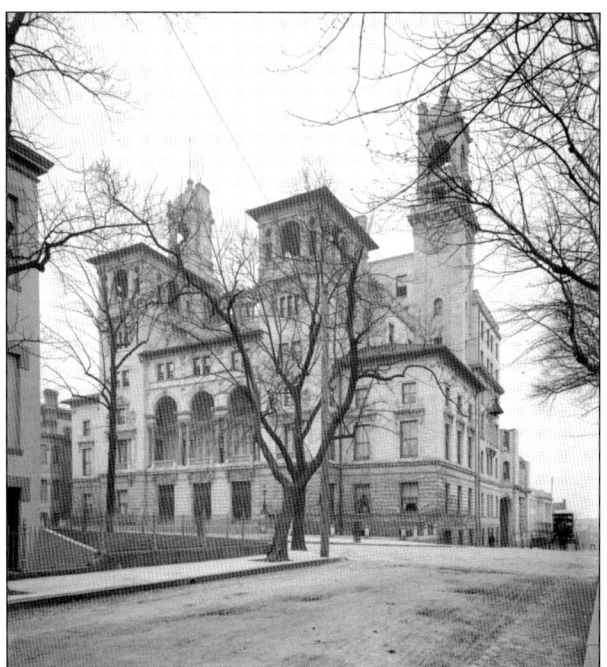

Lewis Ginter commissioned the building of the Jefferson Hotel in 1895, shortly before his death. Ginter was a world traveler and a fan of the arts and architecture. He also had a love for his adopted city of Richmond. The luxury hotel is located less than a mile from Hollywood Cemetery. Some of its rooms have views of the James River, just as Hollywood does. (Courtesy of the Library of Congress.)

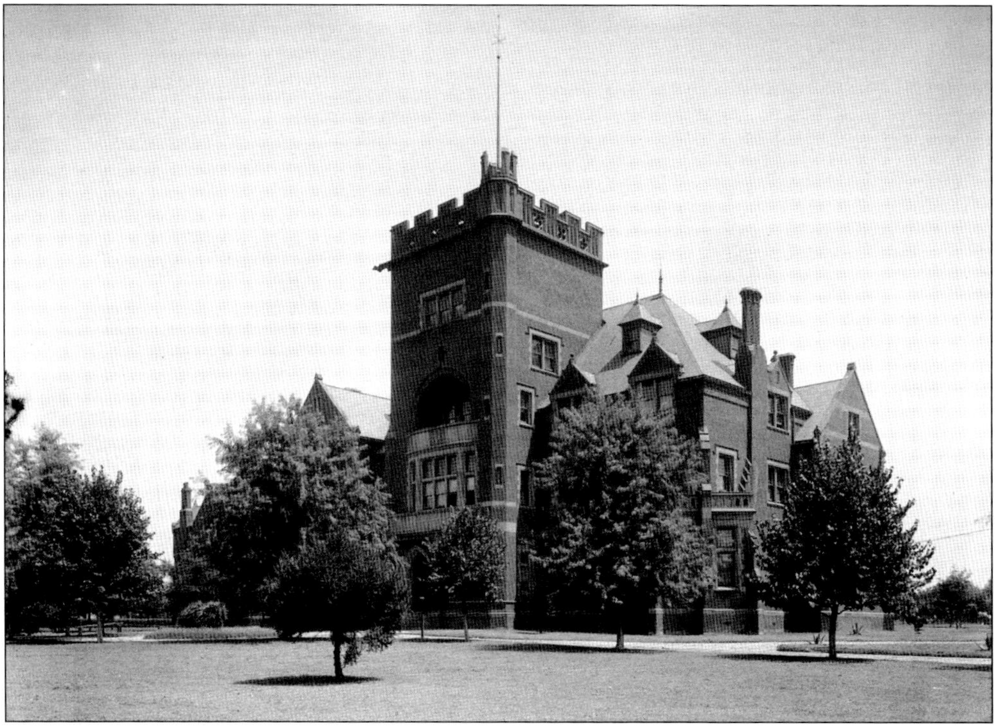

The Union Presbyterian Seminary in Richmond's Ginter Park neighborhood was originally founded in 1812 near Hampden-Sydney College in Farmville, Virginia. Union was built to train men and women to serve as pastors, educators, and scholars. Its Northside Richmond branch was opened in 1898, not long after philanthropist Lewis Ginter—who helped fund the campus—died and was buried at Hollywood Cemetery. (Courtesy of the Library of Congress.)

Hunter McGuire, founder of the schools and hospitals that eventually became the Medical College of Virginia, served as Gen. Stonewall Jackson's surgeon during the Civil War. As chief surgeon of Jackson's corps, McGuire amputated Jackson's left arm after the general was wounded by friendly fire near Chancellorsville. Days later, Jackson died of pneumonia near Richmond. McGuire went on to serve under generals Trimble, Ewell, and Early. He died in 1900. (Courtesy of the Library of Congress.)

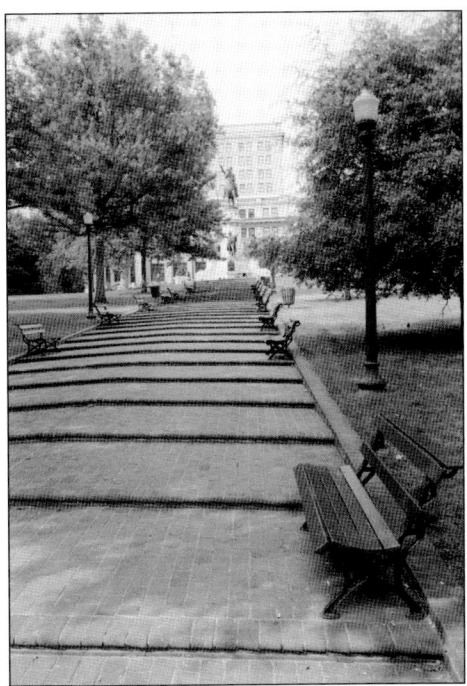

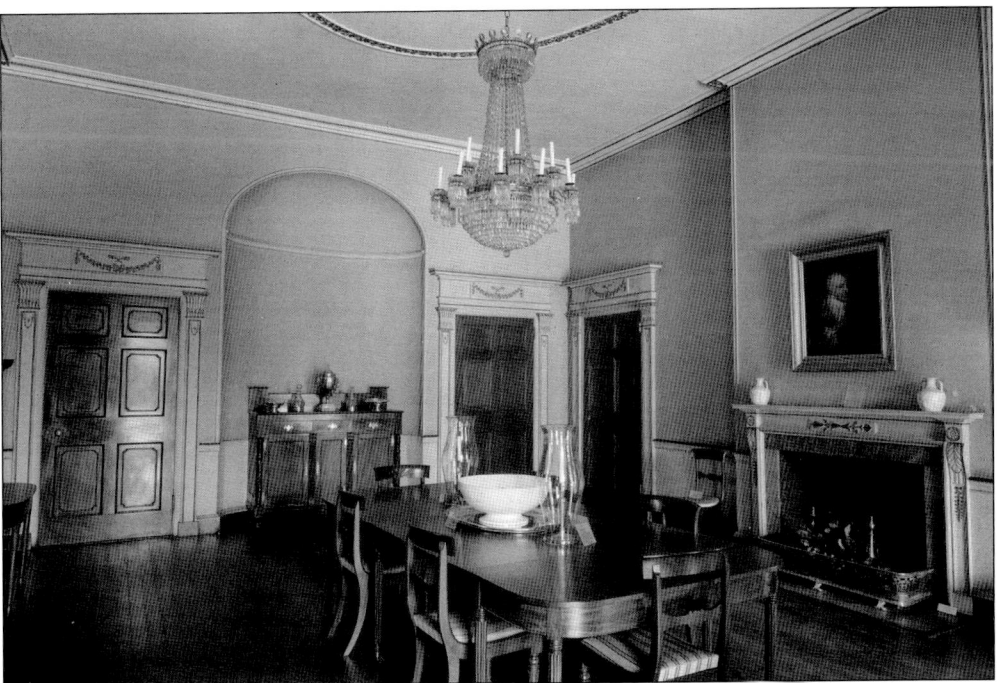

The interior of the Wickham-Valentine House reflects the wealth and influence of Richmond's Valentine family, who built their fortune on the 1871 invention of Valentine Meat Juice, a popular beef bouillon marketed as a multivitamin. Several members of the Valentine family are buried in Hollywood Cemetery, including Mann II, who donated his home to the City of Richmond. The property is known as the Valentine Richmond History Center and 1812 Wickham House. (Courtesy of the Library of Congress.)

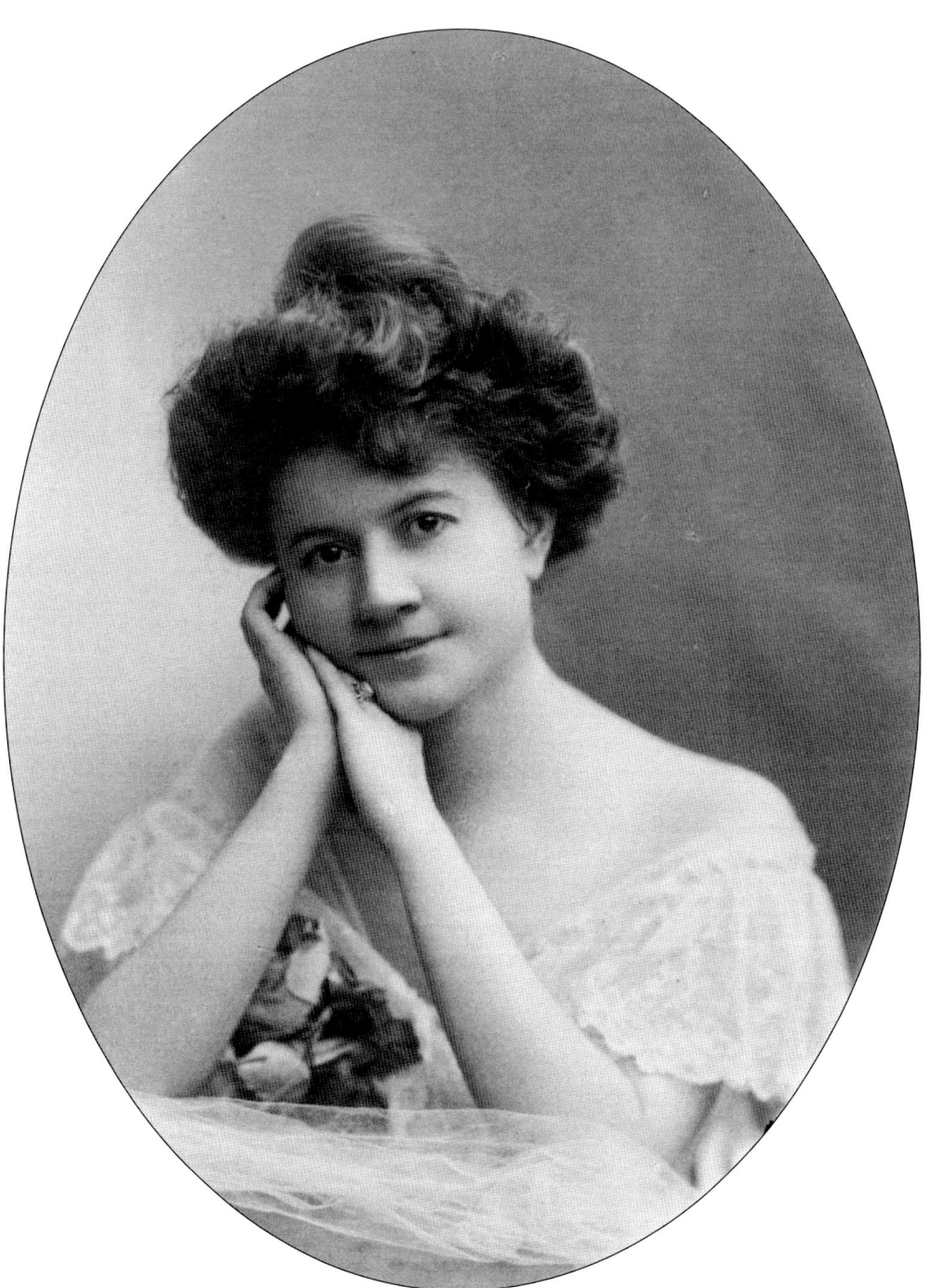

Richmond-born novelist Ellen Glasgow earned renown for portraying the contemporary South in her stories. Because of childhood illness, Glasgow was educated at home and spent a lot of time reading rather than training for the social and domestic life typical for young women of her class. She published 18 novels during her lifetime, earning the Pulitzer Prize in 1942 for *In This Our Life*. On November 21, 1945, Glasgow died. She was buried in Hollywood Cemetery. (Courtesy of the Library of Congress.)

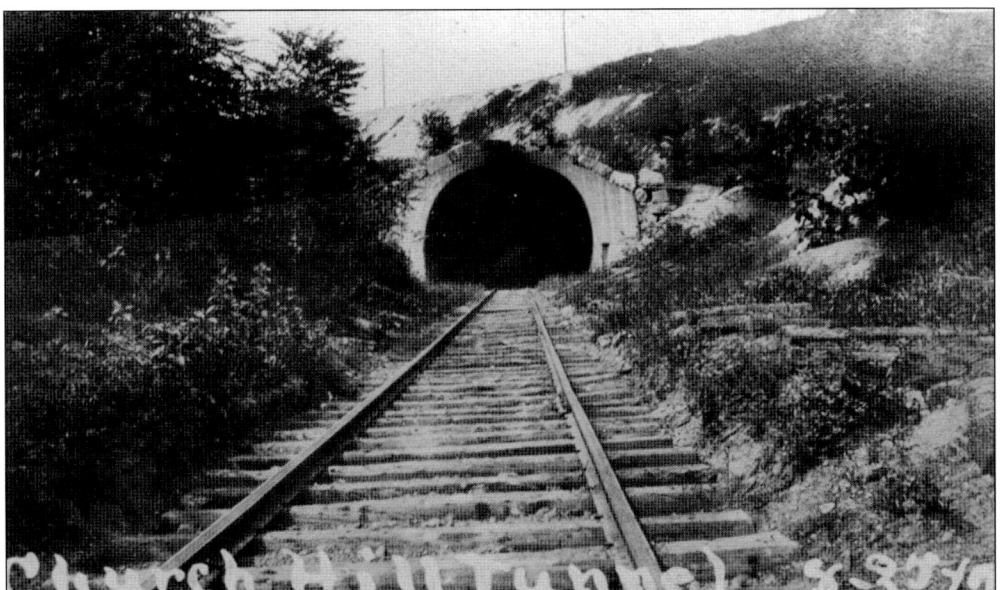

A vampire is believed to inhabit the tomb of W.W. Poole in Hollywood Cemetery. This urban legend spread purely by word of mouth. Poole had no heavy affiliation with the Church Hill Tunnel (shown here). His elaborate gravesite is at the front of the cemetery. To this day, the tunnel is one of the most popular sites for tourists, who pose for photographs in hopes of feeling the presence of the vampire. (Courtesy of the Library of Congress.)

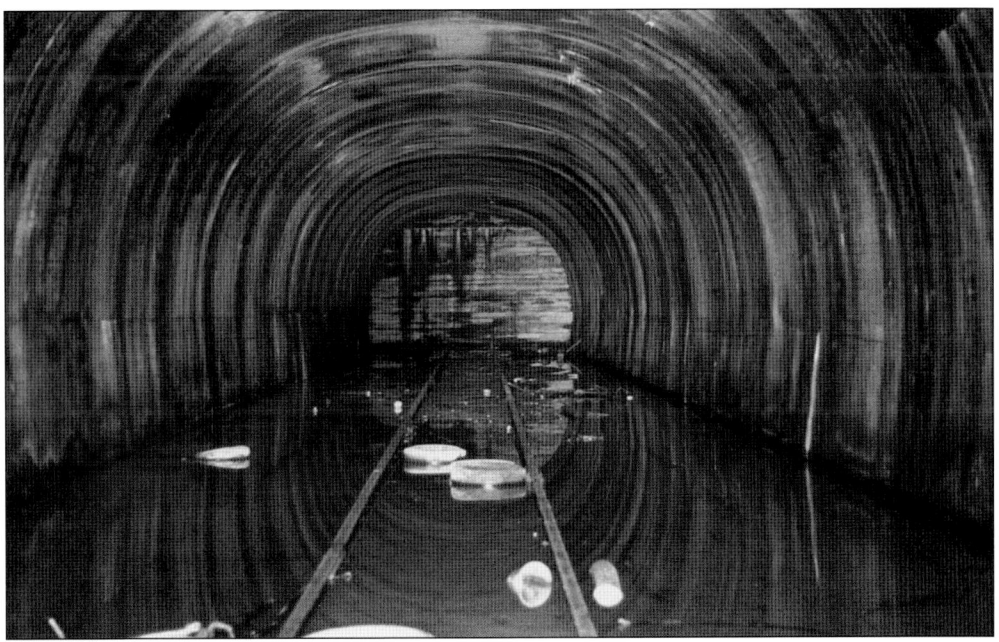

Urban legends fill a city like Richmond, and the Church Hill Tunnel was one of the first. After the collapse of the tunnel in 1925, a legend spread about a vampire that emerged from the tunnel. When running from the tunnel, Benjamin Mosby was thought to be a vampire. His mouth had been so damaged that he appeared to have fangs. This photograph depicts the interior of the tunnel. (Courtesy of the Library of Congress.)

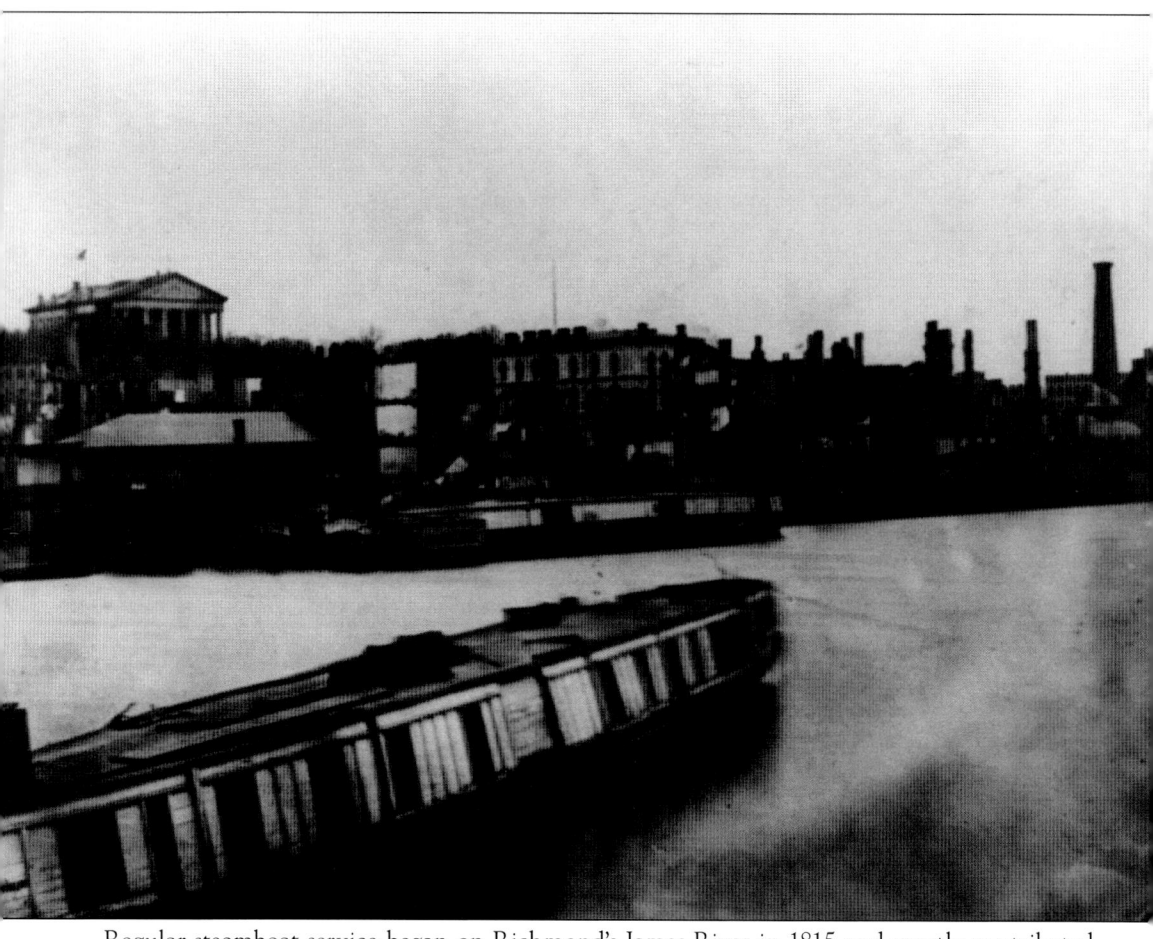

Regular steamboat service began on Richmond's James River in 1815 and greatly contributed to the wealth of the city during the antebellum period. Tobacco, railroads, and flour mills were among other great contributors to the city's prosperity. This wealth is what allowed for the funding of large-scale architecture and public works projects like Hollywood Cemetery. (Courtesy of the Library of Congress.)

Two

Evergreen and Oakwood Cemetreries

Evergreen Cemetery was one of the first African American cemeteries in Richmond—a designation that includes many slave burial grounds. Located on Evergreen Road near Richmond Road and Stony Run Parkway, the cemetery dates to 1891. Many famous and respected African Americans are laid to rest within the cemetery's nearly 60 acres. This cemetery was to be the African American equivalent to Richmond's Hollywood Cemetery. Evergreen was mapped out to be located on a very high ridge to overlook the city. Sometime in recent memory, the cemetery has become overgrown with weeds and kudzu, making it difficult to read many of the tombstones that are still intact.

Among the famous residents of Evergreen Cemetery is Maggie Walker, a teacher and businesswoman who was also the first African American bank president. Confined to a wheelchair, she was a great example of how those with disabilities can prevail. Another famous Richmond businessman buried in Evergreen is John Mitchell. A banker, politician, and civil rights activist, he was also the editor of the *Richmond Planet* and organized boycotts of Richmond's segregated trolley system. He ran unsuccessfully as a Republican candidate for governor in 1921.

Along with Walker and Mitchell, Alfred "A.D." Price is also buried in Evergreen Cemetery. He was born into slavery in 1860 and moved to Richmond to begin his own blacksmith shop. He expanded the shop and turned it into a stable and funeral home. He became the first funeral director in Virginia to become state-certified in embalming.

Evergreen Cemetery is a privately owned cemetery. The most recent burial dates to the 1980s. Over 5,000 people are buried at Evergreen, which is made up of four cemeteries—Evergreen, East End, Oakwood Colored Section, and Colored Pauper's Cemetery. Oakwood Cemetery is a city-owned facility in the East End of Richmond. In 1862, Oakwood opened to help to bury more of the Confederate soldiers who lost their lives in the Civil War. Oakwood was set as the final resting place for those who died at Chimborazo Hospital.

Many members of the Walker family are buried at Evergreen Cemetery, one of the forgotten African American cemeteries in Richmond. Shown here are Maggie Walker's younger son, Melvin, along with his wife, Ethel, and their son Armstead. Members of the Walker family would visit the family plot to show their love and pay their respects. (Courtesy of the Maggie Walker Historic Site.)

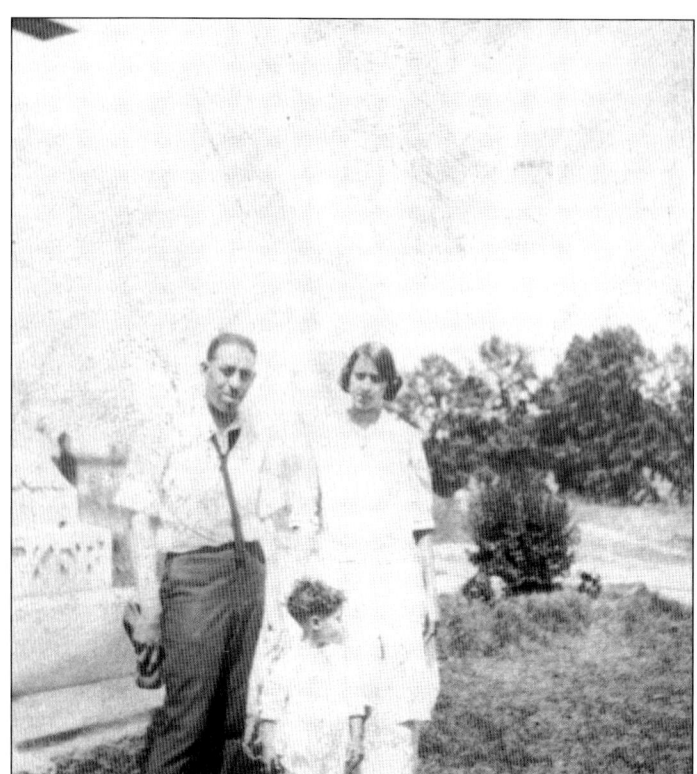

Maggie Walker always presented herself in the most luxurious ways, even when her family was struggling. She was known for her perseverance when things got rough. Even when bound to a wheelchair, she never gave up. When her husband, Armstead, was killed tragically, he was buried in Evergreen Cemetery. She would visit his grave to help maintain it and grieve for the love of her life. (Courtesy of the Maggie Walker Historic Site.)

Located in Richmond, the St. Luke Bank and Trust was made famous by Richmond's own Maggie Walker. In 1903, the bank opened on James Street. The opening of this institution led to many new jobs for African Americans and also helped to prove that members of the community were able to open their own successful businesses. Evergreen Cemetery is proud to have the successful Walker resting on its grounds. (Courtesy of the Maggie Walker Historic Site.)

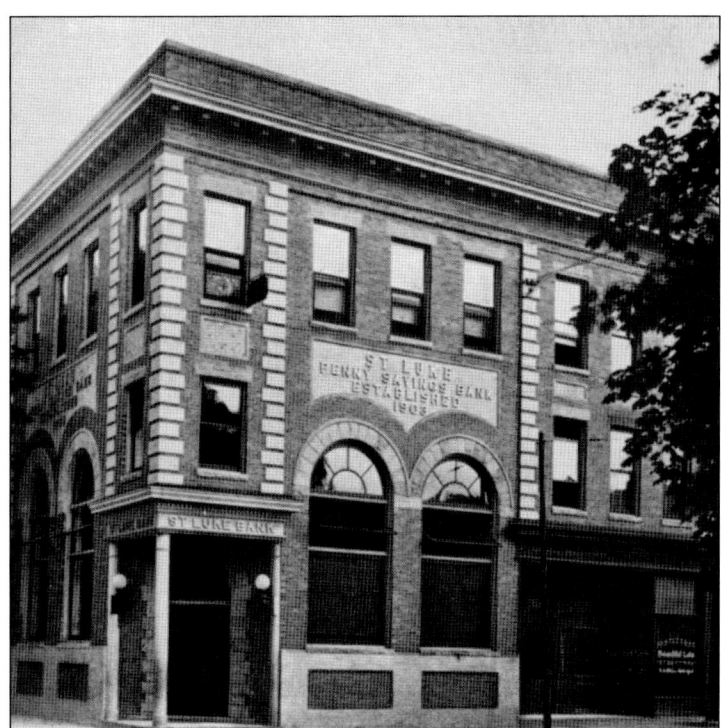

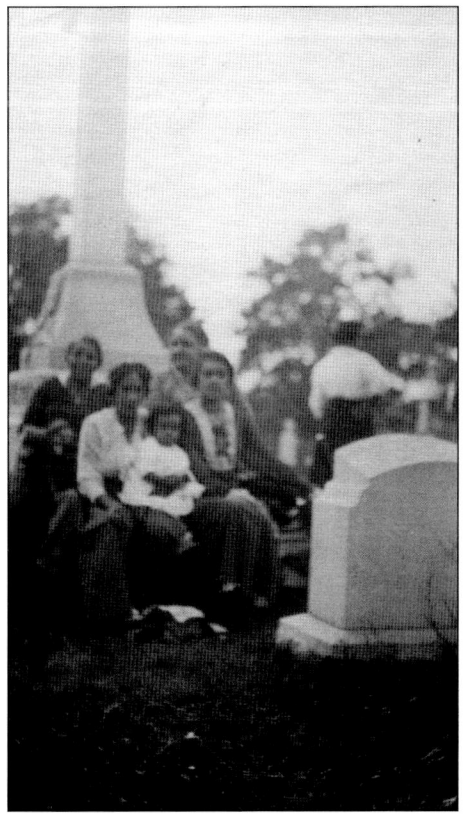

The Walkers were an incredibly close family. They would often be found visiting Evergreen Cemetery in groups to help to pay their respects to the many that were already buried there. Maggie Walker (far right) is seen here with her daughter-in-law, Hattie (middle), her granddaughter Maggie Laura (far left), and a few other women from Richmond. (Courtesy of the Maggie Walker Historic Site.)

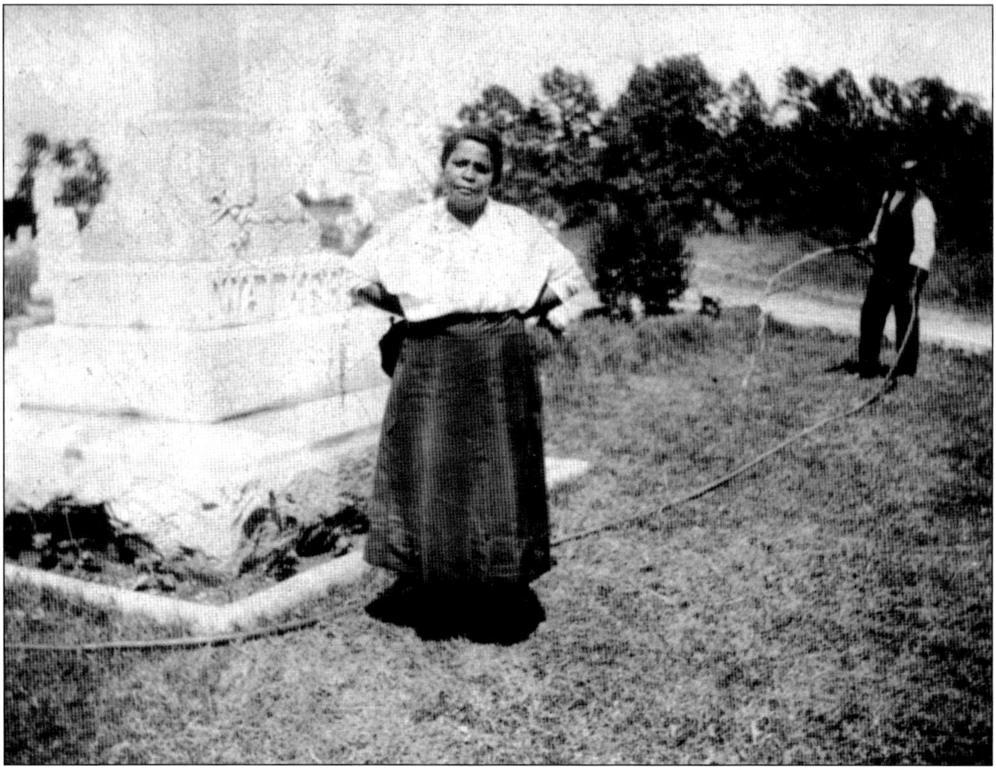

The Walker family plot saw many visitors come through and place flowers or clean up the site. The Walkers were a popular family in Richmond because of their kindness and their efforts to pave the road for many African Americans' successes. Seen here are two unidentified African Americans; one has taken on the task of watering the grass and helping to landscape the plot. (Courtesy of the Maggie Walker Historic Site.)

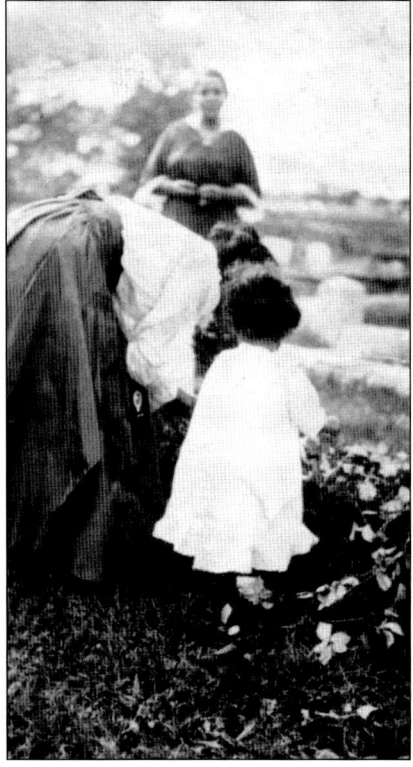

Maintaining Evergreen Cemetery was very important in its early days. Many African American cemeteries were neglected by the city. It was not until recently that volunteers and the families of those buried there began to maintain the grounds and tombstones. Seen here are people trying to help to beautify a tombstone. (Courtesy of the Maggie Walker Historic Site.)

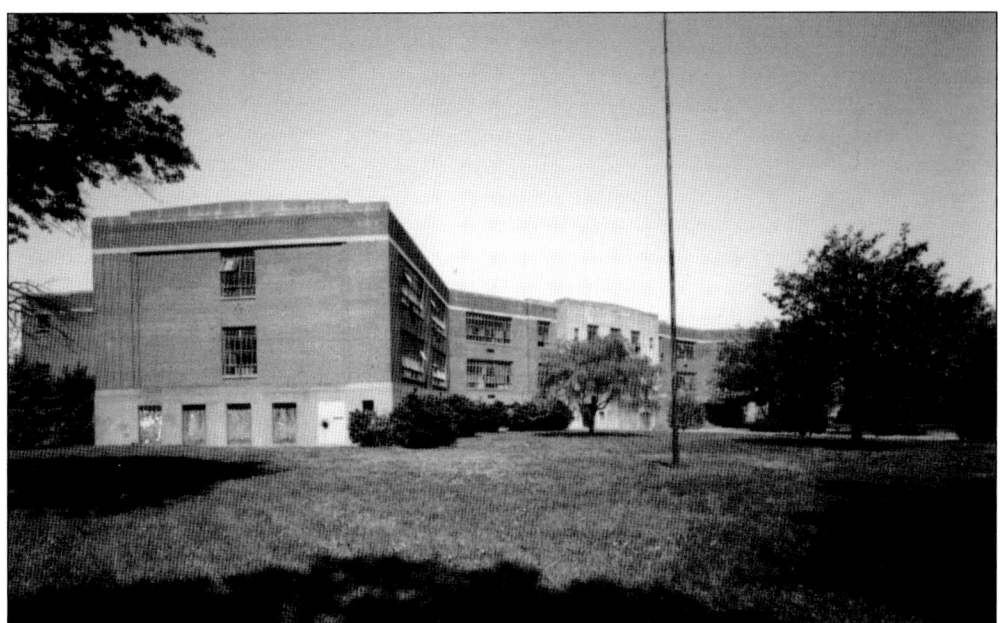

The Maggie Walker Governor's School was the first vocational high school built for African American youth and the only one named after a famous citizen of Richmond. Located on Lombardy Street, it remained a solely black school until the civil rights movement. It was desegregated in 1964. Finally, in 2002, it went through a renovation and is now a school for gifted high school students. (Courtesy of the Library of Congress.)

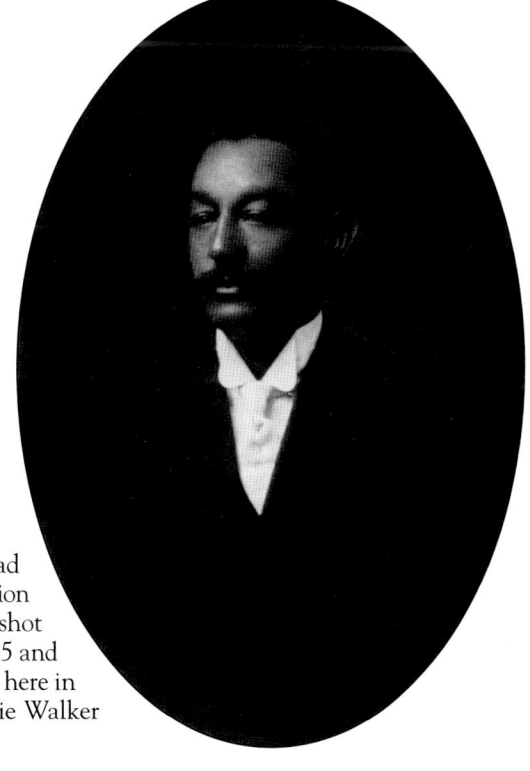

In 1886, Maggie Mitchell married Armstead Walker. A member of a family in the construction trade, he worked as a bricklayer. After being shot accidentally by his son, Armstead died in 1915 and was buried in Evergreen Cemetery. He is seen here in the prime of his life. (Courtesy of the Maggie Walker Historic Site.)

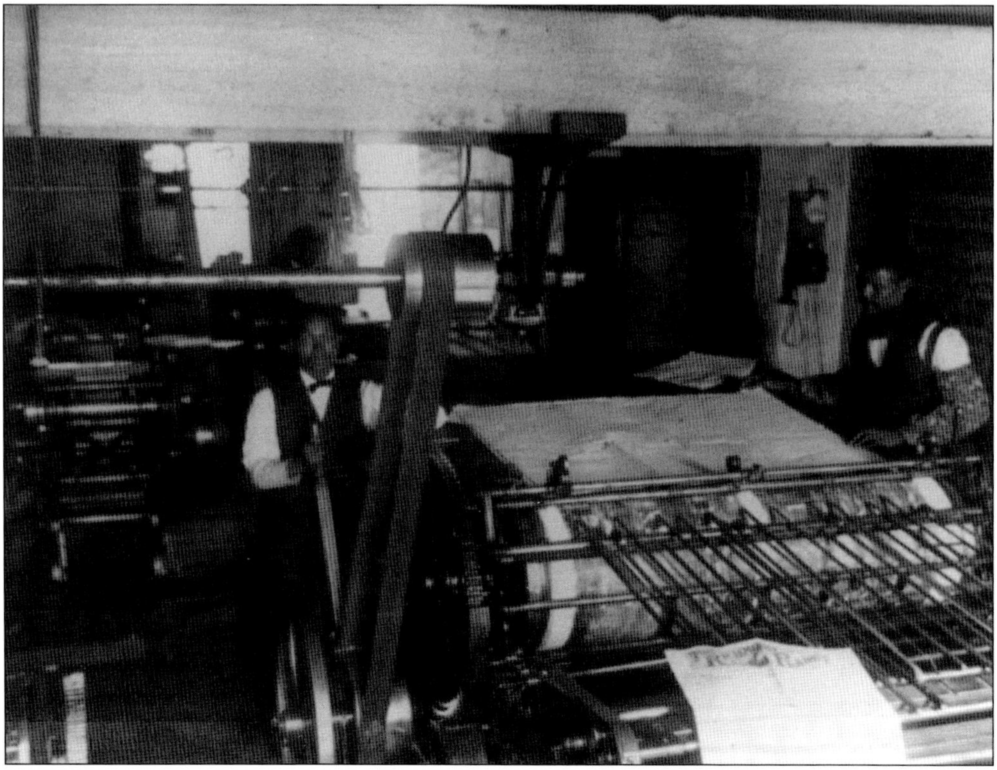

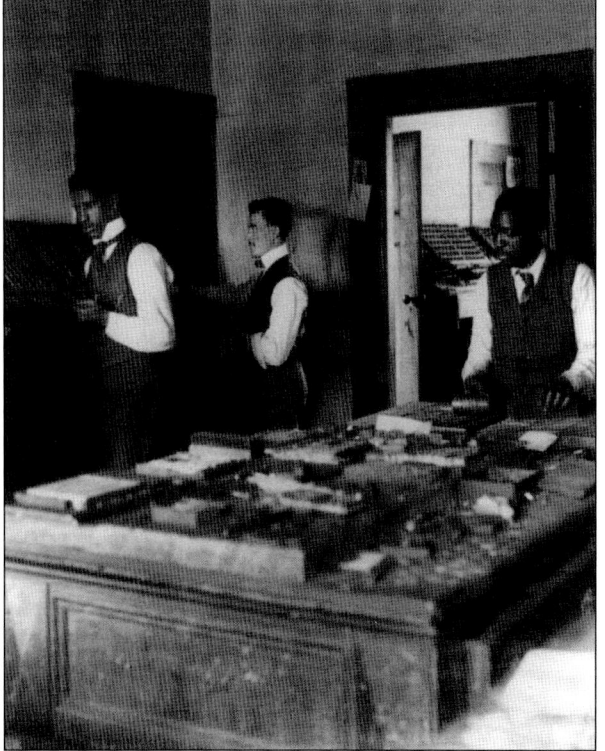

The *Richmond Planet*, first published in 1821, was founded by 13 former slaves from Virginia. John Mitchell Jr. took over as editor when he was a mere 21 years old. He died at his desk in 1929 and was buried in Evergreen. His marker quotes the Book of Isaiah. (Courtesy of the Library of Congress.)

John Mitchell Jr. was one of the first African American editors of a Richmond publication. The newspaper, born in the wake of freedom, opened many doors to African Americans. It pushed for racial equality and set the standard for black journalists and editors. Mitchell is one of Evergreen's most influential men laid to rest here. (Courtesy of the Library of Congress.)

The Walkers were a very large and close-knit family. They all supported each other and had many successes. Maggie Walker began as a teacher who later became the grand secretary of the Independent Order of St. Luke, an organization that set out to better the financial lives of African Americans. Walker is one of the most well-known and successful women buried in Evergreen Cemetery. (Courtesy of the Maggie Walker Historic Site.)

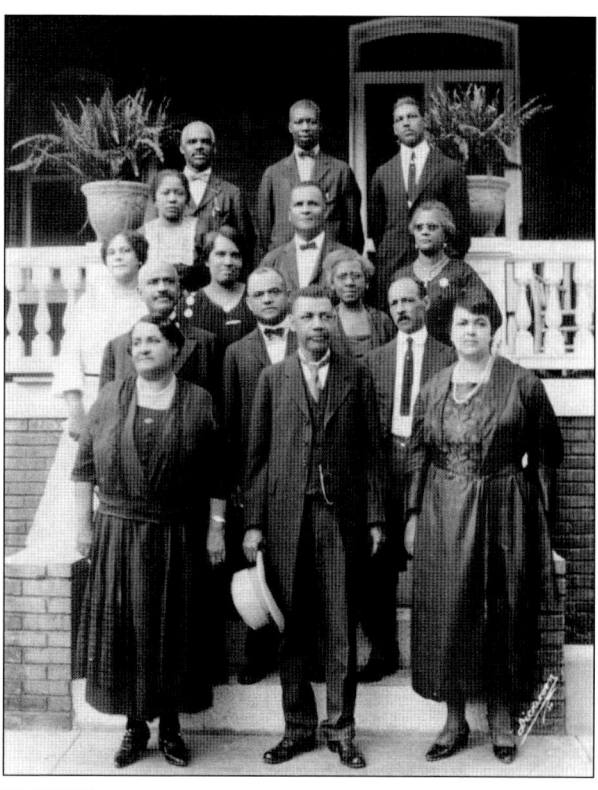

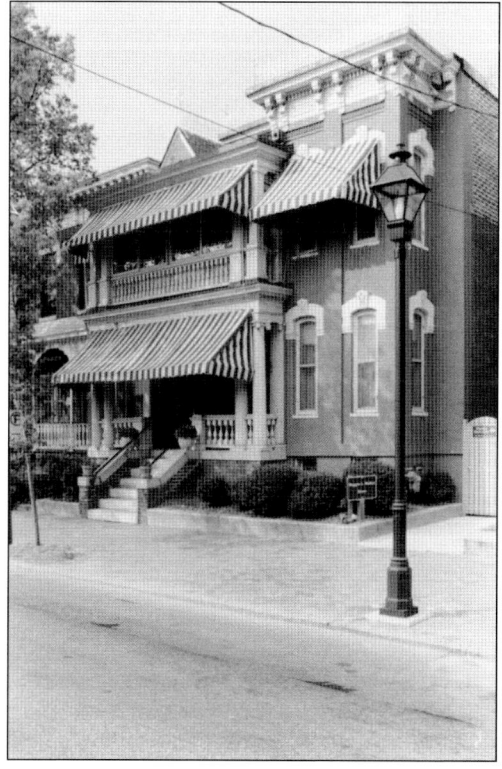

The Walker home is located in the heart of downtown Richmond, in Jackson Ward. This part of the city was once called the "Harlem of the South." It found much success as a home to the *Richmond Planet* and St. Luke Bank and Trust, and became a historic landmark in 1978. (Courtesy of the Library of Congress.)

51

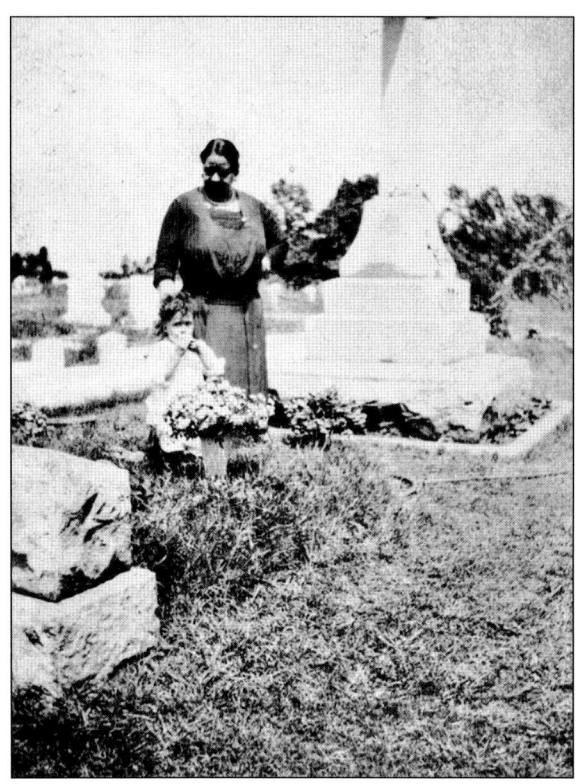

Maggie Walker is shown here with one of her two sons. She was a very strong figure in the African American society in Richmond and helped open many doors for black women in the city. She helped to supply jobs and social activities for them. She and her family would often visit the Walker family plot in Evergreen to pay respects to loved ones lost. (Courtesy of the Maggie Walker Historic Site.)

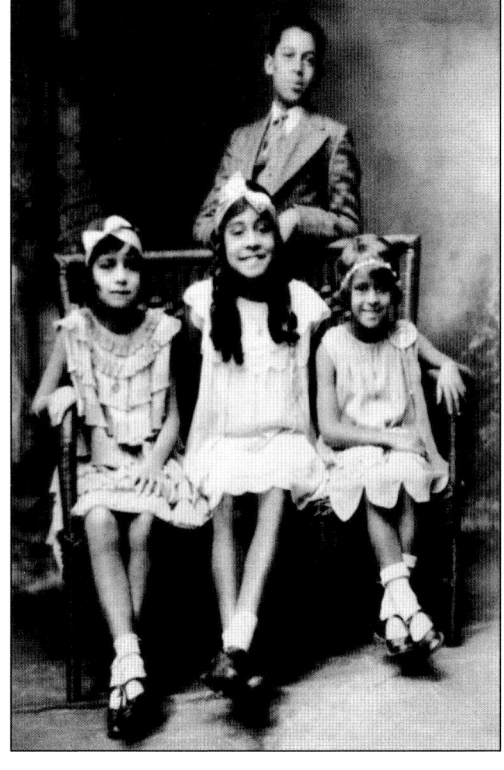

While slavery was tearing many African American families apart in Richmond, the Walker family always stayed incredibly close. Maggie Walker made it a point to display all of her children's diplomas and achievements in the family library. She was a very proud mother and was always pushing her children to achieve the goals that they had set in life. Her sons Melvin and Russell are both buried at Evergreen Cemetery. (Courtesy of the Library of Congress.)

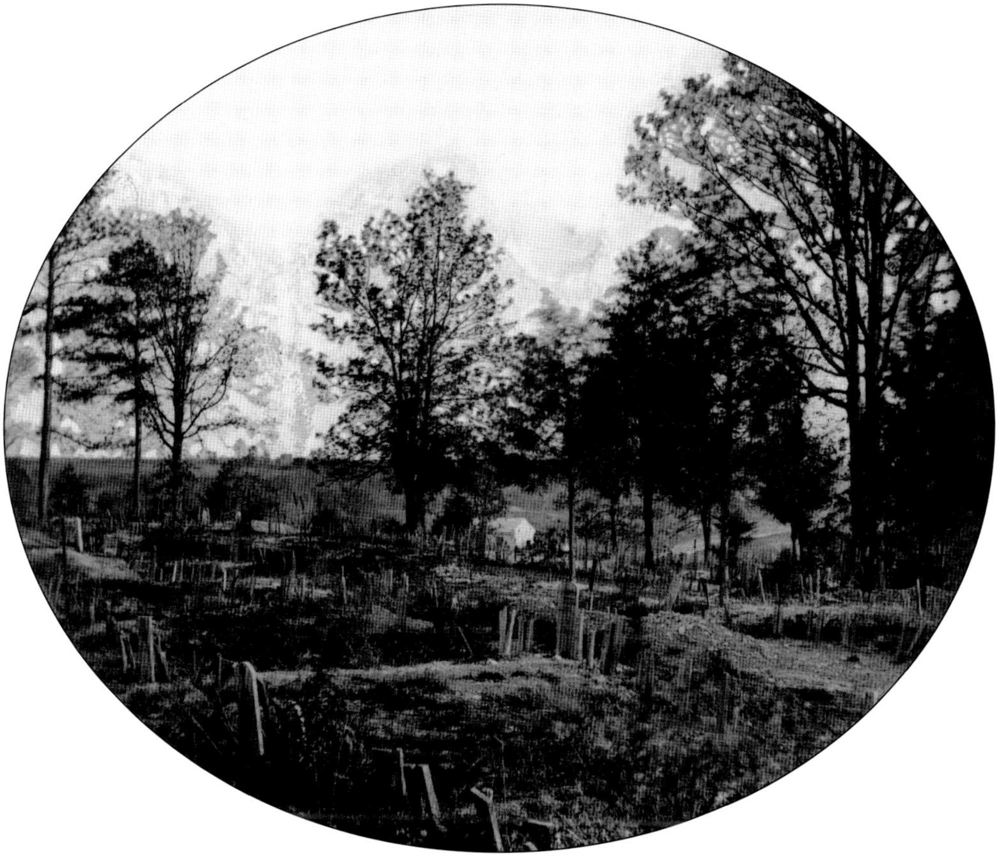

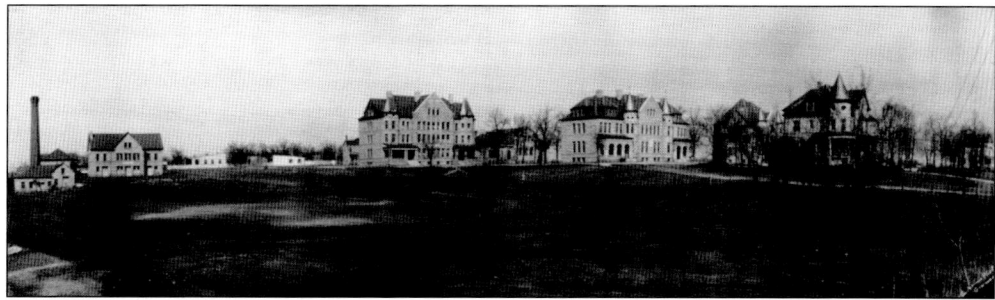

There are many historic African American cemeteries in the city of Richmond. Evergreen Cemetery is one that has been forgotten. The families of those buried here are solely in charge of the upkeep of their relatives' plots. Evergreen is seen here at its very beginning. The landscaping was well kept then. Today, volunteers are the ones to maintain it. (Courtesy of the Maggie Walker Historic Site.)

Located near Maggie Walker Governor's School is Virginia Union University. It is a historically black university with many famous Richmond alumni. It was once called the Richmond Theological Institute. John Andrew Bowler, buried in Evergreen, was an alumnus of VUU and became a deacon at the first African American Baptist church in Richmond. He also helped to organize one of the first black schools in Church Hill. (Courtesy of the Library of Congress.)

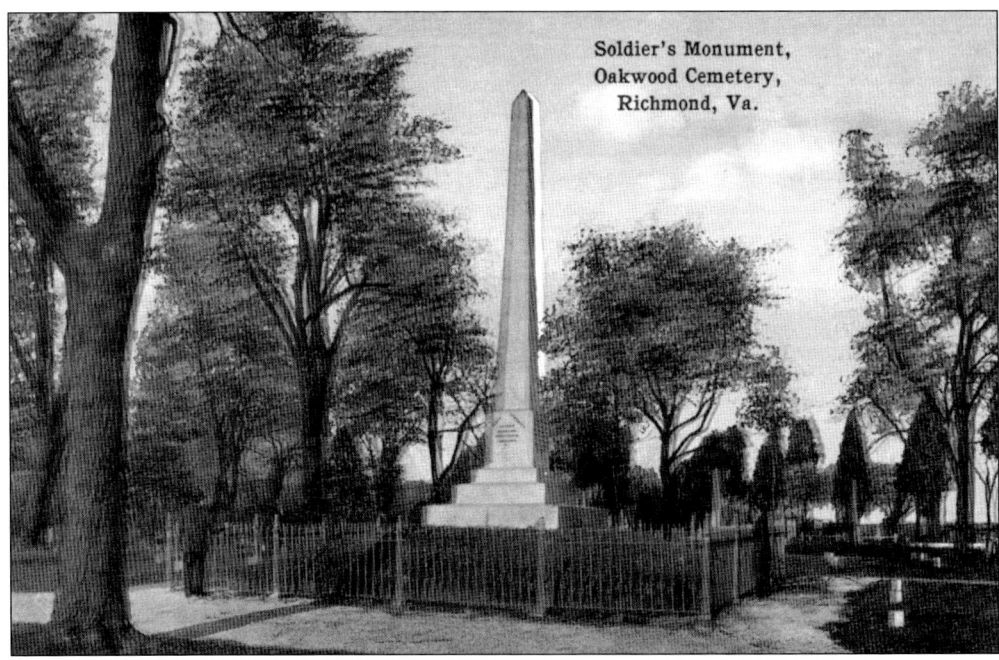

The Soldier's Monument at Oakwood Cemetery pays homage to the estimated 16,000 Confederate soldiers who rest there. Many of them were soldiers unsuccessfully treated at nearby Chimborazo Hospital. Chimborazo opened on October 17, 1861. As one of the largest hospitals of its time, it could accommodate 3,000 patients. Medical staff had reportedly treated more than 75,000 patients at the facility by the end of the Civil War. Shown here are two views of the monument. (Both, courtesy of VCU James Branch Cabell Library Special Collections.)

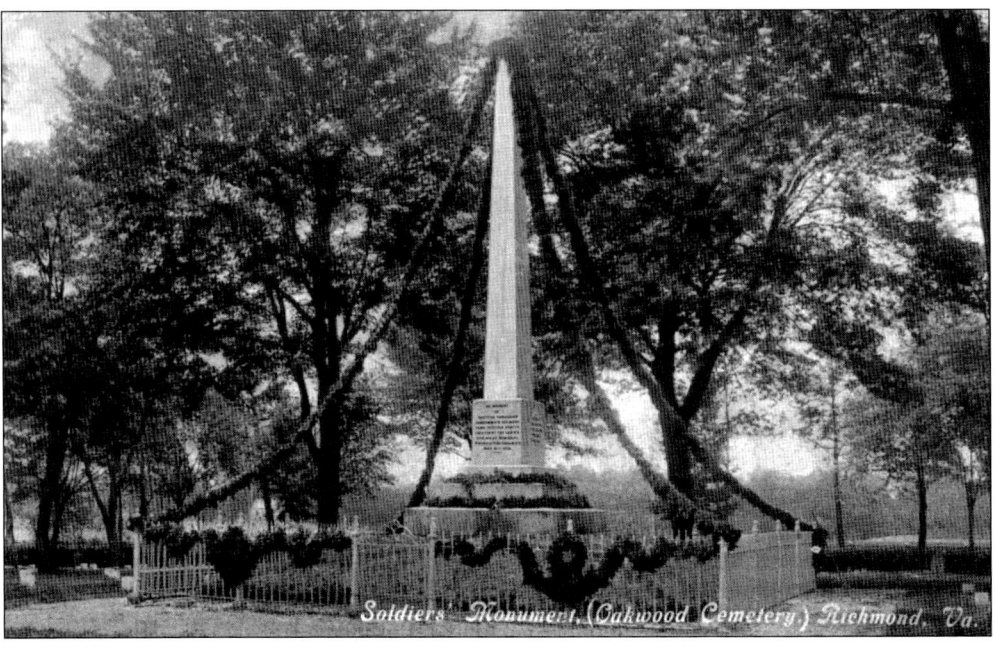

Three

CHURCHES AND GRAVEYARDS

Cemeteries and graveyards are often confused with one another. A cemetery, by definition, is an area set apart for containing graves, tombs, or funeral urns that is not located in a churchyard. A graveyard is a burial ground that is associated with smaller, rural churches. Richmond is known for many of its church graveyards.

Once called Richmond Church, St. John's Church is one of the most famous national landmarks in American history. There are 1,300 persons buried in its graveyard. Located in the heart of downtown Richmond, the church was made famous by American politician Patrick Henry. In 1775, he delivered his "Give Me Liberty or Give Me Death" speech to the Continental Congress there. The speech would change history for every American. History is found not only inside the church, but also on the grounds in the graveyard. St. John's graveyard holds many influential residents of Richmond.

A famous statesman buried in the graveyard is Edward Carrington. He was a member of the Continental army and a delegate to the Continental Congress. According to legend, Carrington listened to Henry's speech outside one of the windows of the church and was so affected by the speech that he proclaimed that the spot on which he stood should be his burial site. His grave marker lies outside the window on the eastern side of the church.

Among other famous persons buried here is Elizabeth Poe, Edgar Allan Poe's mother. A famous actress in Richmond, she and became ill and died in an actor's boardinghouse. Her memorial marker is near the eastern border of the cemetery.

Richmond's church graveyards can also be found at Mount Calvary, Holy Cross, and St. Joseph. The latter was built as a seminary campus on Anniston Street. In the mid-1850s, it was decided that it would be used as a cemetery. In the 1970s, the graves there were transferred to Holy Cross and Mount Calvary. Holy Cross continues to be used today by many Catholic Richmonders. Mount Calvary houses many deceased Richmond priests and is the final resting place for many Richmond bishops.

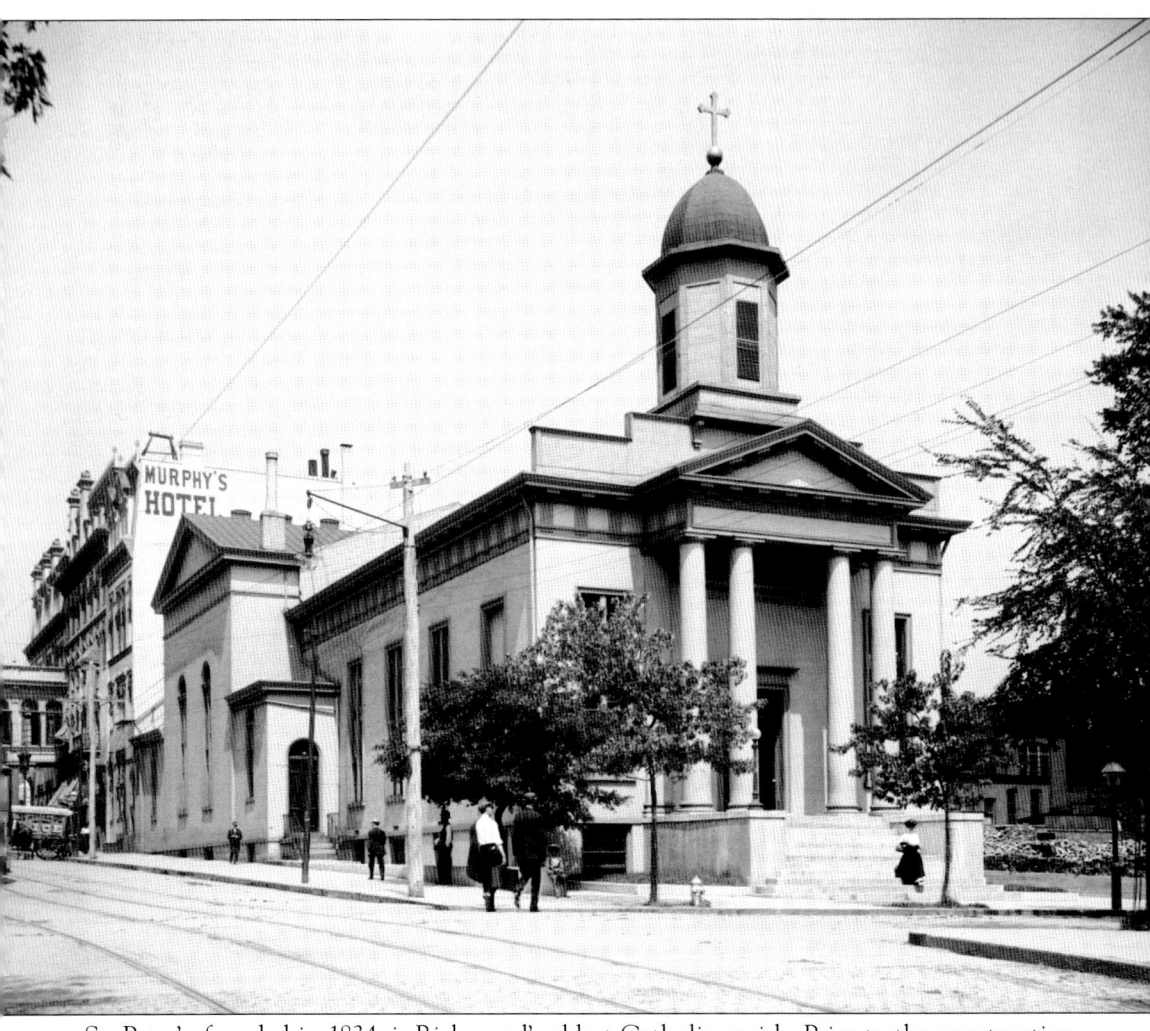

St. Peter's, founded in 1834, is Richmond's oldest Catholic parish. Prior to the construction of the Cathedral of the Sacred Heart in 1906, the church served as the seat of the Richmond Diocese. Mount Calvary has been the Catholic cemetery of Richmond since 1880. (Courtesy of the Library of Congress.)

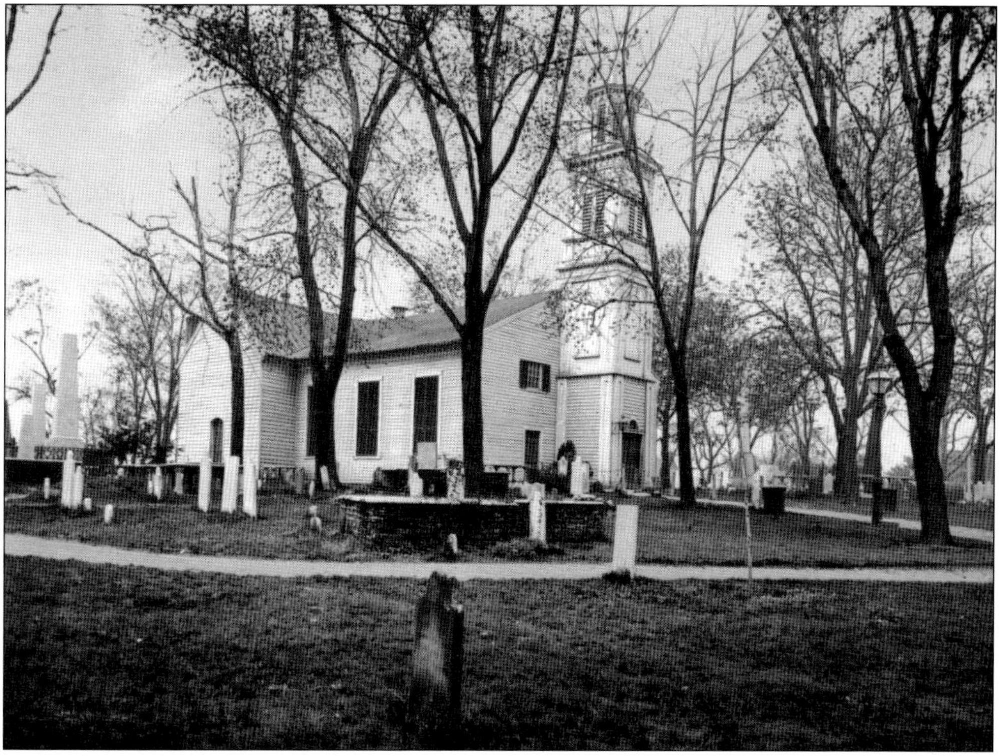

Located in Richmond's Church Hill district, St. John's Church is a very popular landmark and visitor destination. The church has seen its share of history in the pews as well as in its graveyard. Politicians, including George Wythe, one of the first signers of the Declaration of Independence, are buried here. These views depict St. John's Church, as seen from the east (above) and from the west (below). (Both, courtesy of VCU James Branch Cabell Library Special Collections.)

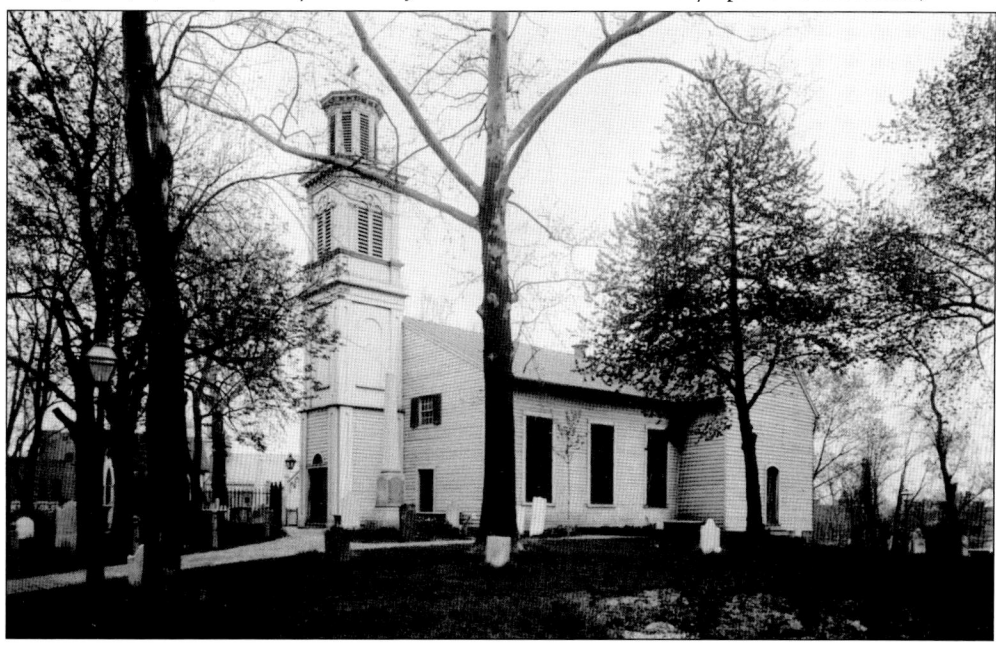

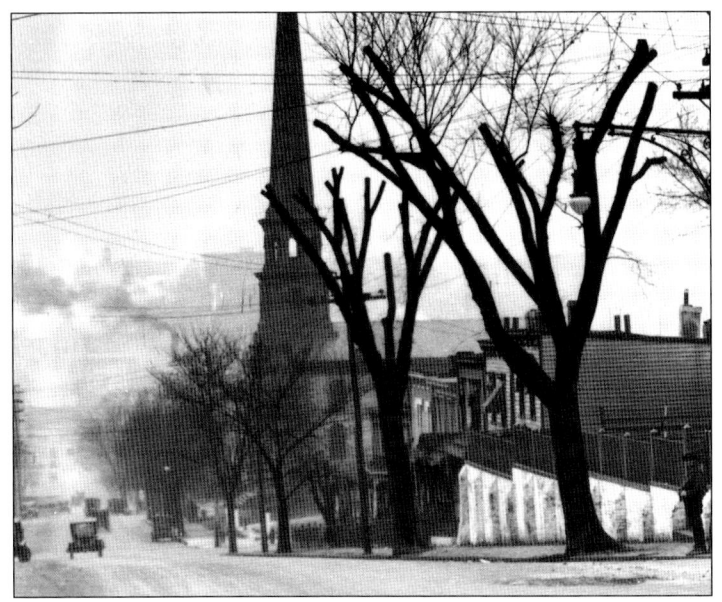

Made famous by Patrick Henry's speech, St. John's Church, located in the heart of Richmond in the Church Hill community, was established in 1741. The church's graveyard is the final resting place for many of the wealthiest and most affluent residents of Richmond. To this day, the church remains a National Historic Landmark and a popular tourist attraction. (Courtesy of the Library of Congress.)

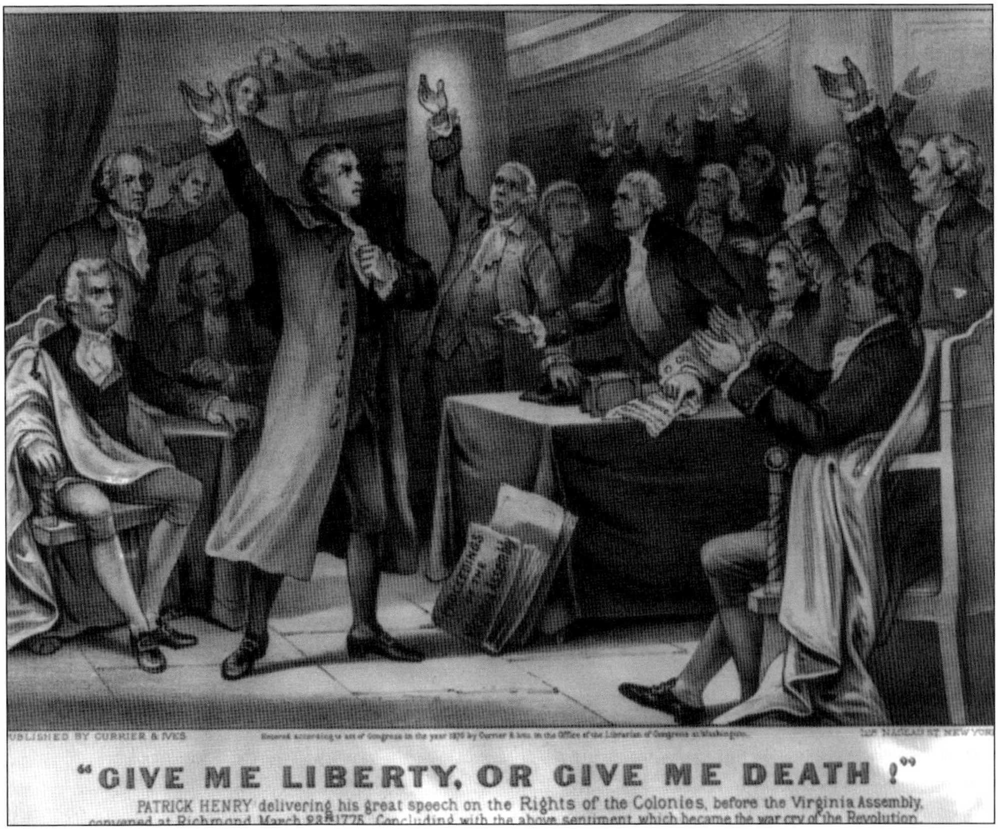

St. John's Church was made famous by the "Give Me Liberty or Give Me Death" speech of Patrick Henry to the Virginia Convention in 1775. Quite a few politicians were present for this speech, including John Carrington, who is buried in the graveyard at St. John's Church. (Courtesy of the Library of Congress.)

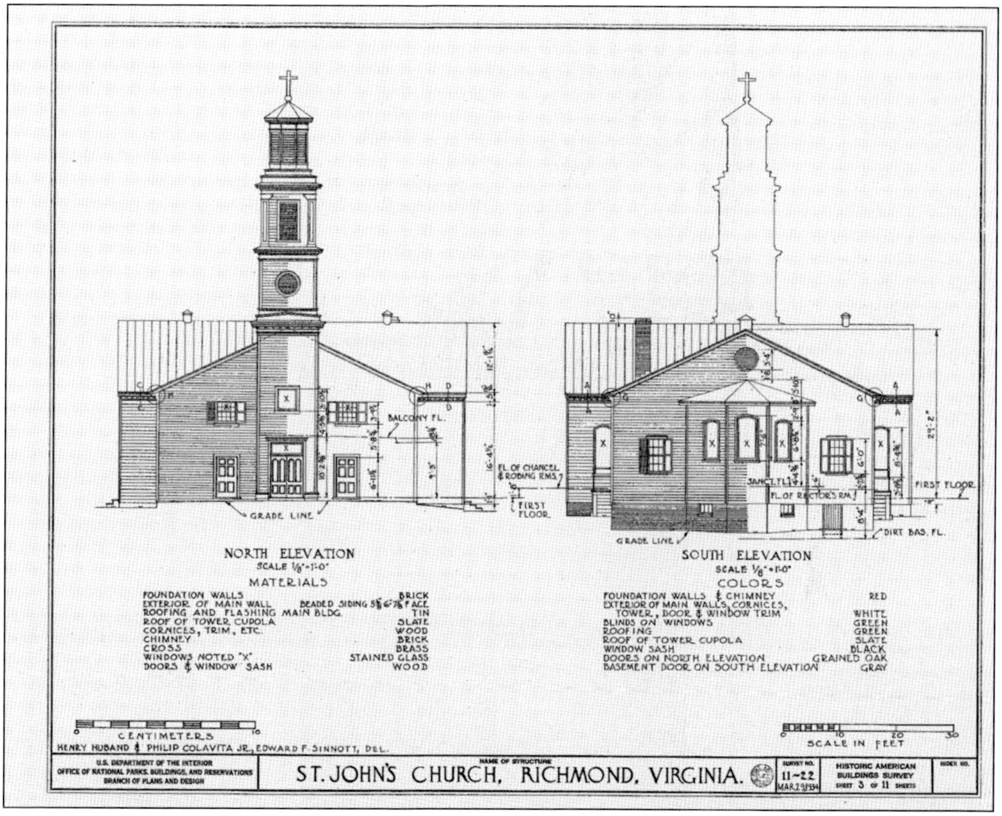

St. John's Church is quite possibly one of the most historic buildings in Richmond, Virginia. Located in the heart of the Church Hill neighborhood, the church has seen famous politicians like George Washington, Thomas Jefferson, Richard Henry Lee, and George Wythe, one of the signers of the Declaration of Independence. (Courtesy of the Library of Congress.)

Dating to 1741, St. John's Church was one of the first Anglican churches in Richmond. It was originally known as the Church on Richmond Hill and was later named St. John's in the early 19th century. It remains open to the public to attend services on Sundays and also holds public tours on a daily basis. (Courtesy of the Library of Congress.)

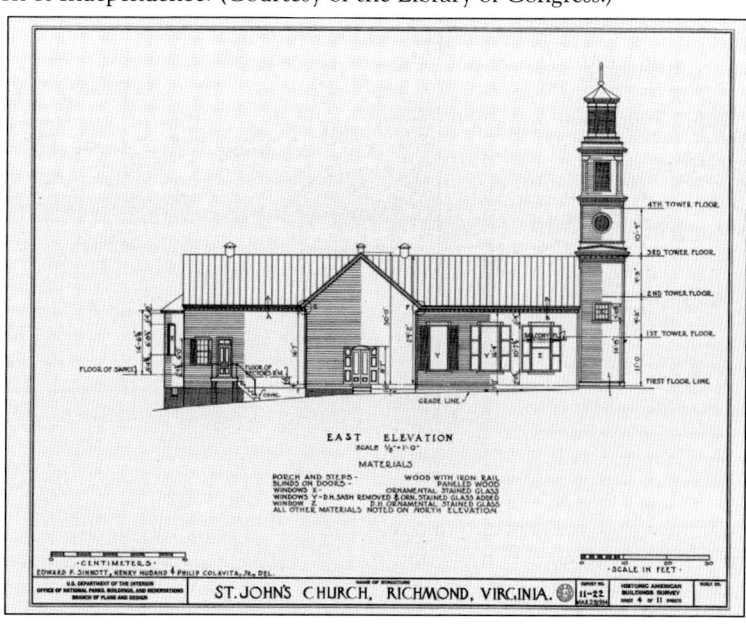

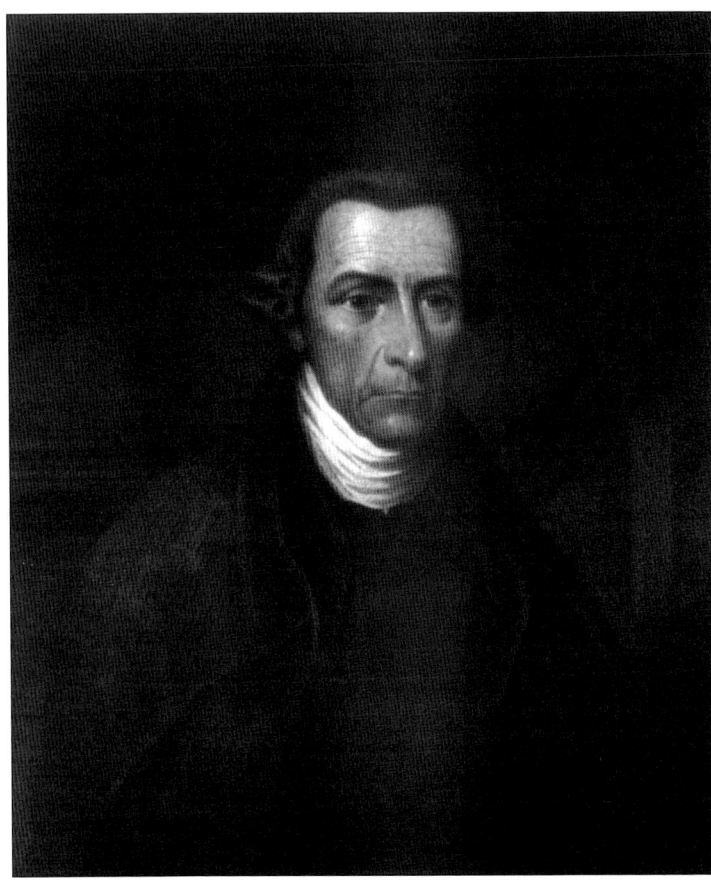

In 1775, Patrick Henry (pictured) made St. John's Church a famous place. Statesman Edward Carrington was in attendance, and legend has it that the church was so packed that he had to stand outside, by one of the windows, to hear Henry's speech. It is also said that Carrington was so moved by the speech that he requested to be buried by that same window. (Courtesy of the Library of Congress.)

The graveyard located at St. John's Church was originally used for members of the church and Richmond aristocratic society. Church burials were reserved for the wealthy. The burials at St. John's include Elizabeth Poe, Edgar Allan Poe's mother, who was a Richmond actress. It is said that no one knows her exact burial spot at St. John's, but a marker speaks to her importance there. (Courtesy of the Library of Congress.)

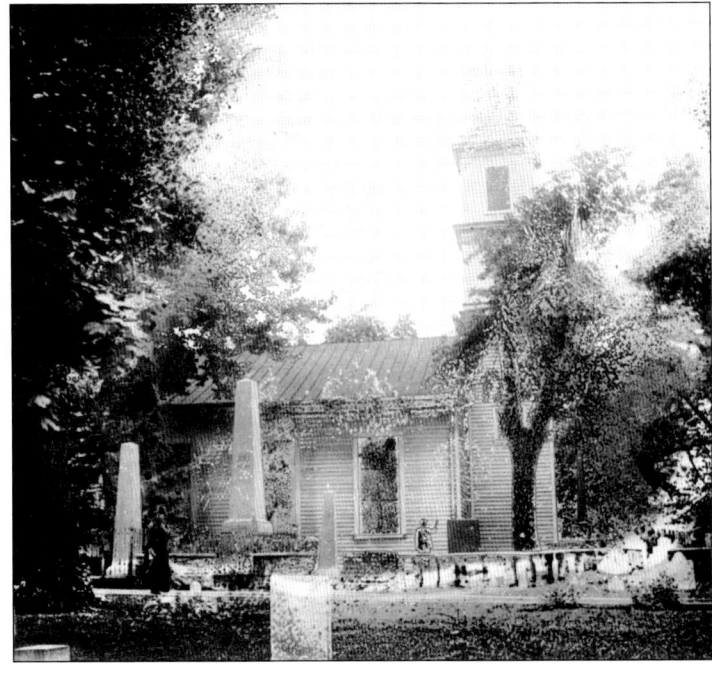

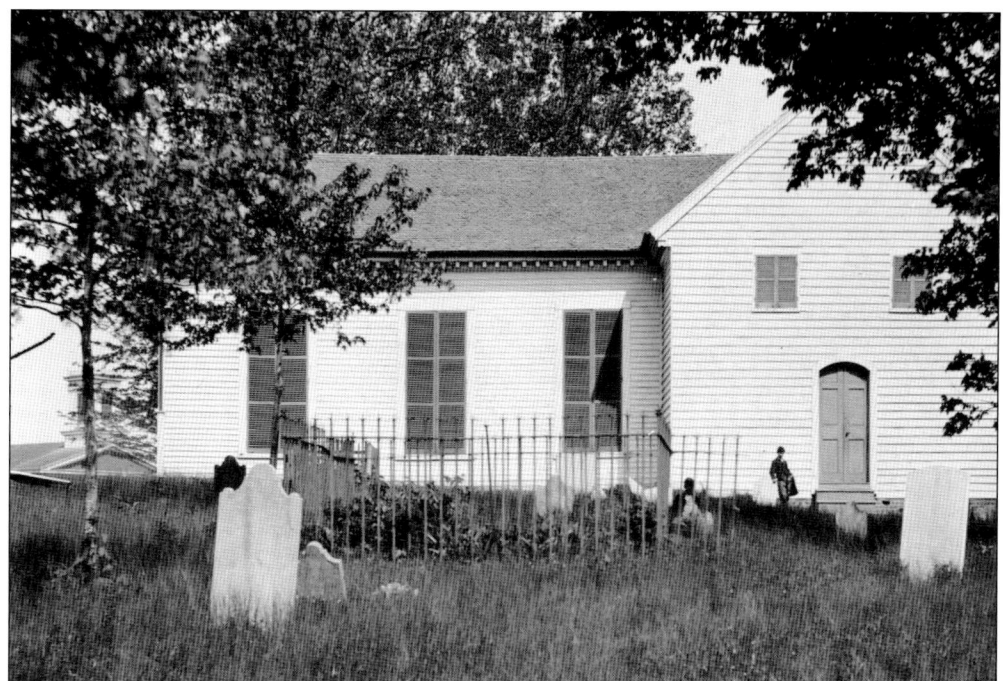

St. John's Church is one of the most important places in the city of Richmond and in the United States as a whole. Over 100 leaders and politicians from all over the country were in attendance for what would become one of the greatest speeches of all time. Patrick Henry's "Give Me Liberty or Give Me Death" speech would forever change Richmond and the country. It is seen by many as the beginning of the American Revolution. (Courtesy of the Library of Congress.)

The burial grounds at St. John's were full by the beginning of the 19th century. The walls that surround the church and graveyard are incredibly extensive and remained strong throughout the Revolutionary War and the Civil War. The gates of St. John's Church remain undamaged and forever strong, along with the history there. (Courtesy of the Library of Congress.)

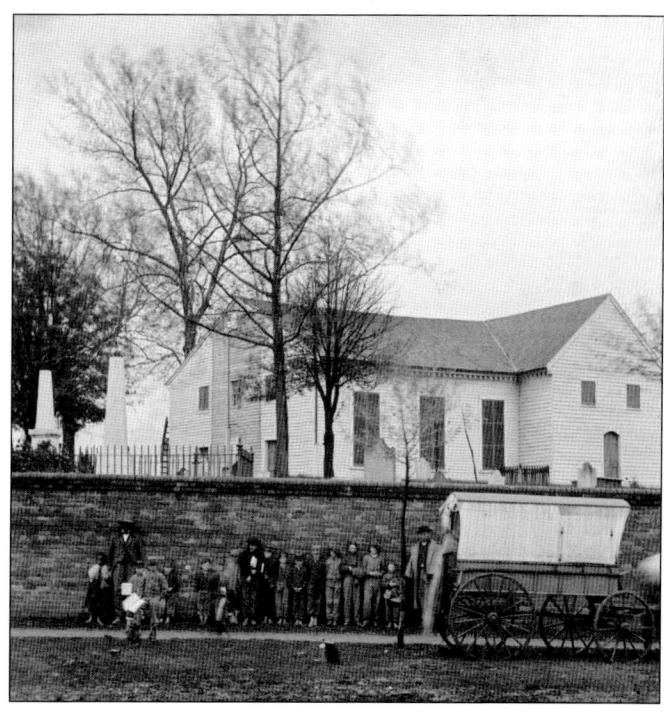

Though made famous by Patrick Henry, St. John's Church has ties to quite a few memorable members of Richmond society buried there. Once called Richmond Church, the church was renamed in 1829. Its graveyard remained a public burial ground until 1822. Elizabeth Poe, biological mother of Edgar Allan Poe, is buried in the graveyard. Her tombstone is near the church where Henry gave his speech. (Courtesy of the Library of Congress.)

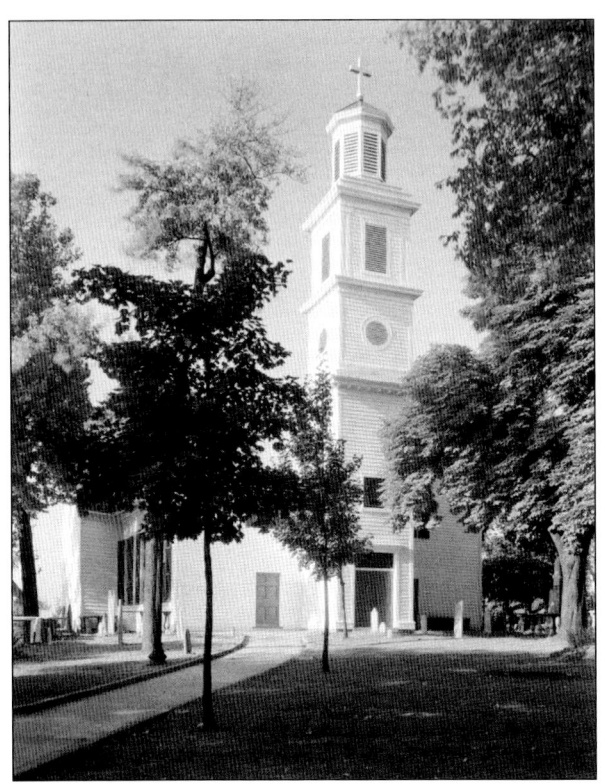

Elizabeth Poe, buried at St. John's Church, was the biological mother of Edgar Allan Poe. An actress in Richmond, she died of tuberculosis at a very early age. Frances K. Allan, seen here, was Poe's adopted mother. She is buried in Shockoe Hill Cemetery in Richmond. (Courtesy of the Library of Congress.)

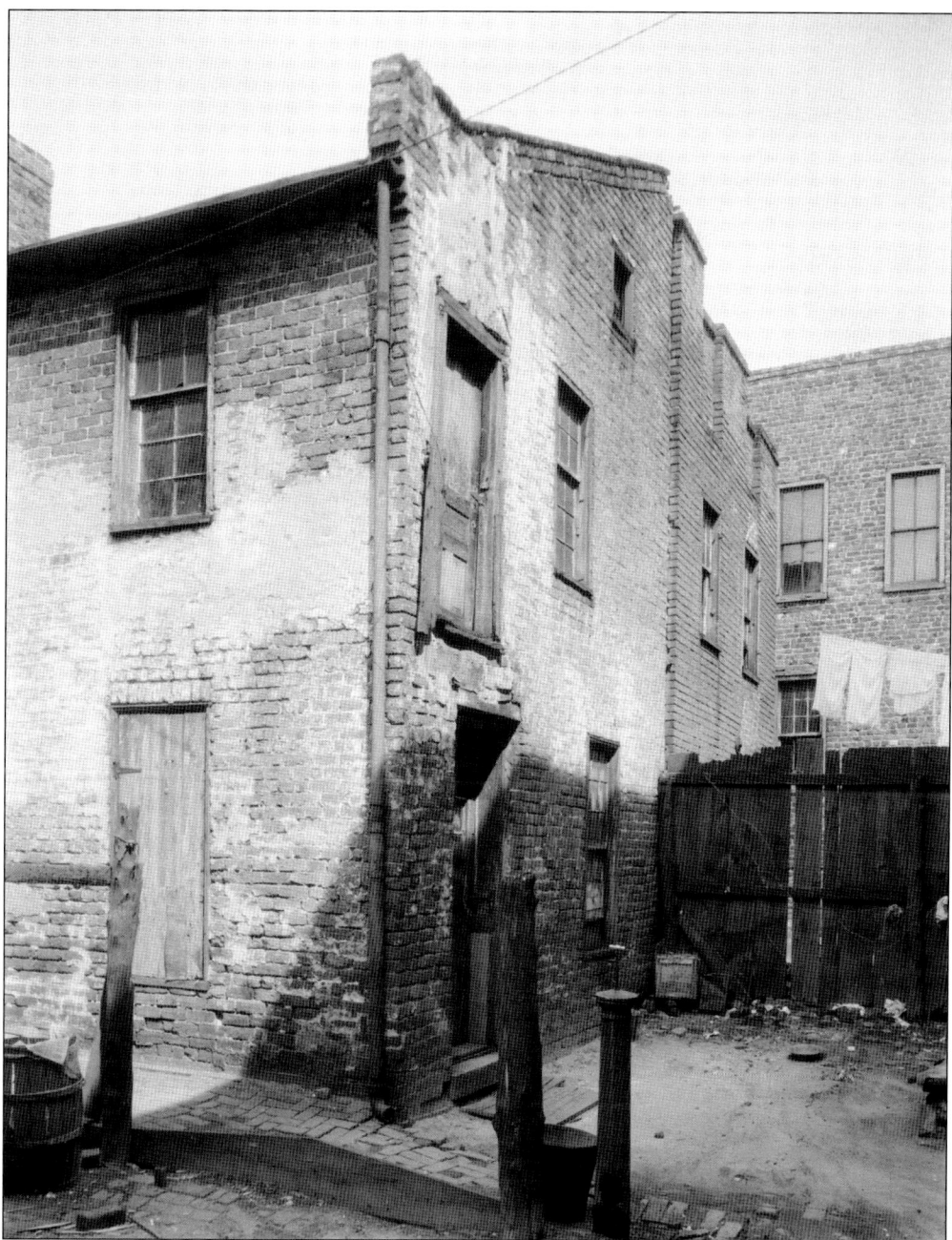

Elizabeth Poe, one of the many notable people buried at St. John's Church, lived in Richmond for most of her life. This photograph depicts the boardinghouse where she last lived. Legend has it that she died in the Richmond Theatre fire of 1811, since she was an actress there. But she actually died of an illness prior to the fire. (Courtesy of the Library of Congress.)

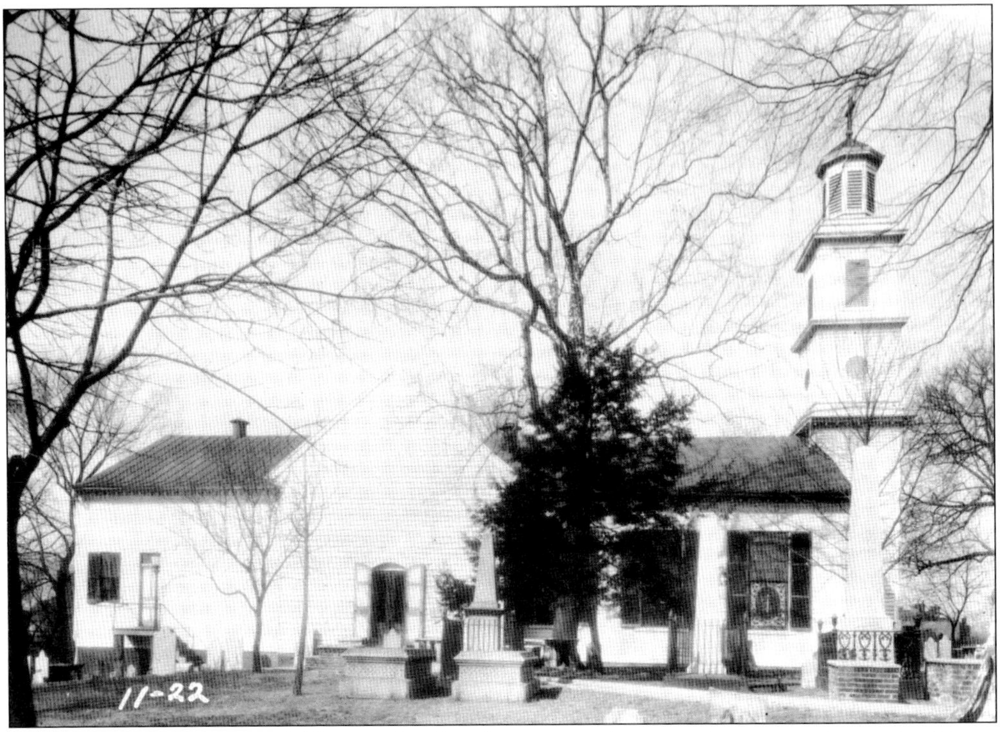

St. John's Church, a beautiful historic landmark, captures the eyes of many tourists and residents in Richmond. The history of the church is vast, as is that of graveyard, with over 3,000 people buried there. From paupers to theater actors and politicians, St. John's still welcomes families to bury their dead here. (Courtesy of the Library of Congress.)

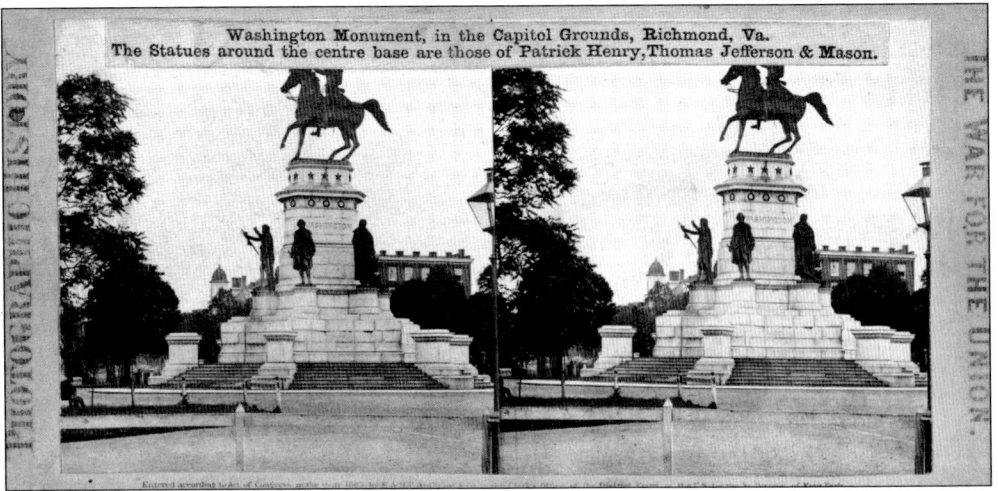

The grounds at the capitol in Richmond are a living landmark to Virginia and early European American history. Home to the Virginia General Assembly since 1788, the neoclassical capitol building was designed by Thomas Jefferson. The Washington statue in the middle of the capitol's entrance is made of granite and represents freedom and the history of Virginia. There is also a statue of Patrick Henry, who made St. John's Church famous. (Courtesy of the Library of Congress.)

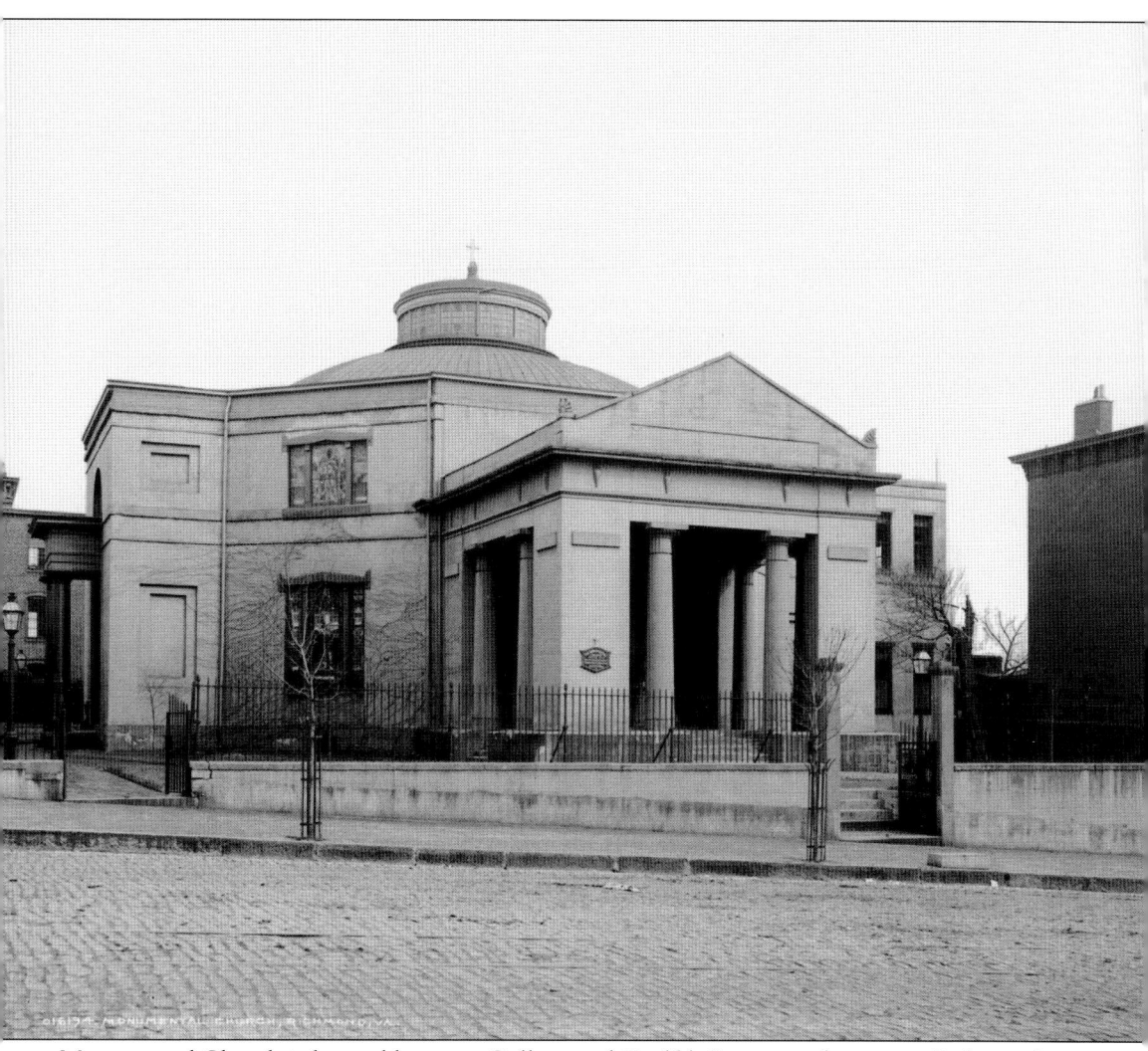

Monumental Church is located between College and Twelfth Streets in downtown Richmond. It was built between 1812 and 1814 as a monument to those who were killed in the Richmond Theatre fire in 1811. The structure now serves as both a church and a crypt. The crypt is located beneath the sanctuary and holds the remains of those who died in the fire. (Courtesy of the Library of Congress.)

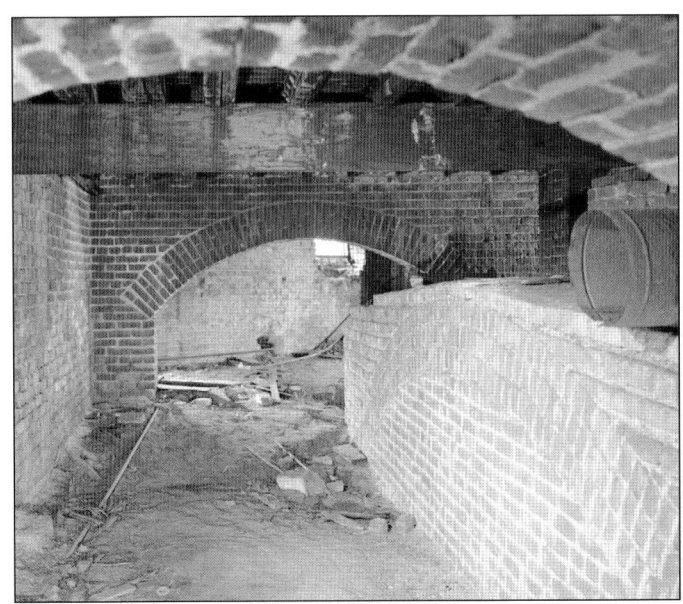

The site of Monumental Church was initially the Richmond Theatre. Many notable people attended plays in the theater, including Patrick Henry, James Madison, James Monroe, and John Marshall. When a fire broke out in the theater in 1811, a total of 72 people were killed. Most of their remains are located in the brick crypt located beneath the church's sanctuary. At the time, the fire was considered one of the worst urban disasters in American history. (Courtesy of the Library of Congress.)

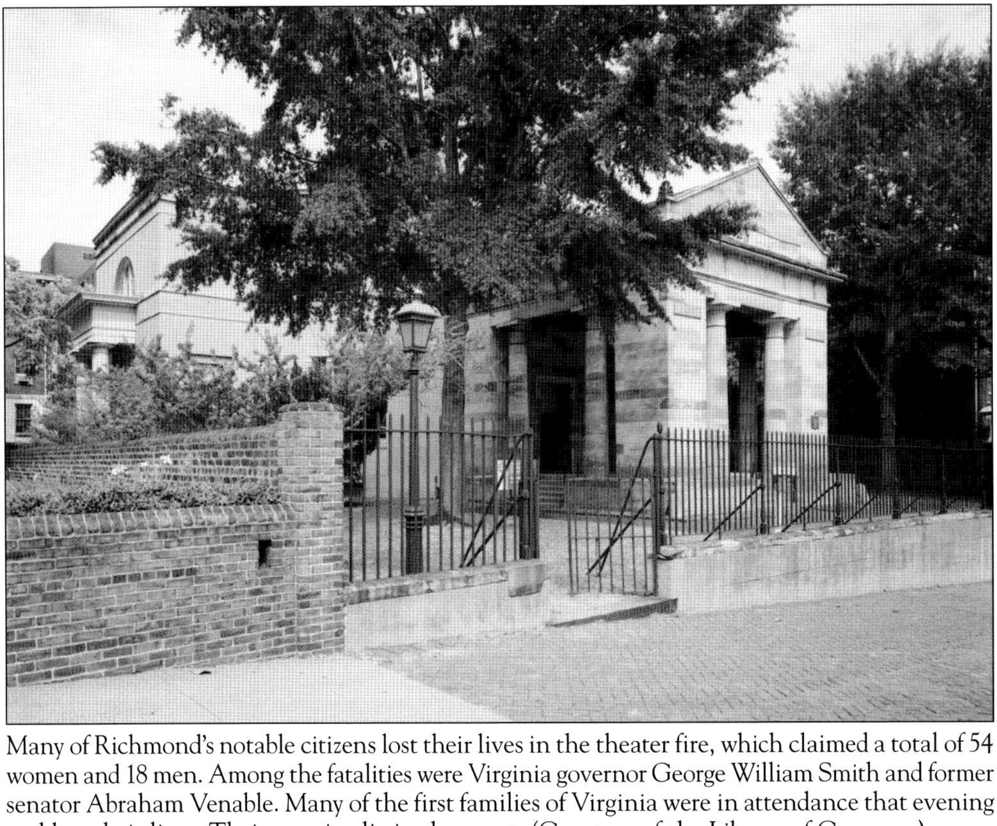

Many of Richmond's notable citizens lost their lives in the theater fire, which claimed a total of 54 women and 18 men. Among the fatalities were Virginia governor George William Smith and former senator Abraham Venable. Many of the first families of Virginia were in attendance that evening and lost their lives. Their remains lie in the crypt. (Courtesy of the Library of Congress.)

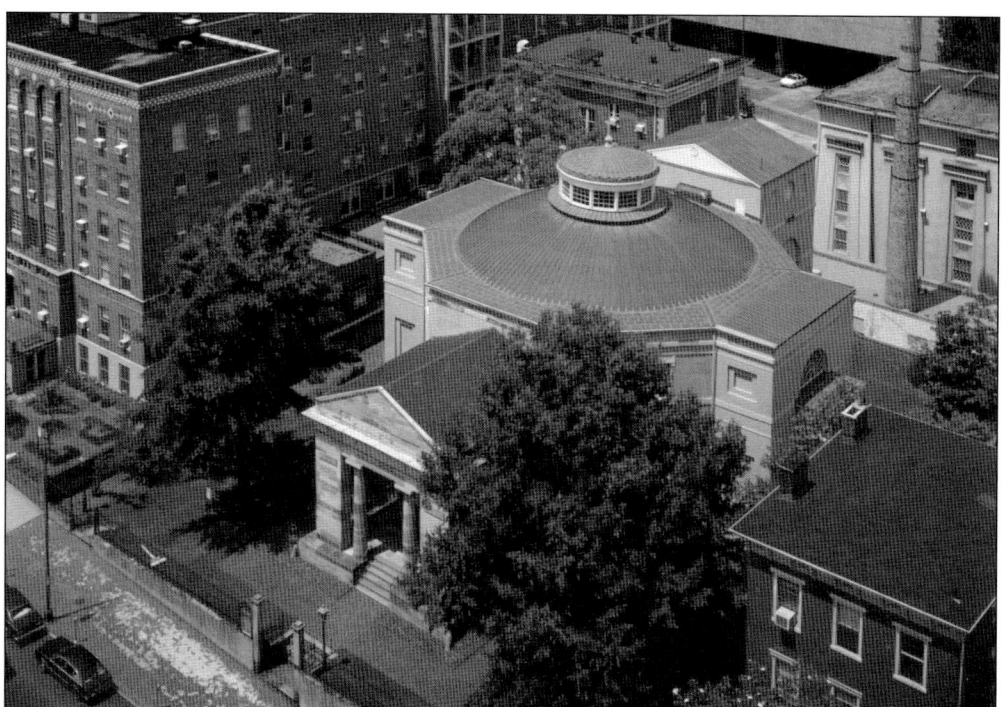

Controversy surrounded the building of Monumental Church. Many citizens of Richmond were not happy with the idea of building a church on top of a crypt, on the site where many people lost their lives. After much debate, eventually, the decision to build was made. The church was intended as a memorial to those who lost their lives. Justice John Marshall commissioned the church. (Courtesy of the Library of Congress.)

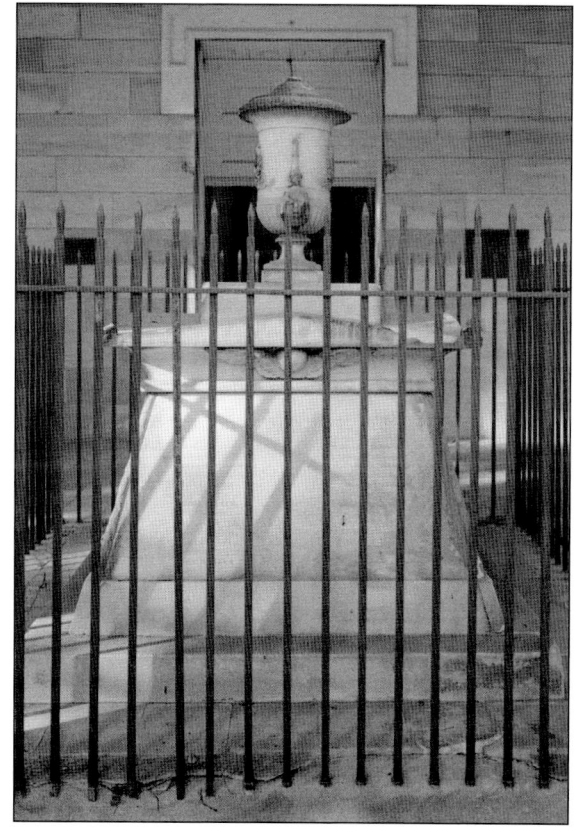

Monumental Church was one of the first churches in Richmond to offer a Sunday school program. Edgar Allan Poe and his family were often in attendance here. This was one of the most popular churches for the well-to-do citizens of Richmond. Serving as a place of worship as well as a site for social gathering, it is now a National Historic Landmark and is listed in the National Register of Historic Places. (Courtesy of the Library of Congress.)

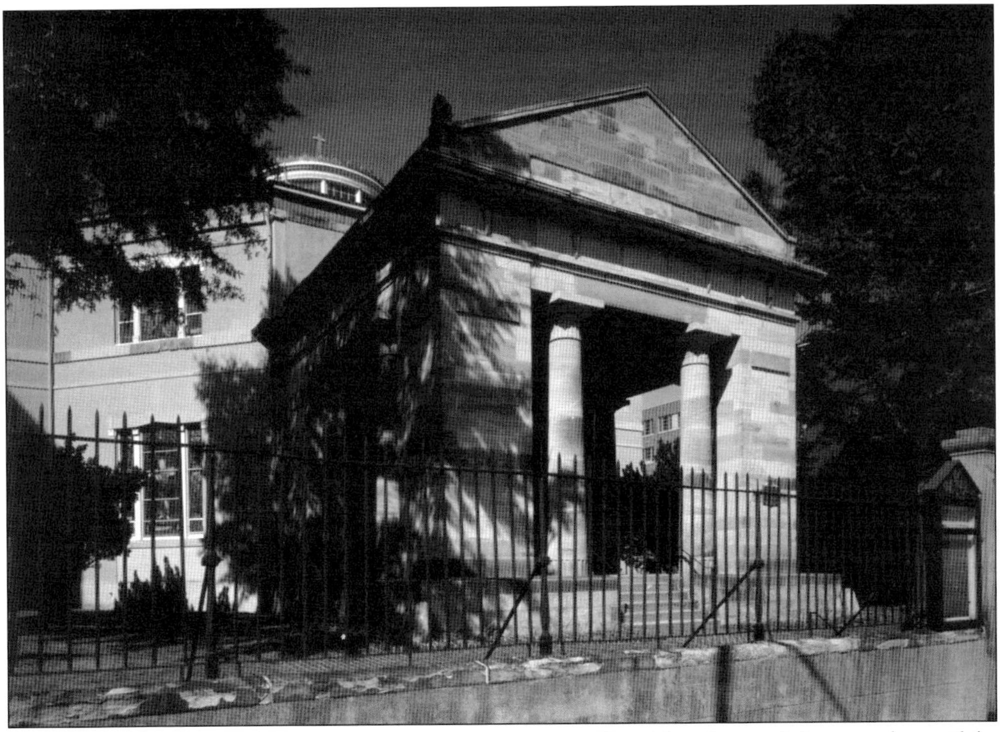

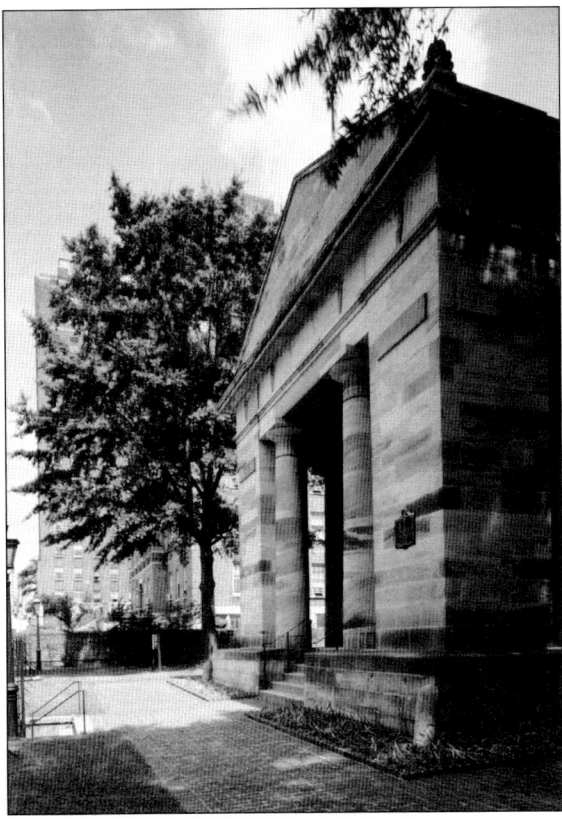

Considered one of the most beautiful churches in Richmond, Monumental Church has also been said to be one of the most haunted places in the city. The remains of those who lost their lives on the night of the fire are contained in beautiful mahogany boxes that are walled into the basement of the church. This is where many of the legends and stories began. (Courtesy of the Library of Congress.)

There have been quite a few ghost stories associated with the Richmond Theatre fire of 1811. Many church workers and paranormal experts have confessed to having eerie experiences at Monumental Church. Voices have been heard coming from the balcony of the church, as have unexplained noises. Many of the doors slam shut without anyone being near them, and some of the doors will open and close freely. (Courtesy of the Library of Congress.)

Church workers have told stories of leaving their tools in one spot, only to have the tools disappear and reappear in a different place. Some workers have heard heavy footsteps in the church, scaring some workers to the extent that they never again returned to Monumental Church. Caretakers have mentioned that motion detectors have gone off at random times without a person in sight. (Courtesy of the Library of Congress.)

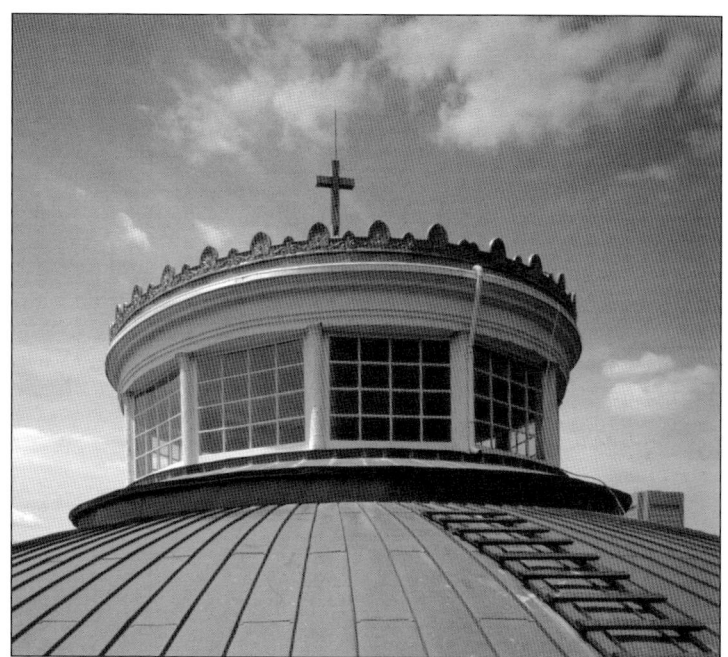

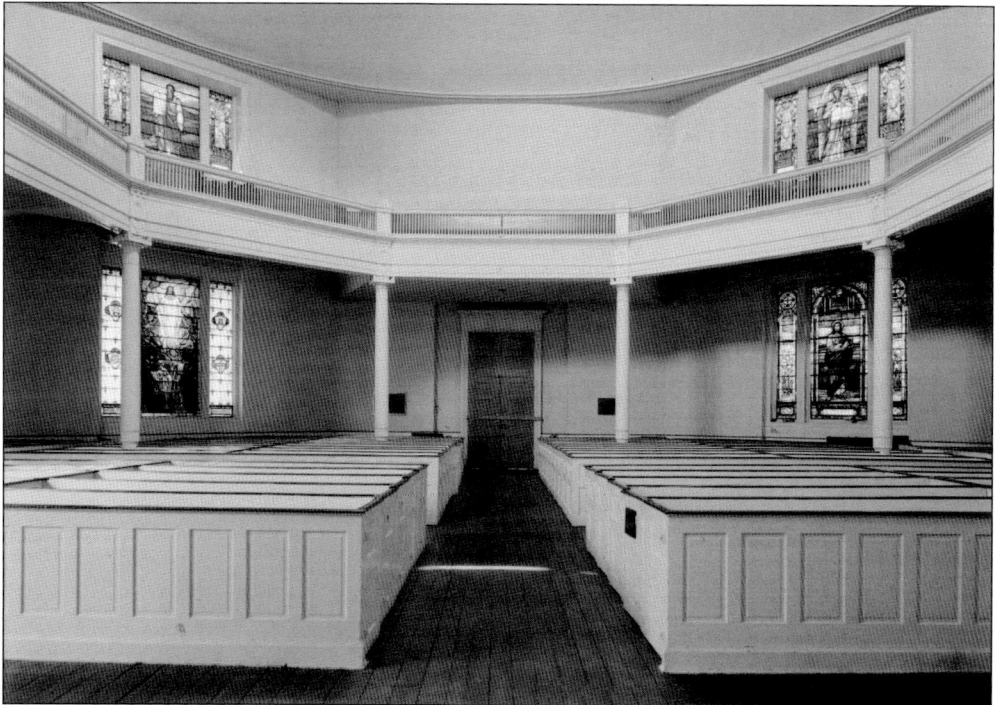

Monumental Church is still open to the public, and many ceremonies still take place inside. Whether or not the church is really haunted will remain a mystery; only those who have seen or heard anything similar to a spiritual encounter can attest to their experiences. Many workers have confessed to seeing people and objects appear out of thin air and of hearing noises, but these remain legend, as none of the accounts have been written down. (Courtesy of the Library of Congress.)

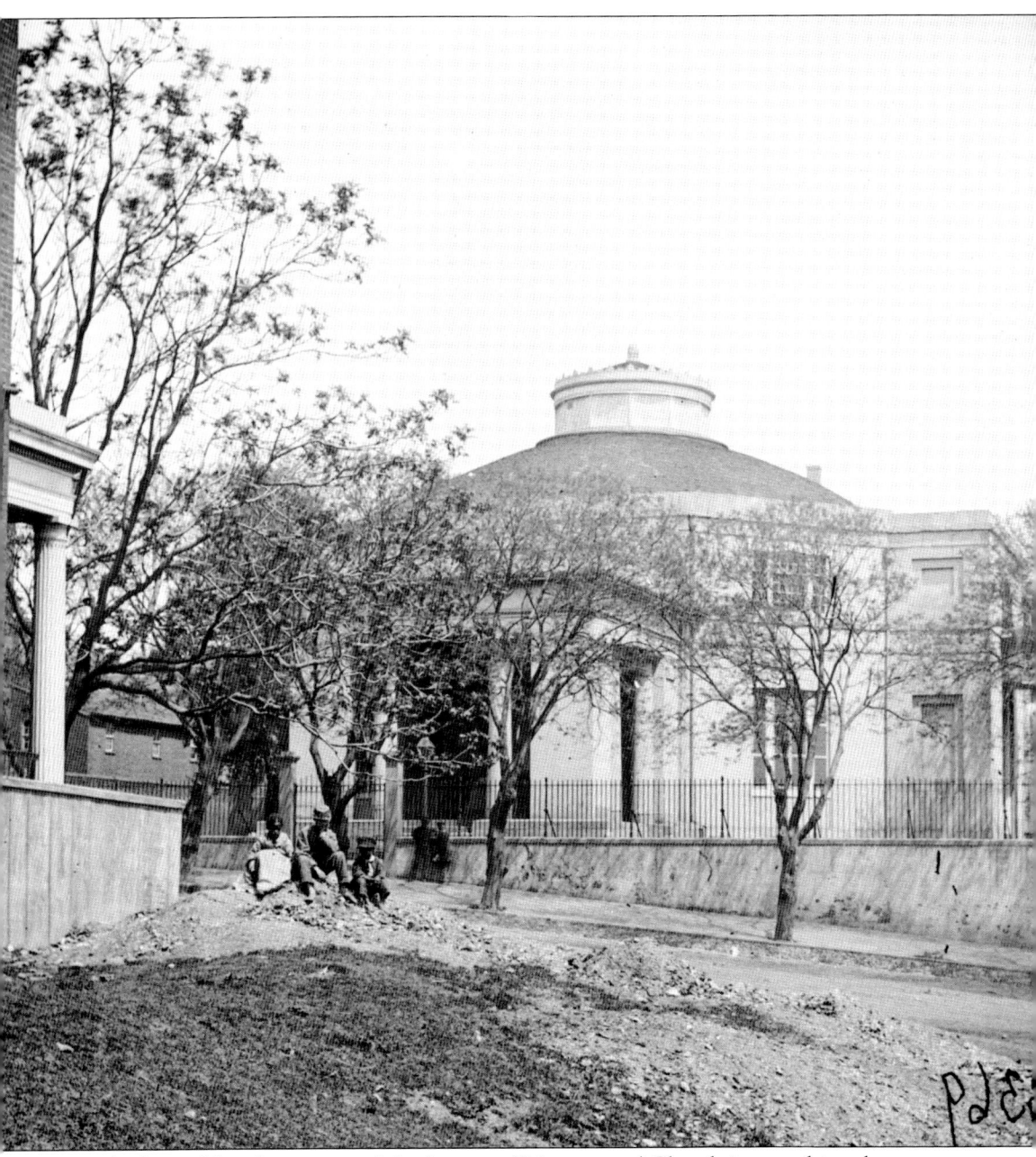

The beautiful architecture and the history of Monumental Church is something that everyone who visits Richmond must witness. The church hosts many types of ceremonies, including weddings and funerals. Visitors frequently explore the church in order to see if any of the legends of hauntings are true. (Courtesy of the Library of Congress.)

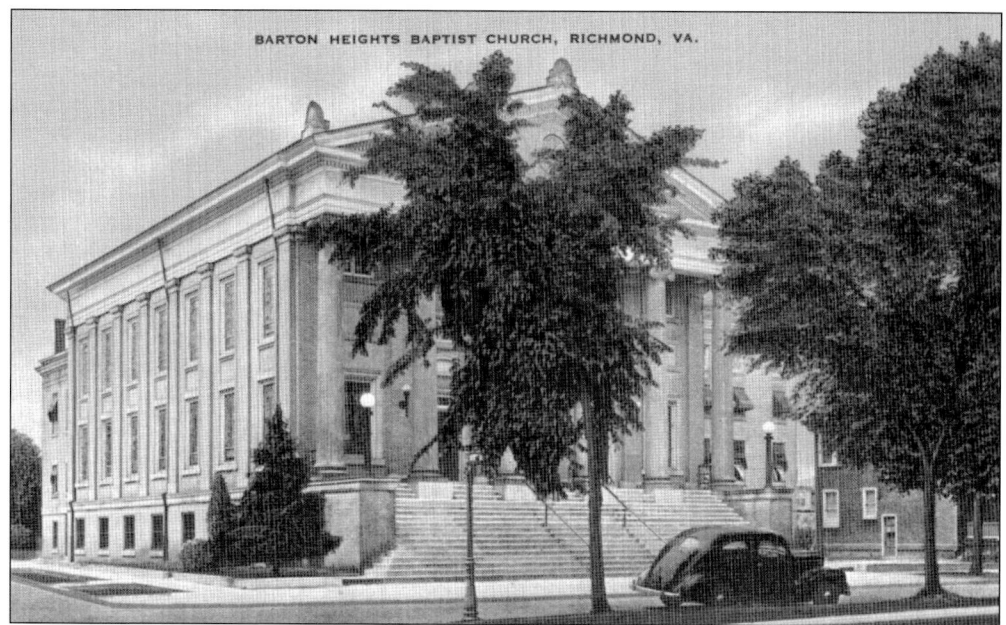

Barton Heights is one of the most historic cemeteries in Richmond. It is made up of six contiguous burial grounds that African American churches began to establish in 1815. Many notable African Americans are buried in these cemeteries. Ebenezer Baptist Church was one of the first churches to purchase land in one of these burial grounds, around 1858. The City of Richmond is now making improvements to the cemetery. (Courtesy of the Library of Congress.)

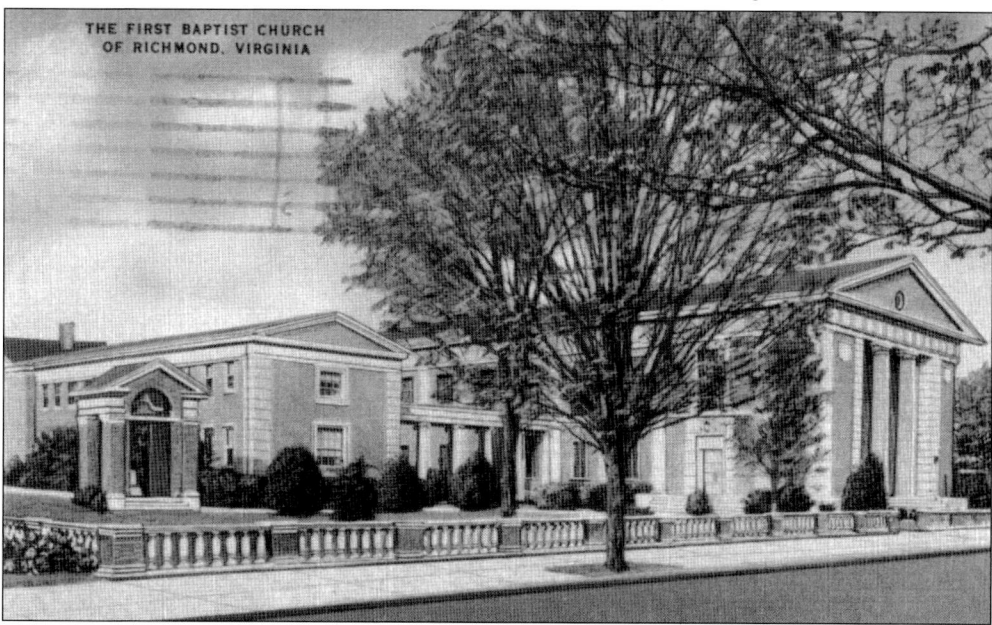

Richmond founder William Byrd II donated the land and timber necessary to build St. John's Church. Its graveyard is the first public cemetery in Richmond. The brick schoolhouse that is in the churchyard was used as a Sunday school for African American children. The records of the church and graveyard are located in the parish office, on the grounds of the church. (Courtesy of the Library of Congress.)

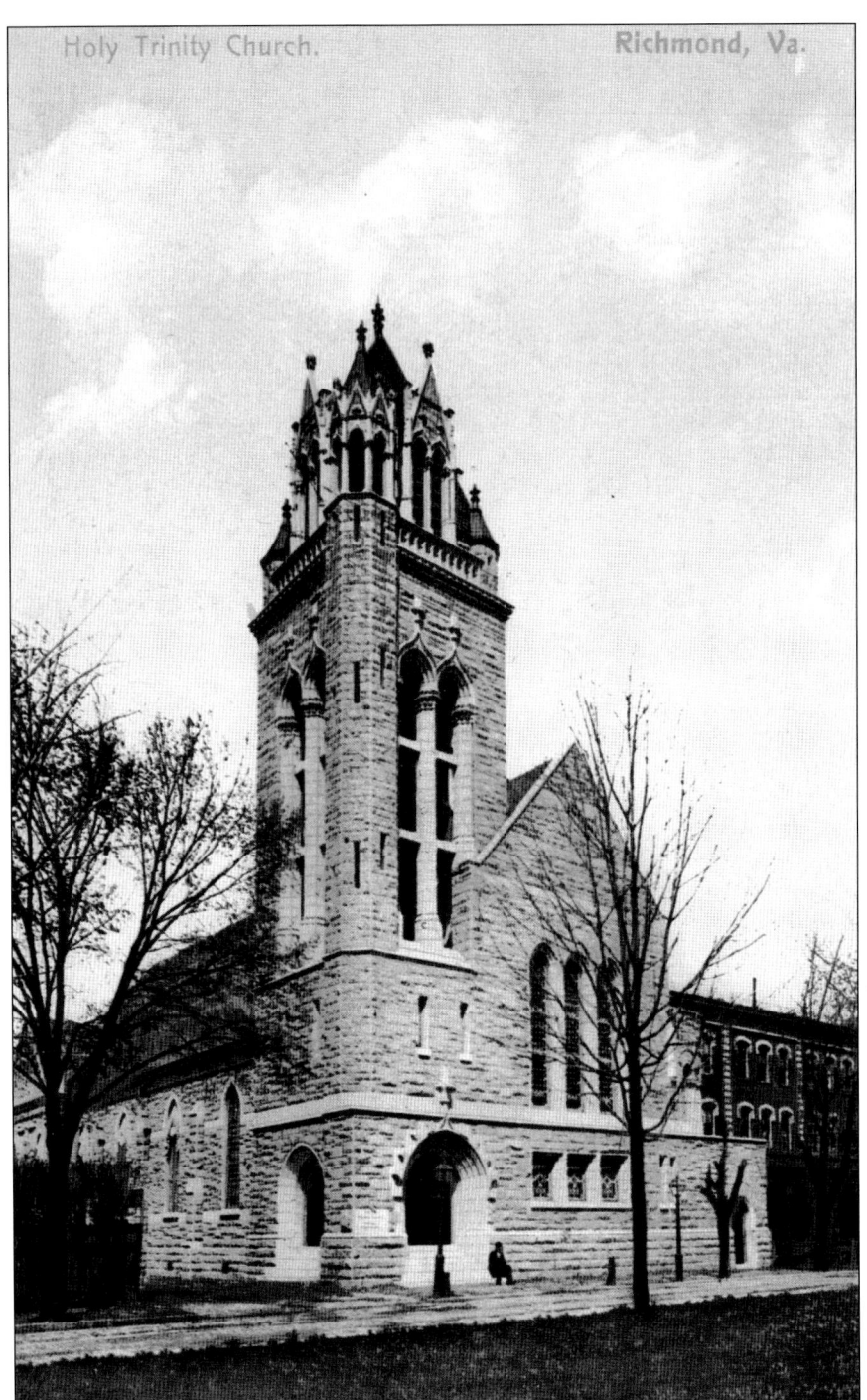

Grace and Trinity Church, built in the French Gothic Revival style, has been a landmark in the city since its construction. Many parishioners have worshipped there, and thousands have had their memorial services and their last hymn played under the great arches. None has been as elegantly memorialized as Indie Wray Gravatt, wife of the first rector. A stained-glass window was built in her honor, symbolizing faith, nature, love, and God. (Courtesy of the Library of Congress.)

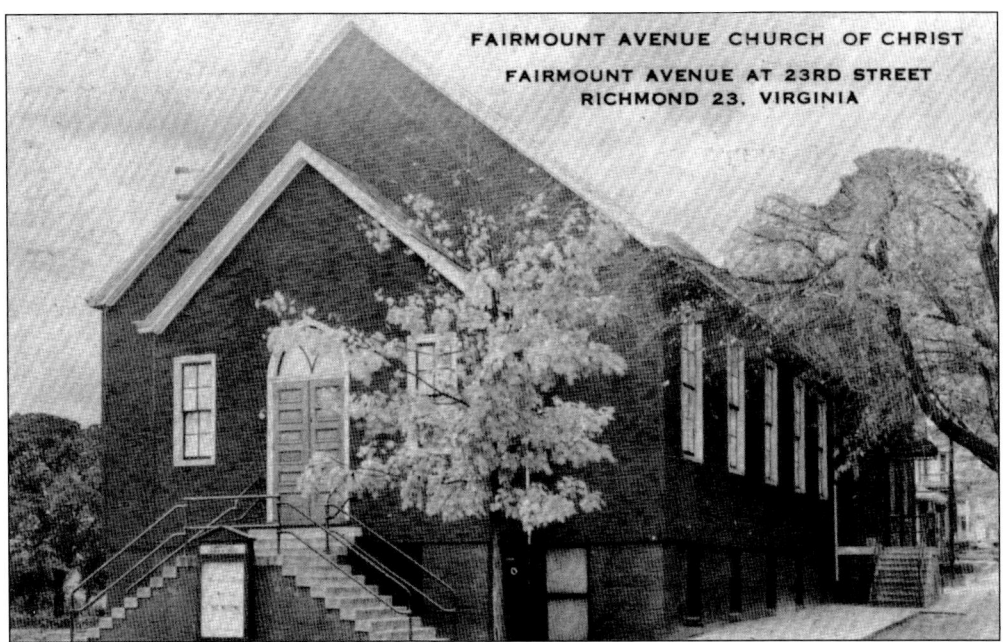

The steep steps leading into the Bethlehem Baptist Church at Fairmount Avenue give promise to the solace, friendship, and peace that lie behind the doors of this Richmond landmark. Like a blackboard that has been erased and washed multiple times, the church's community has changed. But the spirit of the congregation, while its members have perpetually lived and died, has remained the same. (Courtesy of the Library of Congress.)

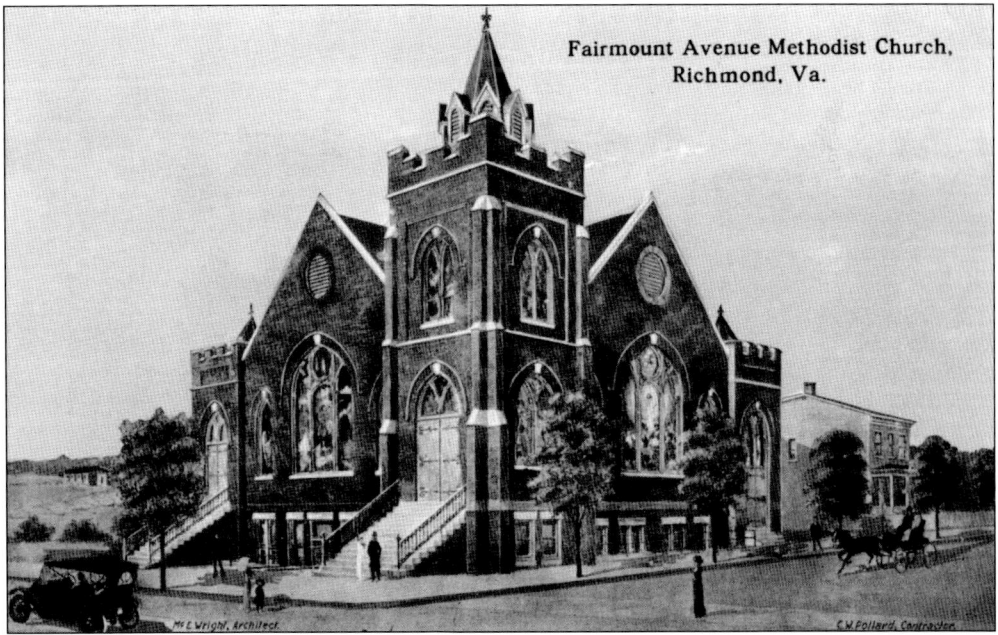

Fairmount Avenue Methodist Church was originally organized in 1889. Now known as Bethlehem Baptist Church, it is located in the heart of Richmond. The African American church originally had only 23 members in the congregation. This church is also associated with Evergreen Cemetery and Barton Heights. (Courtesy of the Library of Congress.)

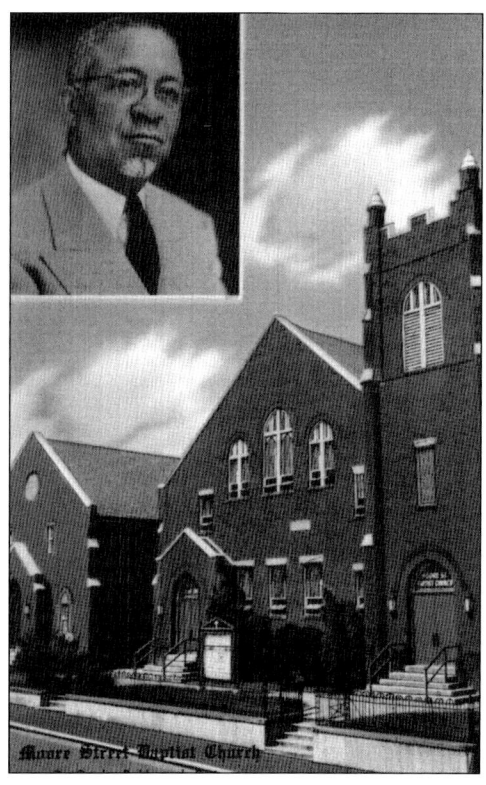

Moore Street Baptist Church is another historic church located in Richmond. Founded in 1875, it is one of the oldest African American churches in the city. The congregation is known for its rich interest in the Christian faith; people of every race and color are always welcome. Many of its deceased members have been buried in Evergreen and Barton Heights. (Courtesy of the Library of Congress.)

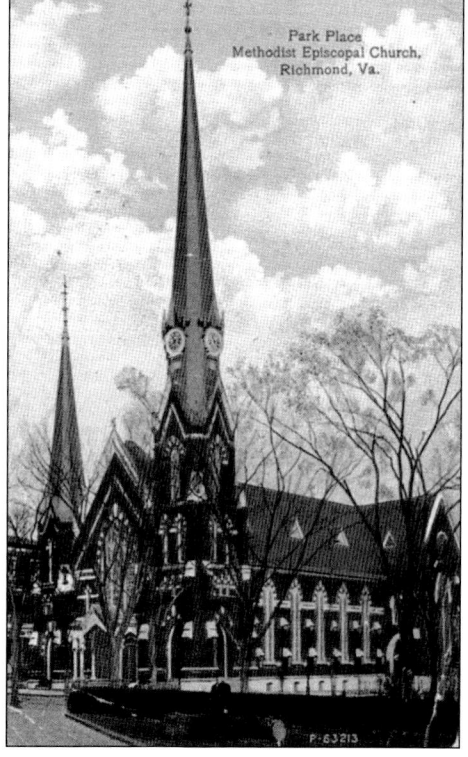

Located near the famous Monroe Park in Richmond on Franklin and Pine Streets, Park Place is one of the oldest churches in the city. Known for its beautiful and extravagant architecture, it is also one of Richmond's most historic places. Many members of the congregation have been buried in Hollywood Cemetery. (Courtesy of the Library of Congress.)

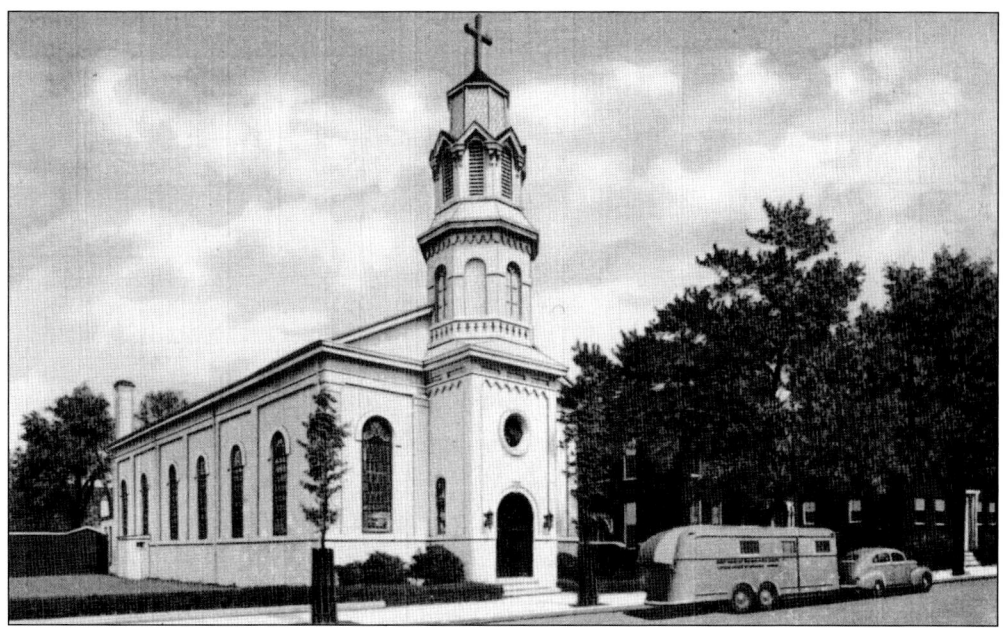

St. Mary's Catholic Church, located in the West End of Richmond, is known for offering an extensive education and worship service. There is a columbarium and consolation garden located directly next to the church's entrance. The church wanted a columbarium to be a part of the daily routine of the members of the church. One can pay respects to those who have passed on a daily basis. (Courtesy of the Library of Congress.)

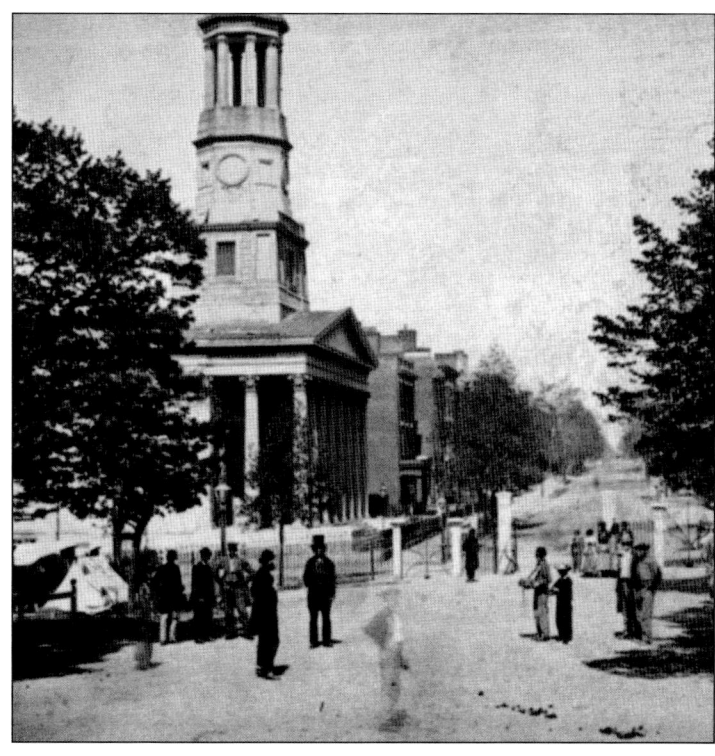

St. Paul's Episcopal Church is located near the capitol building in Richmond. Founded over 150 years ago, it held ceremonies of many kinds for freed and enslaved blacks— an unconventional practice at the time. It has a vast history and was the venue for the General Convention of the Episcopal Church in 1859. The church features a crypt where former bishops are laid to rest. (Courtesy of VCU James Branch Cabell Library Special Collections.)

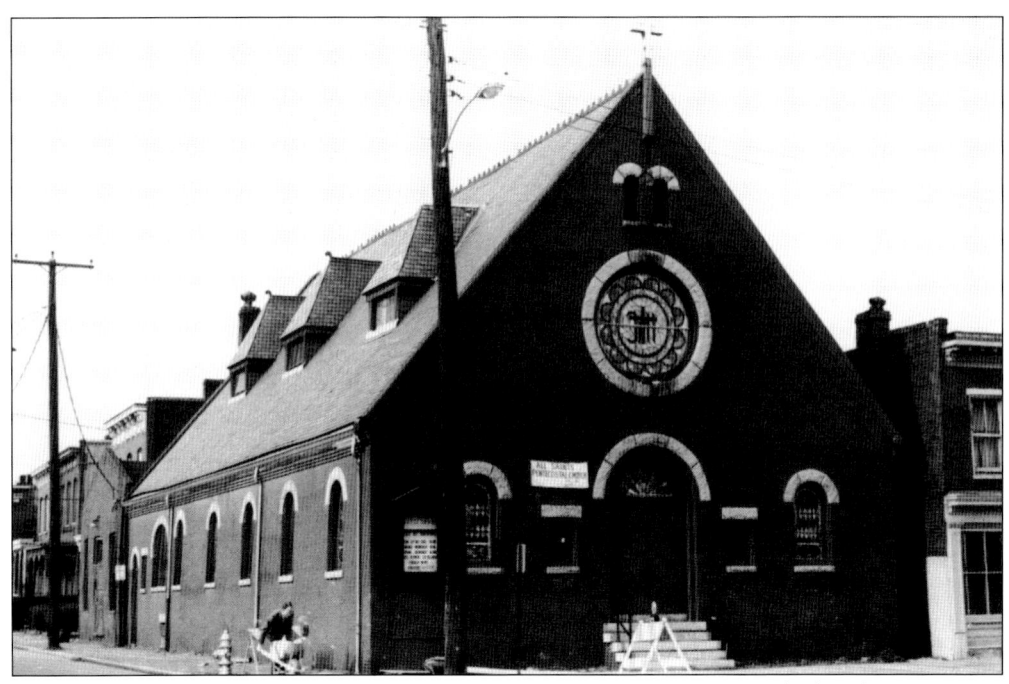

All Saints Episcopal Church was just an idea in 1883. Its mother church, Monumental Church, located in the Church Hill area, was expanding at such a high rate that the members decided to build another location. Monumental Church is known for being unique because of the crypt located in the floorboards of the church. In 1888, on Christmas Day, the church held its very first service. (Courtesy of VCU James Branch Cabell Special Collections.)

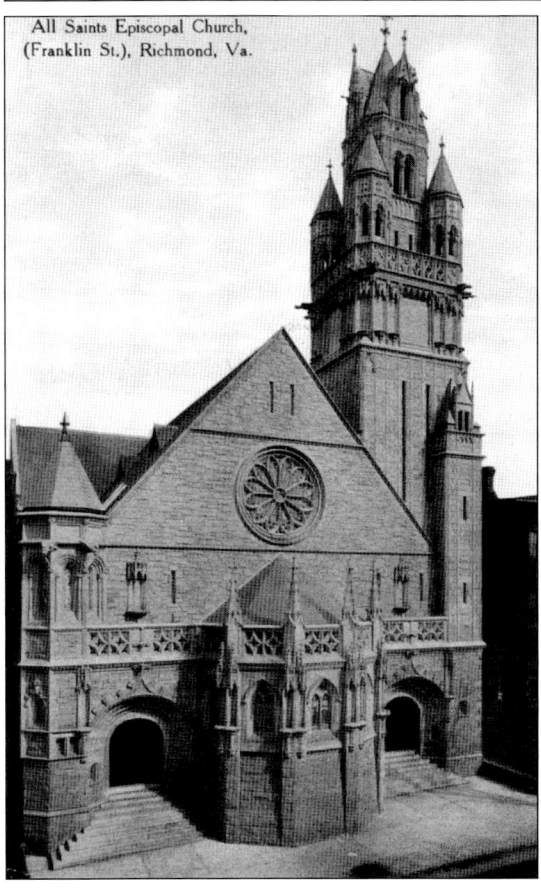

All Saints Episcopal Church, (Franklin St.), Richmond, Va.

All Saints Episcopal Church technically had four founders. One of those founders, Peter H. Mayo, is buried in Hollywood Cemetery. He was among the contributors who gave money to help build this church and then watched it grow. The other founders were J.N. Boyd, T.L. Atkinson, and Thomas Atkinson. All Saints has been affiliated with Hollywood Cemetery and Shockoe Hill Cemetery. (Courtesy of VCU James Branch Special Collections.)

Ebenezer Baptist Church is located in the historic Jackson Ward district of Richmond. The church was founded in 1858 as the daughter church of the First African Baptist Church of Richmond. The church's architect, Charles T. Russell, was the first African American to have a practice in Richmond. One of the church's main focuses was to educate African American children. Members of the church are buried throughout many of Richmond's black cemeteries. (Courtesy of the Library of Congress.)

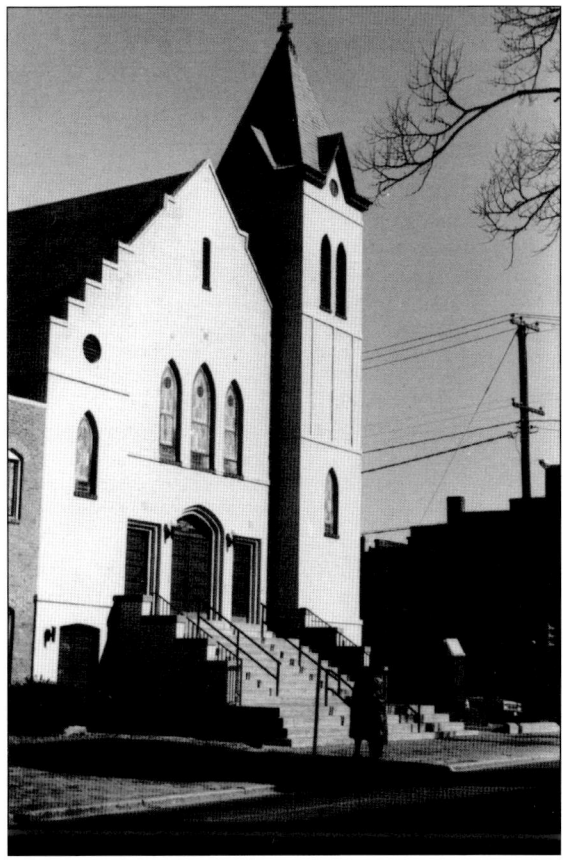

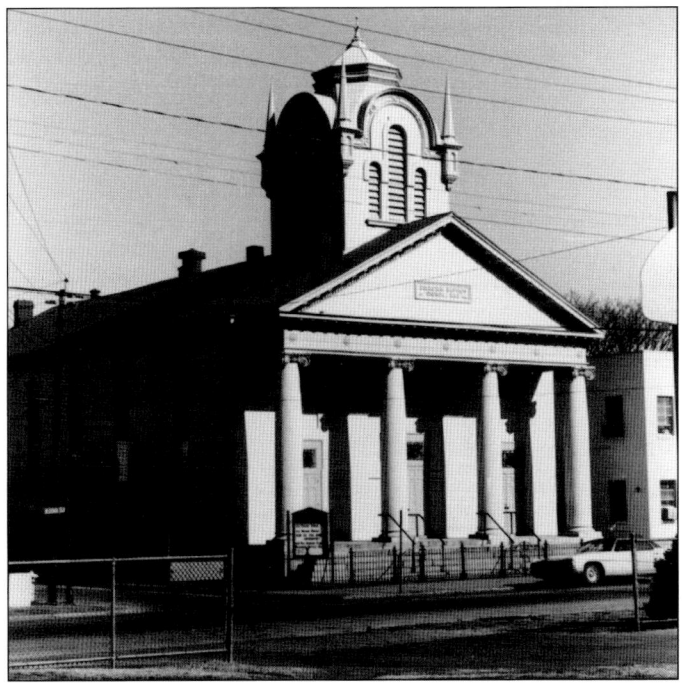

The Sharon Baptist Church is located in downtown Richmond on Leigh Street. It is the daughter church of the Second Baptist Church of Richmond and was established in 1890. Solely an African American church, it has even been visited by Pres. Barack Obama. Funeral ceremonies for members of the church are often held here, and its members are buried in many of Richmond's cemeteries, including Evergreen and Barton Heights. (Courtesy of the Library of Congress.)

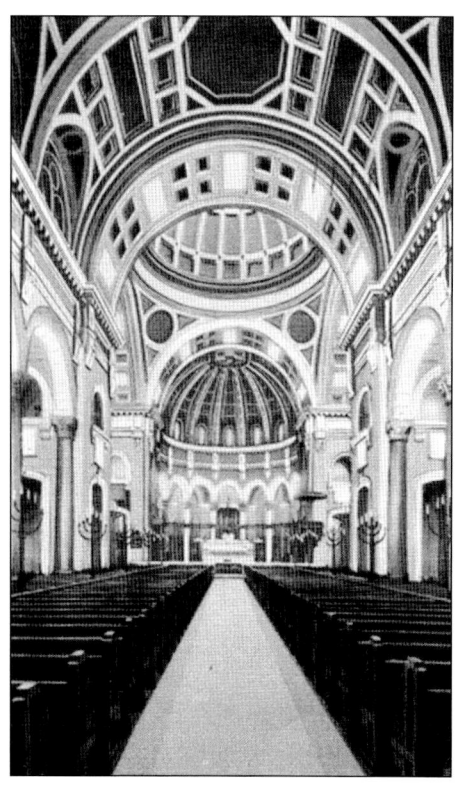

Designed by New York architect Joseph H. McGuire, Cathedral of the Sacred Heart was built in 1906. Sacred Heart remains an active Catholic parish to this day. It is also home to the Museum of Virginia Catholic History and is the official Catholic parish of Virginia Commonwealth University. Sacred Heart's crypt includes three former bishops of the diocese and members of the family of Thomas F. and Ida Barry Ryan, the cathedral's donors. (Courtesy of VCU James Branch Cabell Library Special Collections.)

The Cathedral of the Sacred Heart is the seat of the Catholic Diocese of Richmond. The Ryan family made a grand donation of $250,000 to have the church built. In 2014 dollars, that would equal around $14 million. The newly refurbished crypt and undercroft serves as a museum of the church as well as the resting place for former bishops of the church. (Courtesy of VCU James Branch Cabell Library Special Collections.)

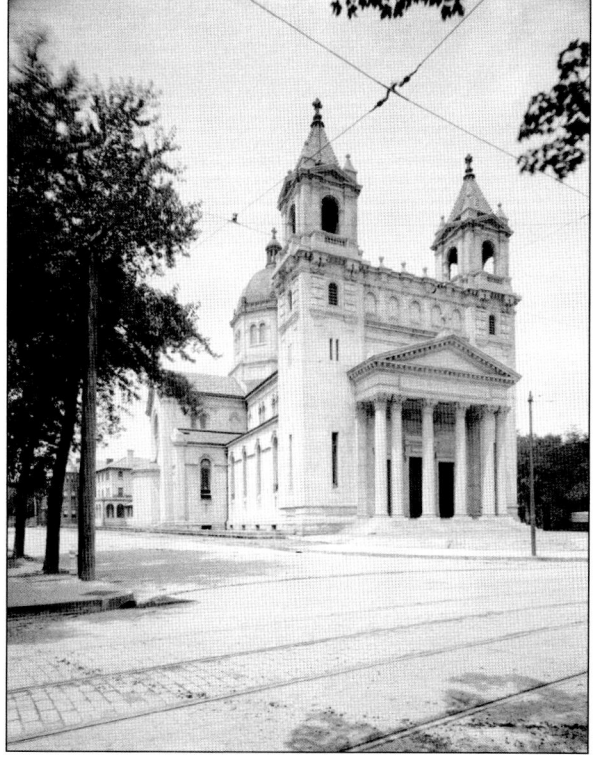

Deep in the crypt of the cathedral, visitors will find some of the original pieces of the cathedral's baptismal font. The church's original bowl was used for all of its baptisms. This baptismal font had been stored in the crypt for over 30 years. It has been returned to the original room where it first stood. (Courtesy of VCU James Branch Cabell Library Special Collections.)

In the crypt of the Cathedral of the Sacred Heart, there is also a museum where visitors can find various artifacts that belong to the cathedral and the Catholic Diocese of Richmond. (Courtesy of VCU James Branch Cabell Library Special Collections.)

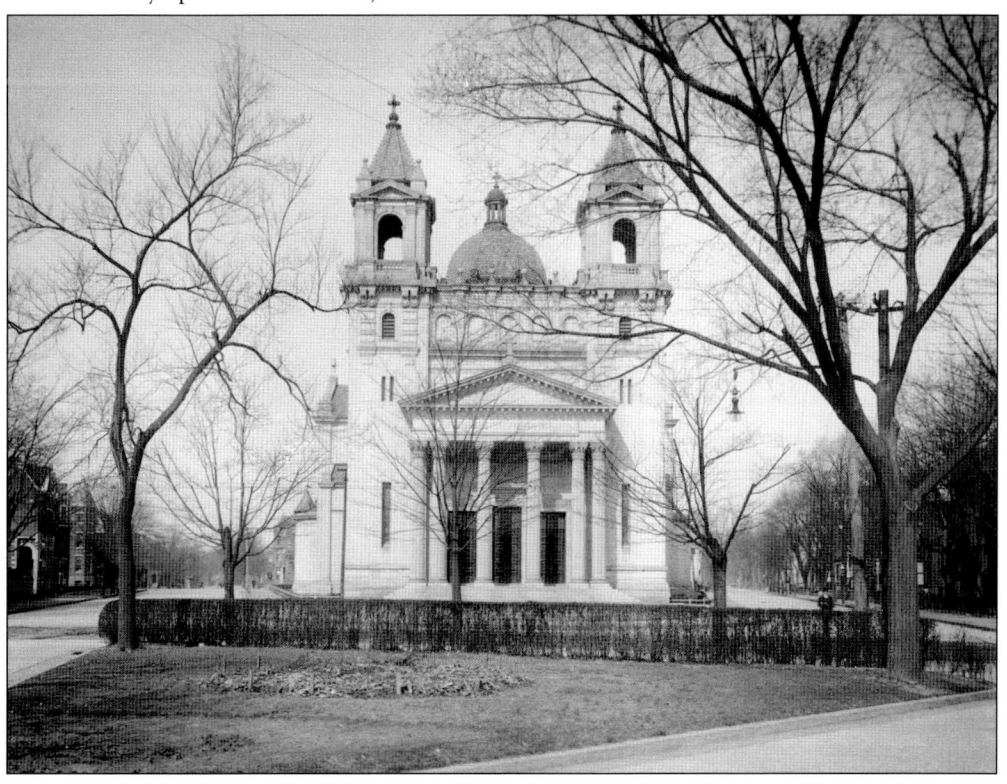

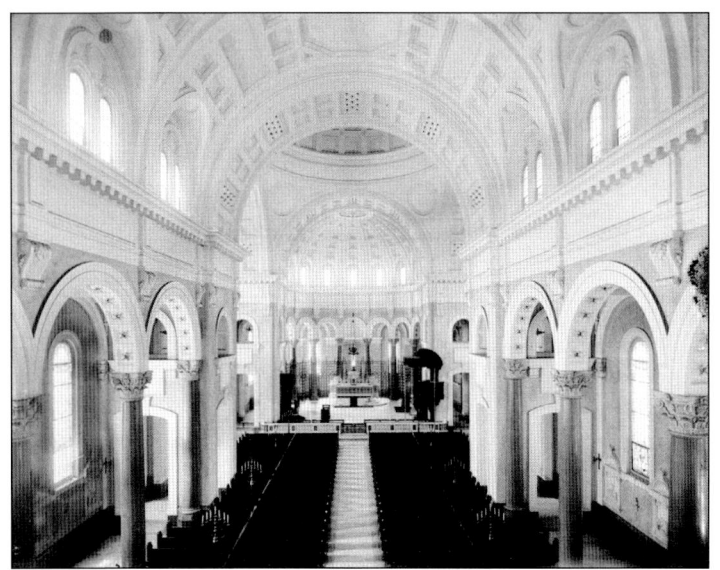

The Cathedral of the Sacred Heart is known for its beautiful organ and stained-glass windows. Masses and concerts are still held in the church, which sees many visitors. Many guests are frightened to find out that there is a crypt located in the lower floor of the cathedral, where three of the former bishops are laid to rest. (Courtesy of VCU James Branch Cabell Library Special Collections.)

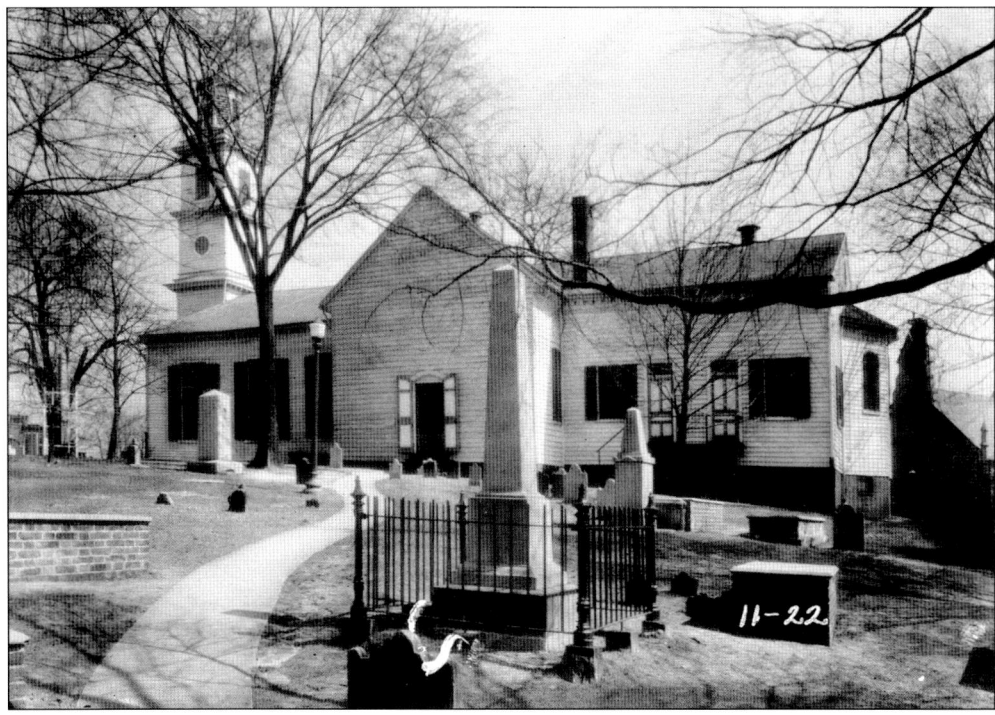

There are many church graveyards in the city of Richmond. The historic legacy of St. John's Church is celebrated and maintained by its active nonprofit foundation. Many Church Hill residents still attend St. John's services on Sundays. Historical and tour groups visit the grounds of the graveyard to learn about the history held inside and outside of these walls. (Courtesy of the Library of Congress.)

Four

THE CIVIL WAR AND NATIONAL CEMETERIES

Throughout the Civil War, soldiers were often buried where it was most convenient. Many tended to be buried where they died, since local cemeteries were not equipped for the hundreds of thousands of deaths in the war. Such burials tended to be hurried affairs involving shallow graves. As a result, soldiers' remains often became exposed in a short matter of time. Natural elements often brought the bodies to the surface. After the war, efforts were undertaken to properly bury these bodies.

   In 1867, Richmond National Cemetery was opened on Williamsburg Road in Richmond's East End. The federal government created the cemetery as one of several established after the Civil War to accommodate the thousands who died as a result of the conflict. Nearly 6,000 Union dead were reinterred at Richmond National Cemetery. They had initially been buried at battlefields, POW camps, and cemeteries throughout the area. Most of the graves remain anonymous. A keeper's lodge was built at Richmond National Cemetery in 1870. Veterans from America's foreign wars are also buried at the cemetery, which is under the care of the National Cemetery Administration in the US Department of Veterans Affairs. The cemetery is closed to new interments.

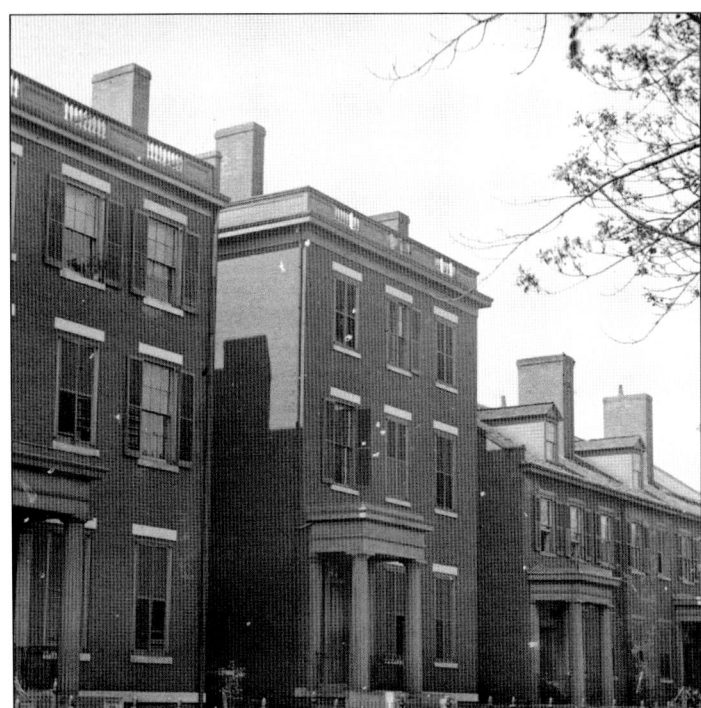

Robert E. Lee marched thousands of Virginians into battle, knowing that many of them would never see their wives, children, or families again. Many bodies were buried in proper military fashion. Hollywood Cemetery and Richmond National Cemetery received their first and final influx of dead soldiers, respectively. Such sacred grounds indicate the destructive power of war, with row after row of inexpensive tombstones. This photograph depicts the home of Robert E. Lee in Richmond. (Courtesy of the Library of Congress.)

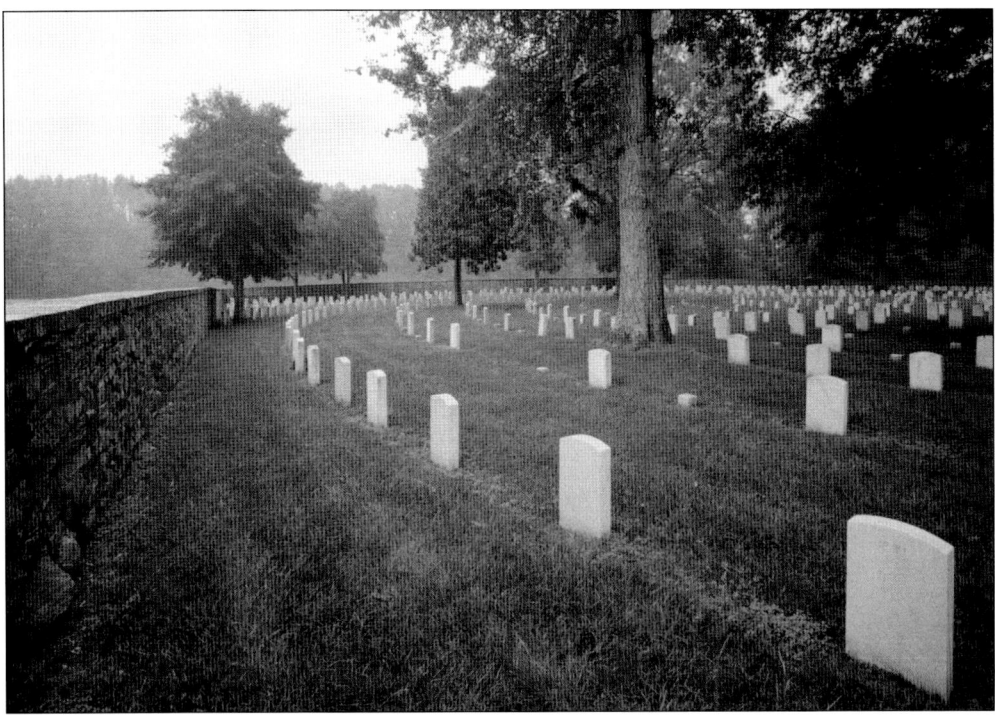

Proper burials for soldiers who died in the Civil War were not always easy. A lot of these men lost their lives in such a manner that their remains were not easy to identify. Monuments throughout the city, in graveyards and cemeteries, indicate how much these men meant to Richmond. The city and its citizens have helped to carry out their legacies. (Courtesy of the Library of Congress.)

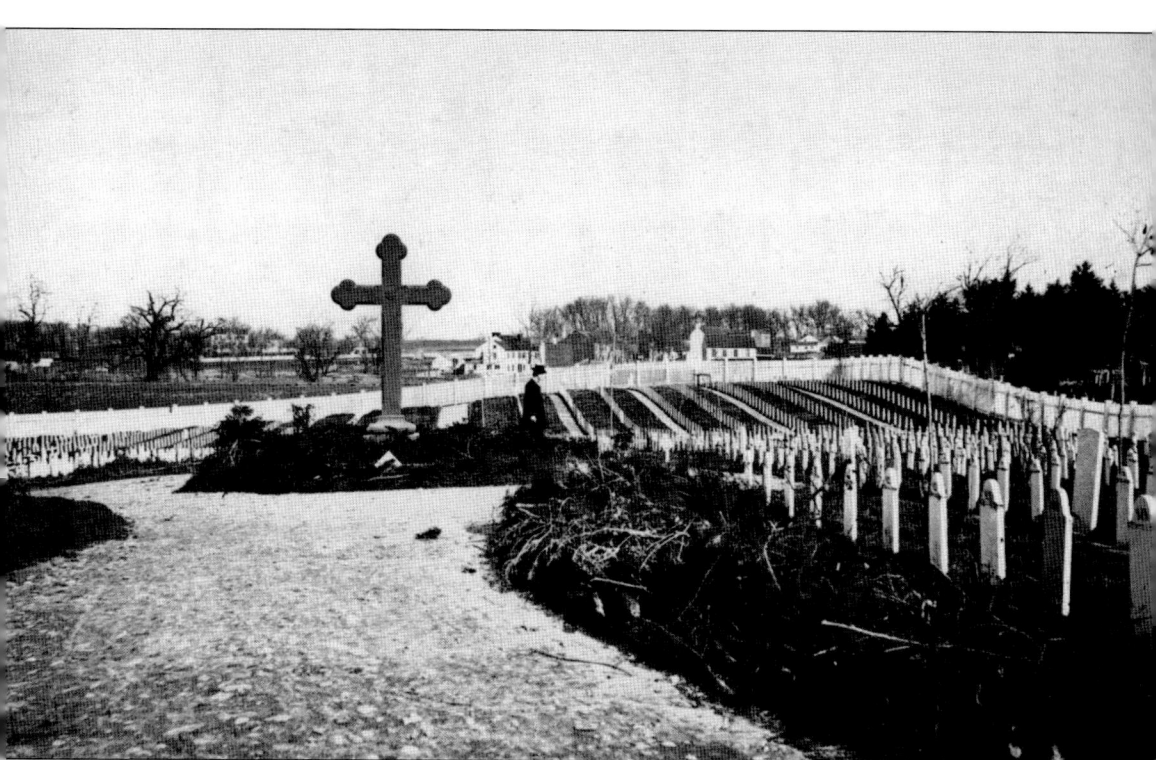

The Union army suffered heavy losses in and around Richmond. Some men died instantly from gunshot wounds, while others died from infections resulting from these wounds. Some soldiers died of exposure, and others succumbed to hunger. Fatalities in the Civil War were also attributed to death by fire and, in some cases, simply losing the will to live in horrendous circumstances. Shown here is a Union cemetery in Alexandria, Virginia, about 115 miles north of Richmond, near Washington, DC. (Courtesy of the Library of Congress.)

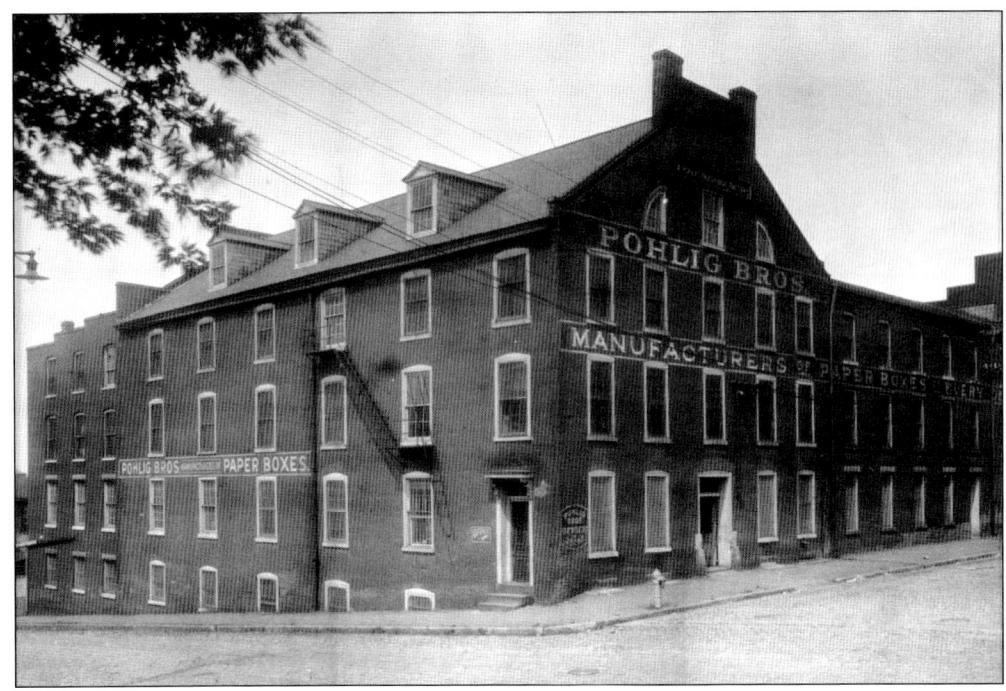

On a cold February day in 1865, Capt. Richard Ewell of the Army of Northern Virginia dispatched orders to burn all of the tobacco warehouses in Richmond, such as this one owned by Pohlig Bros. Manufacturers. The flames took to the tobacco, and the fires spread, eventually incinerating the city. Only the Church Hill neighborhood was spared. The burning went on for almost a month. Citizens still in the city either moved on or stayed to bury their dead. (Courtesy of the Library of Congress.)

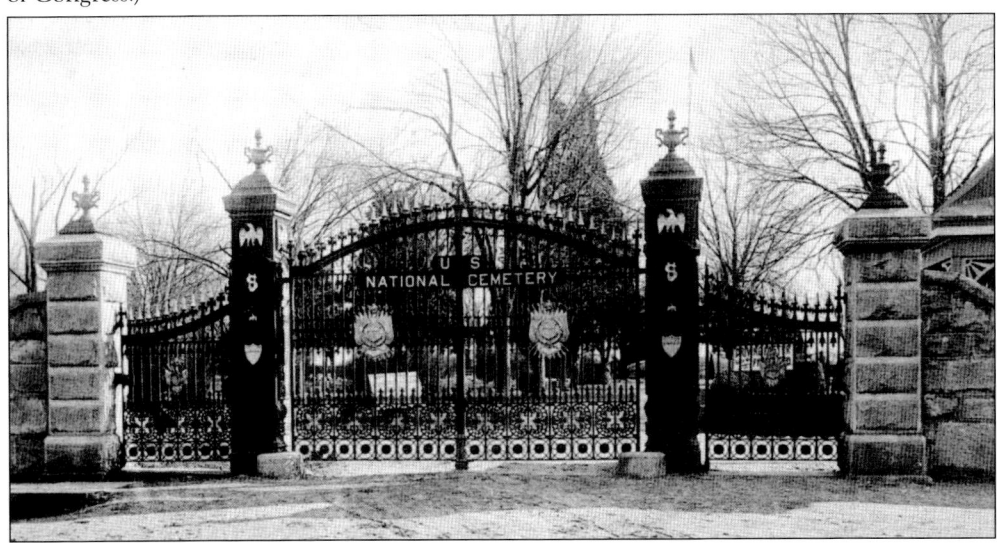

The Civil War was a conflict that will be remembered as one of the bloodiest in American history. There were many hospitals set up all over Richmond to help to heal the wounded. Soldiers who fought in Richmond would camp out in what are now famous parks admired by tourists. Those who did not survive the war were given their recognition in places like Richmond National Cemetery and Seven Pines National Cemetery (pictured). (Courtesy of VCU Special Collections.)

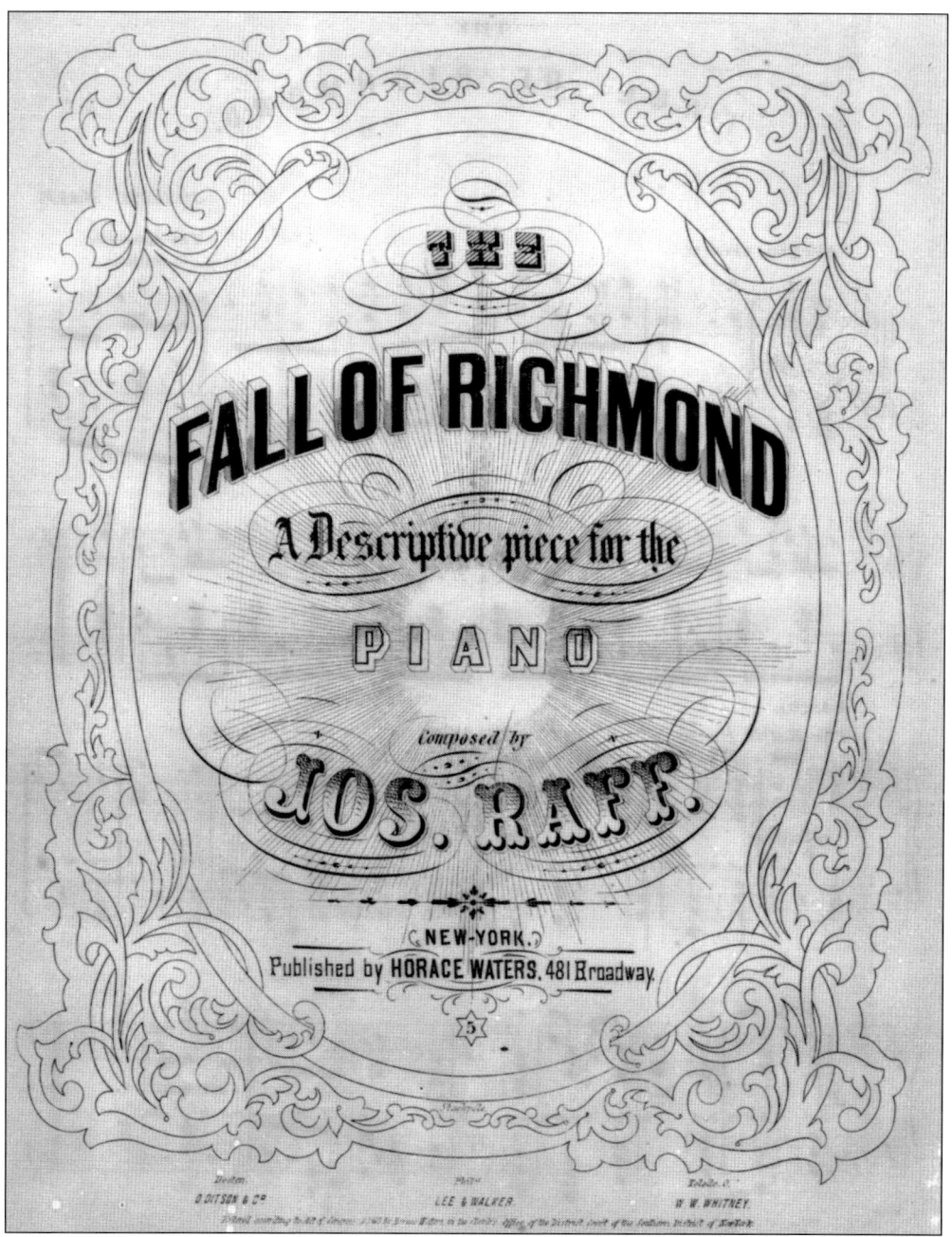

Confederate military hospitals were not stand-alone buildings dedicated to treating soldiers. Hospitals were mostly located in houses and buildings owned by sympathizers and patriots. Many schools were also used as military hospitals, but most did not have the proper resources to help to medicate and cure soldiers of their pains and wounds. The musical piece "The Fall of Richmond," composed by Joseph Raff, commemorates the April 12, 1865, fall of Richmond to Union forces, when the bloodshed finally ended. (Courtesy of the Library of Congress.)

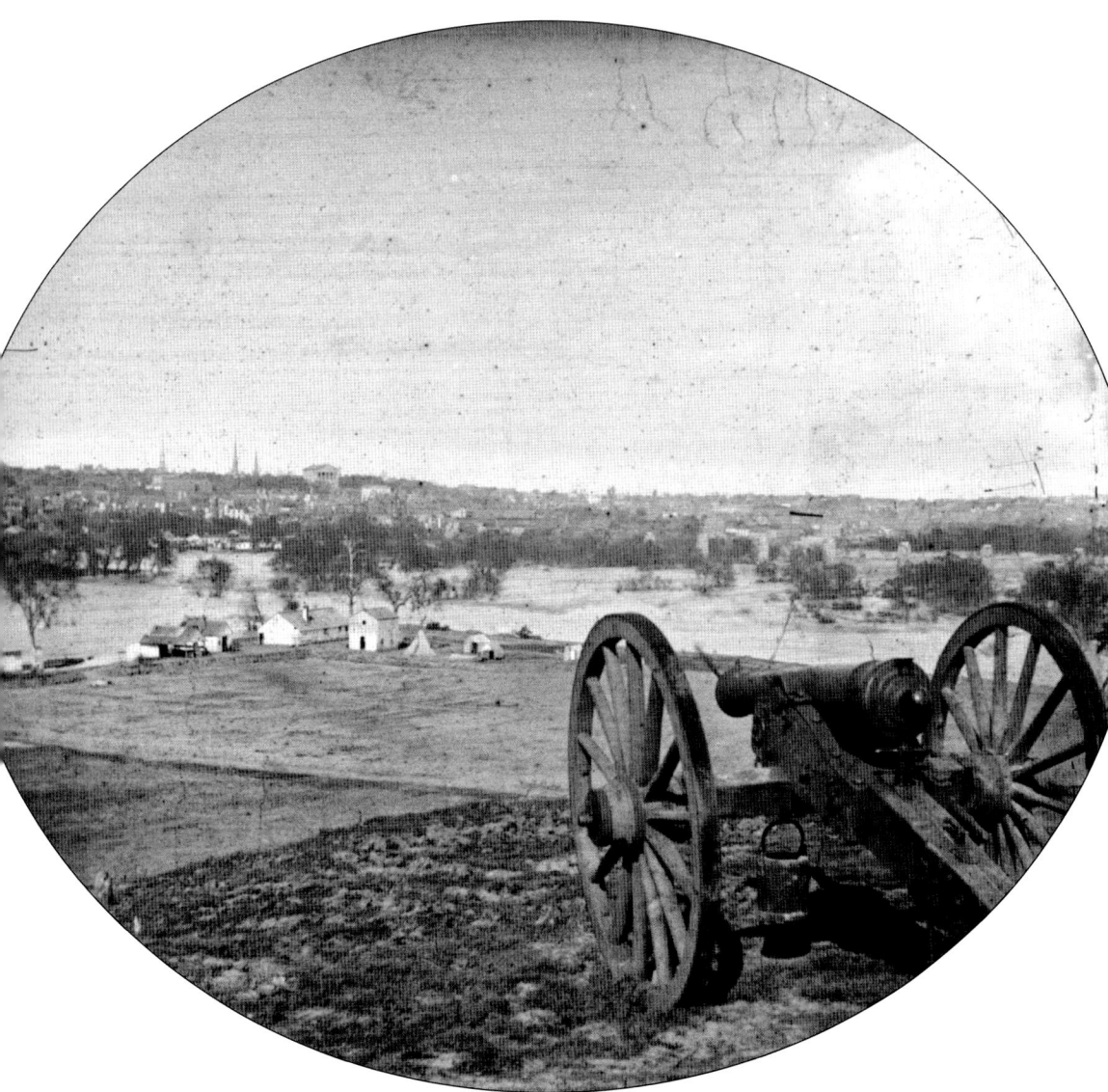

Soldiers who died during the Civil War were lucky if they received a proper burial. Many were not buried, because their bodies were never found. There is a very good chance that the bones of fallen soldiers are buried beneath the feet of strolling tourists on the streets of Richmond. The streets are themselves a graveyard to those who have fallen. (Courtesy of the Library of Congress.)

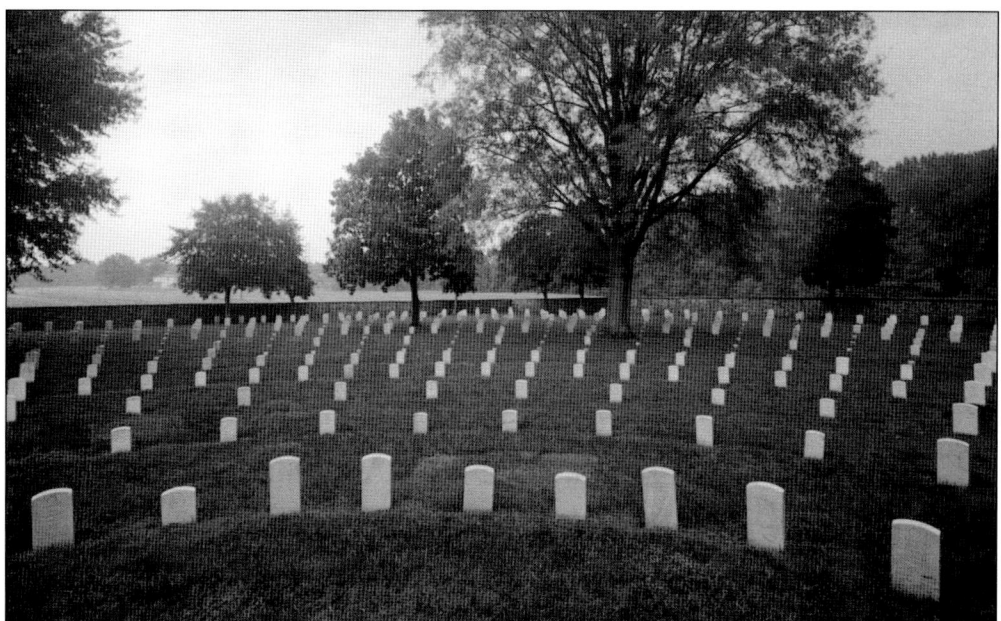

The high wall protecting the 1.9 acres of Seven Pines National Cemetery is proof positive that, even in the nation's darkest times, its citizens still take care of their own. More than 1,300 people are buried in this hallowed ground in Richmond. Many scholars still argue about the reasons behind the Revolutionary and Civil Wars, but their opinions do not matter to those resting here. These photographs depict Seven Pines as a cemetery (above) and as a soldiers' camp (below). (Both, courtesy of the Library of Congress.)

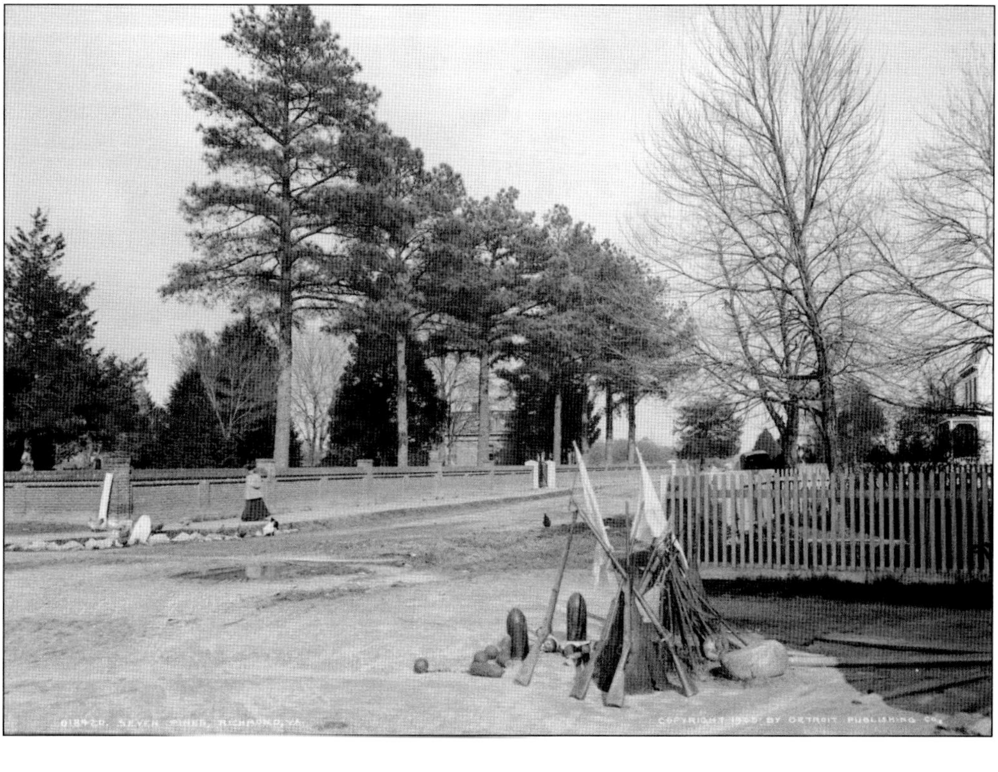

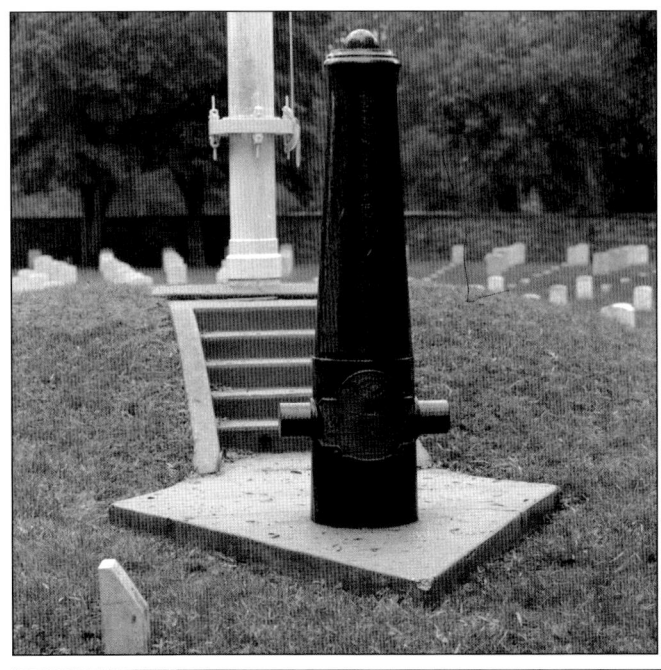

Rich men pay for mausoleums, while some of the men who die in battle are too poor to even pay for a marker. In death, however, all are the same. Visitors to a military cemetery will see this notion plainly illustrated. Seven Pines National Cemetery is a national cemetery in Varina, just outside of Richmond. A poor man's name is engraved on a piece of stone (lower left), paid for by the good citizens who have reaped the bounty of the sacrifices made by all of the soldiers buried here. (Courtesy of the Library of Congress.)

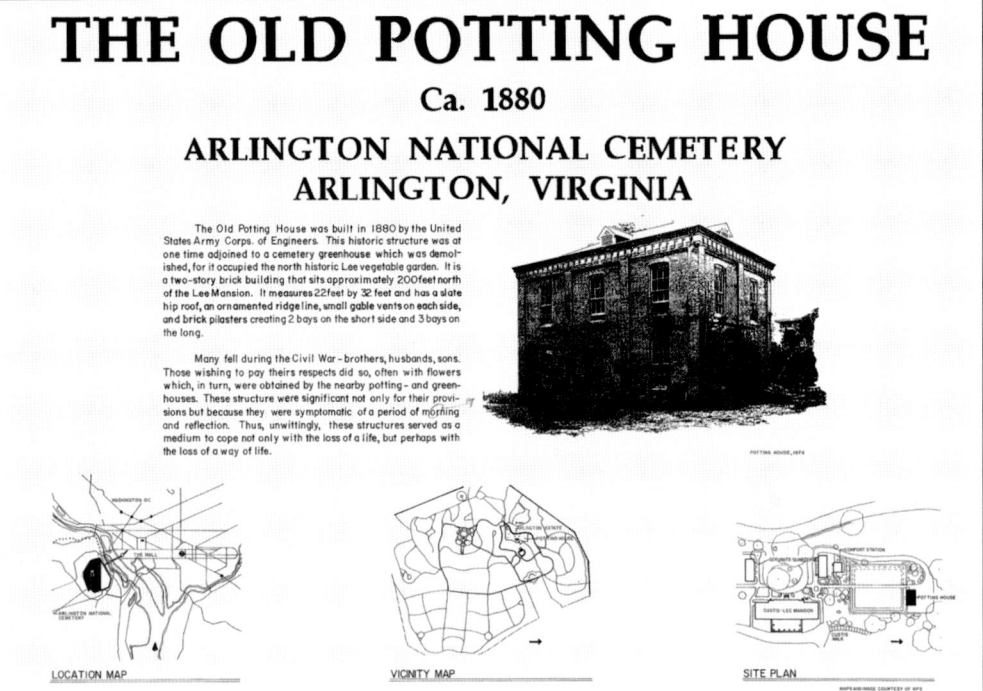

While they are only two years younger than Arlington National Cemetery, more than 150 years have passed since the Richmond National Cemetery and Seven Pines National Cemetery welcomed their first guests. Regardless of one's religious beliefs, national cemeteries are places for loved ones to find that final peace. Picture here is a description and illustration of the Old Potting House at Arlington National Cemetery. The building is used by the grounds' horticultural workers. (Courtesy of the Library of Congress.)

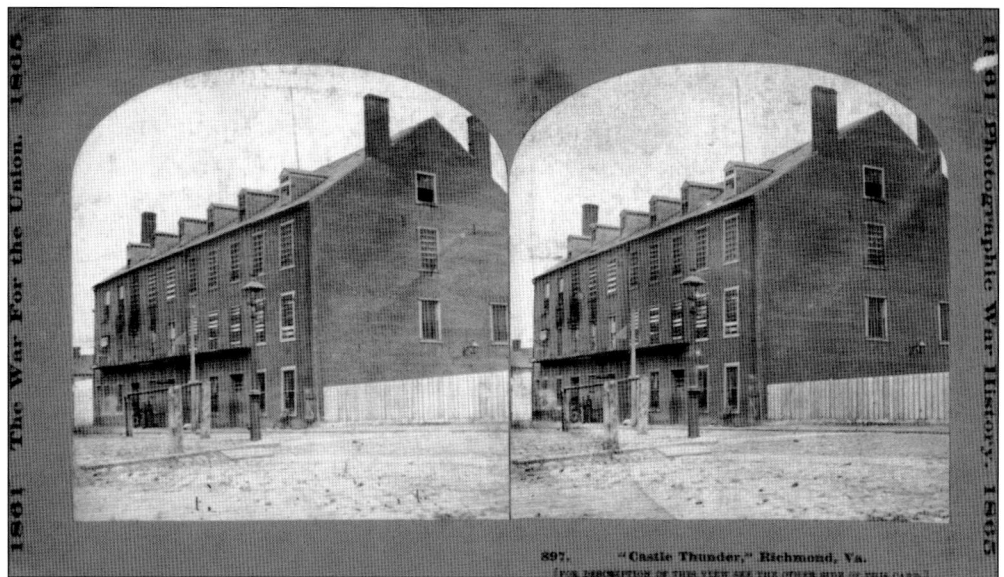

After seeing its citizens sent into war, only to see many of them fall, Richmond was in dire need of a glimmer of hope. Being the capital of the Confederacy, Richmond maintained its strength when the battle got tough. There were many prisoner-of-war camps on Belle Isle and in Shockoe Bottom, including "Castle Thunder" (pictured). (Courtesy of the Library of Congress.)

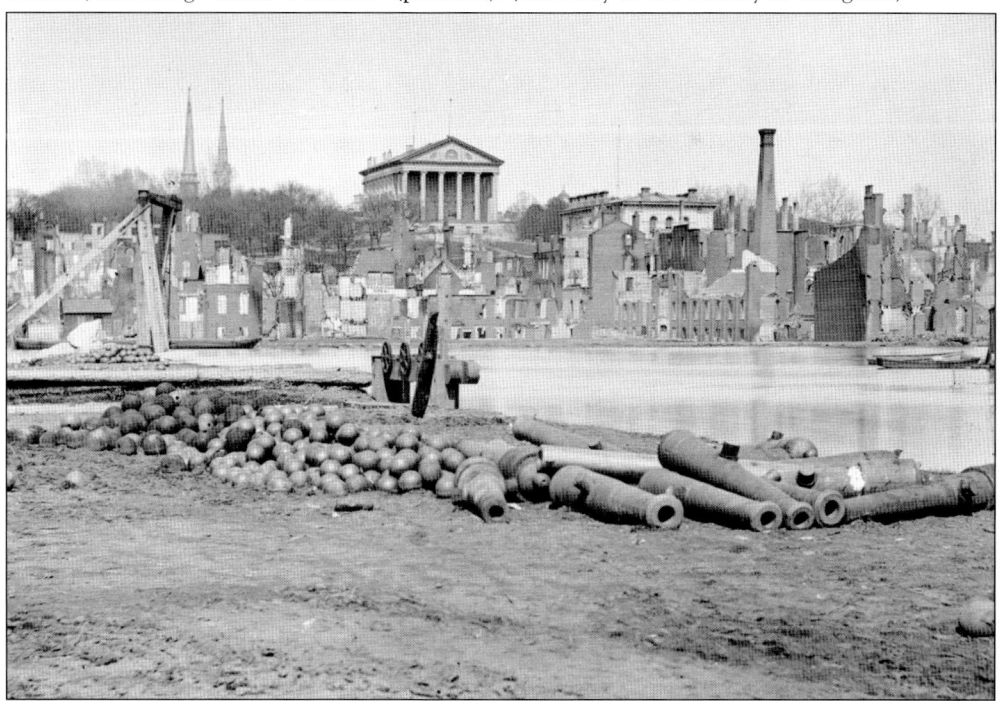

By the start of the Civil War, Confederate citizens were flocking to Richmond because of its blossoming economy, which was diverse and offered many jobs. The Tredegar Iron Works was one of the keystones of the Richmond economy, helping to produce everything from buttons to bullets—items that had the power to kill but also to support life during the war. (Courtesy of the Library of Congress.)

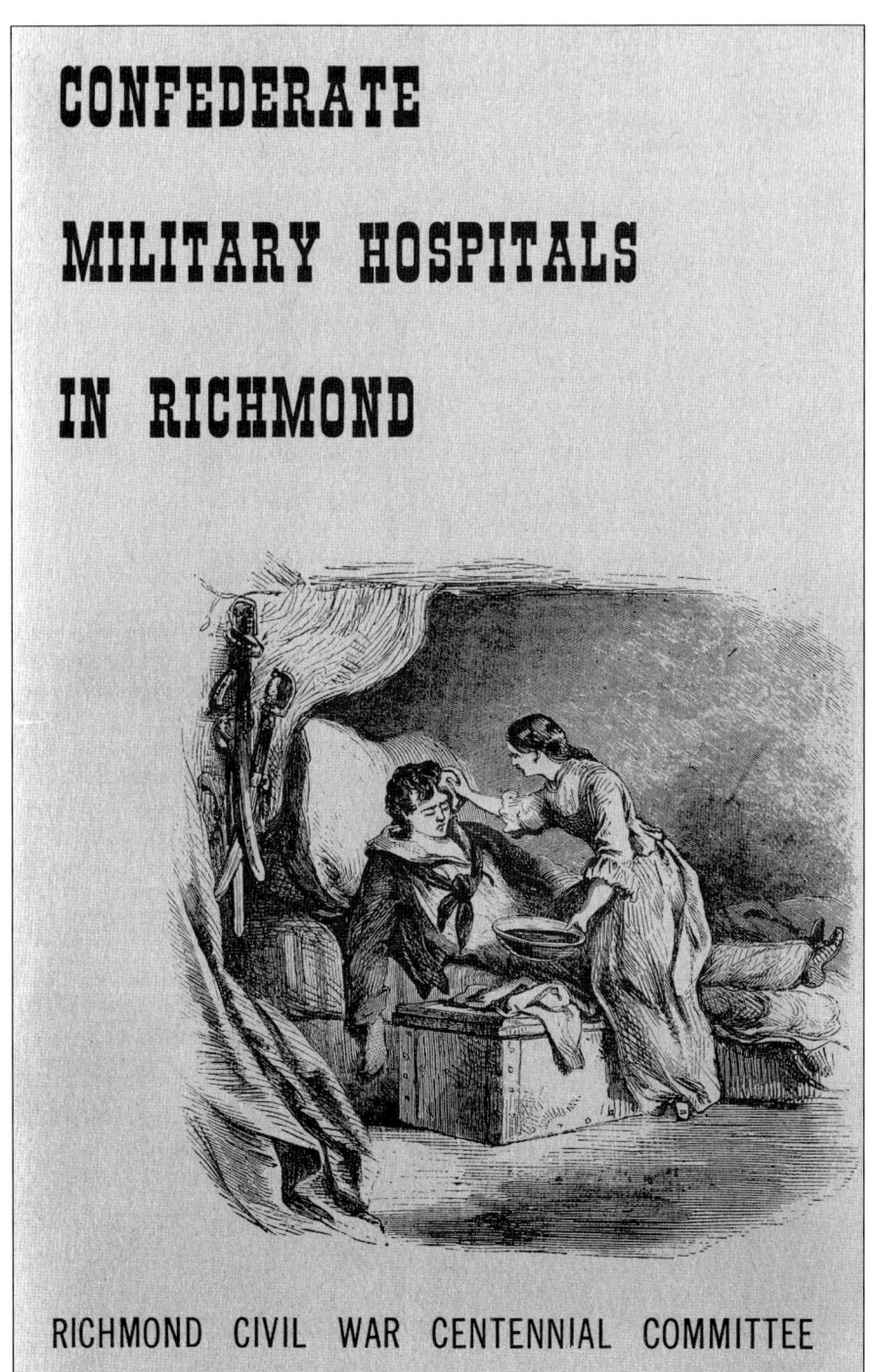

The population of Richmond began to grow with the onset of the Civil War. The city saw laborers, spies, refugees, soldiers, gamblers, and prostitutes move in. With hospitals located all over the city, citizens began to see wounded soldiers being brought in and out of their neighborhoods. Many of the business districts that had once flourished were now sites of military hospitals. (Courtesy of VCU Special Collections.)

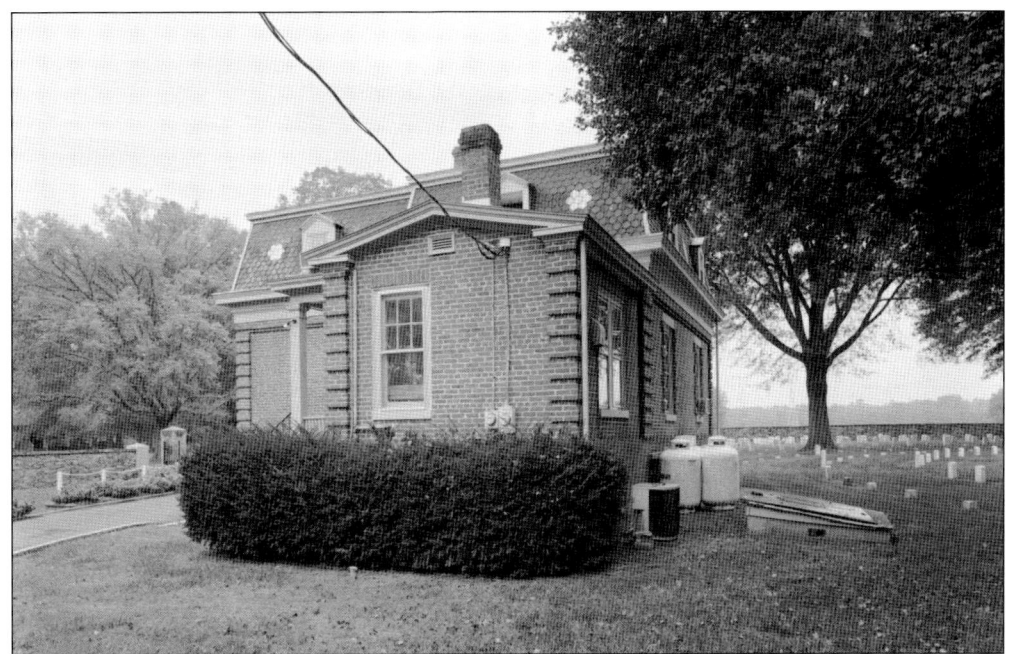

Seven Pines National Cemetery was created in 1866 to accommodate Union casualties from the Battle of Seven Pines. The cemetery is located about eight miles east of the city of Richmond. It is today one of the area's Civil War–era national cemeteries. An administrative building at Seven Pines is pictured here. (Courtesy of the Library of Congress.)

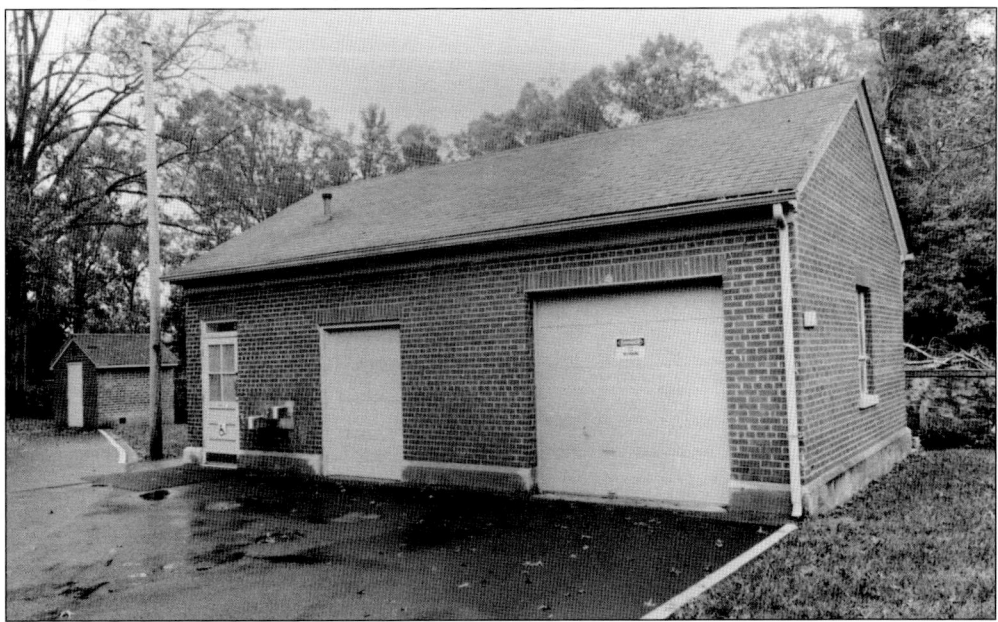

Approximately 1,300 Union soldiers are buried at Seven Pines National Cemetery, though only 150 are identified. They are a small number of the actual number of casualties of the Battle of Seven Pines, also known as the Battle of Fair Oaks Station. Experts estimate that about 6,200 Southern soldiers and 5,000 Northern soldiers died in the battle. This is a building used by groundskeepers at the cemetery. (Courtesy of the Library of Congress.)

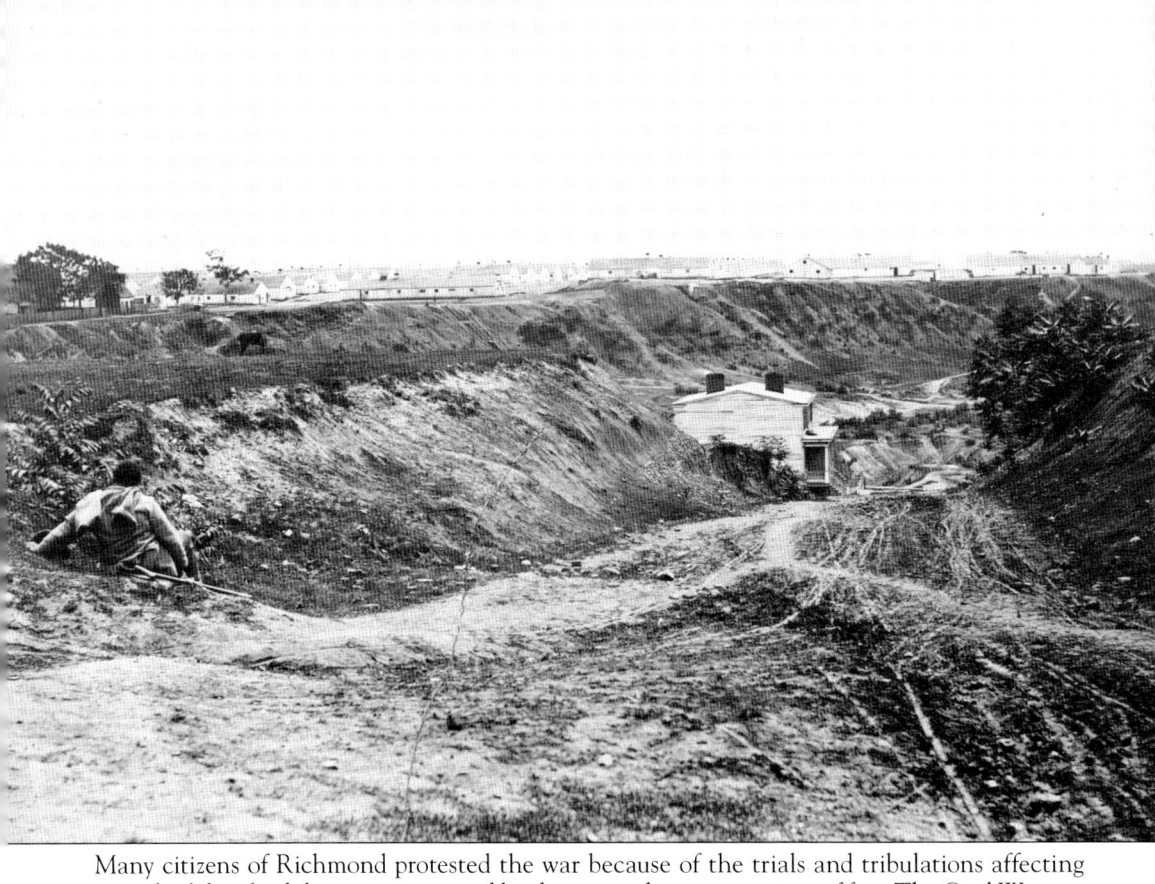

Many citizens of Richmond protested the war because of the trials and tribulations affecting everyday life—food shortages, a ravaged landscape, and a constant state of fear. The Civil War was slowly destroying Richmond's morale. This photograph depicts the desolate environment outside of Chimborazo Hospital, the last place thousands of soldiers saw before they died. (Courtesy of the Library of Congress.)

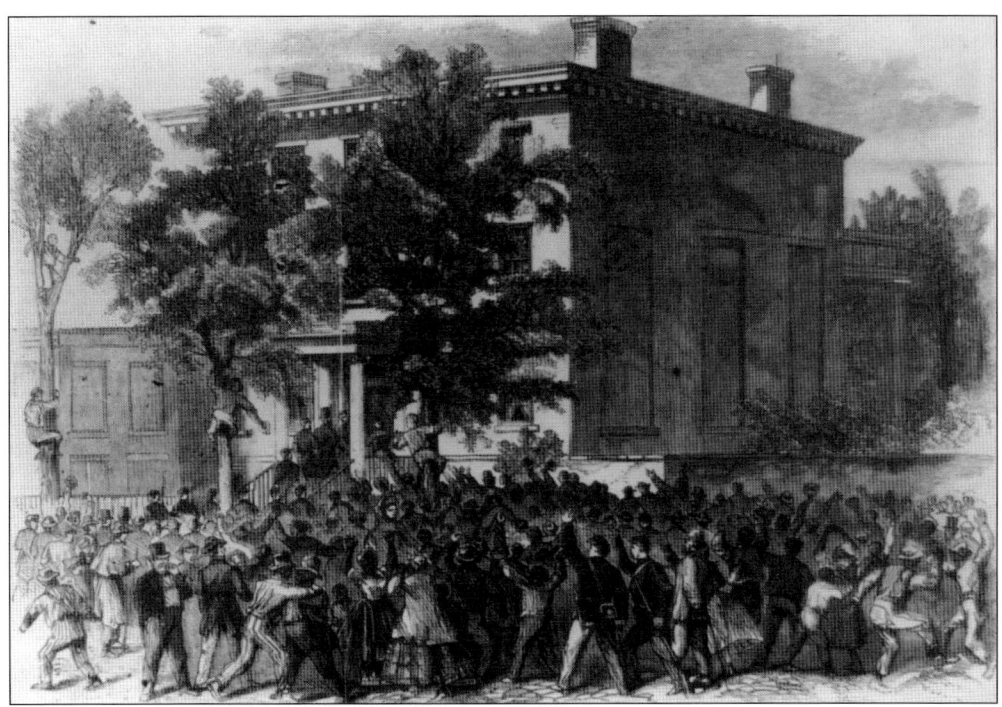

Richmond was at the heart of the Civil War. It became the best-known and longest-running capital of the Confederacy and was constantly under attack. (Danville, Virginia, was the final capital of the Confederate States of America.) The war saw farmers turning their lands into battlefields, shelters, and hospitals. Even President Lincoln visited Richmond to support the city for all that it had done during the war (depicted here). The war cost 620,000 lives, and the battlefields are still open for visitors today. (Courtesy of the Library of Congress.)

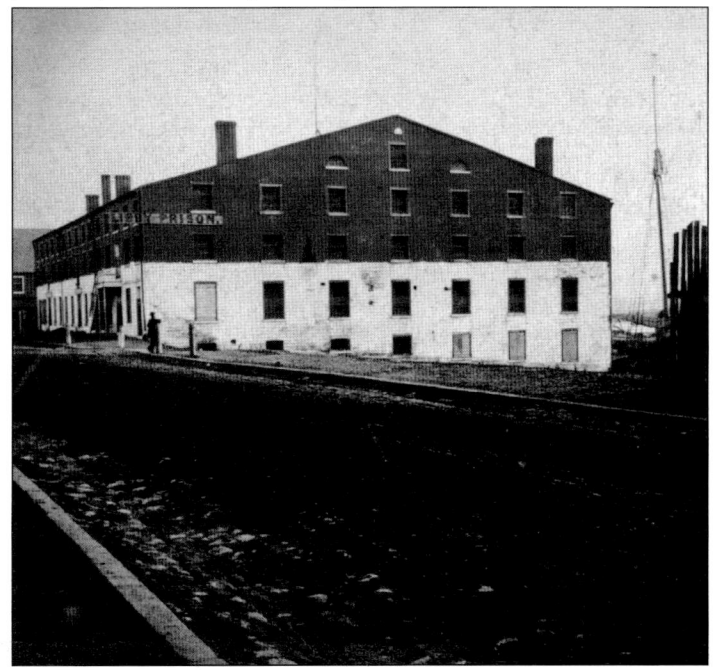

During the war, Richmond was the site of overcrowded prisons that held Union soldiers in inhumane conditions. Many of these soldiers died from malnutrition and disease. There were prisons on what is now known as Tobacco Row, east of Shockoe Bottom, near the Kanawha Canal by the James River. This photograph depicts Libby Prison. (Courtesy of the Library of Congress.)

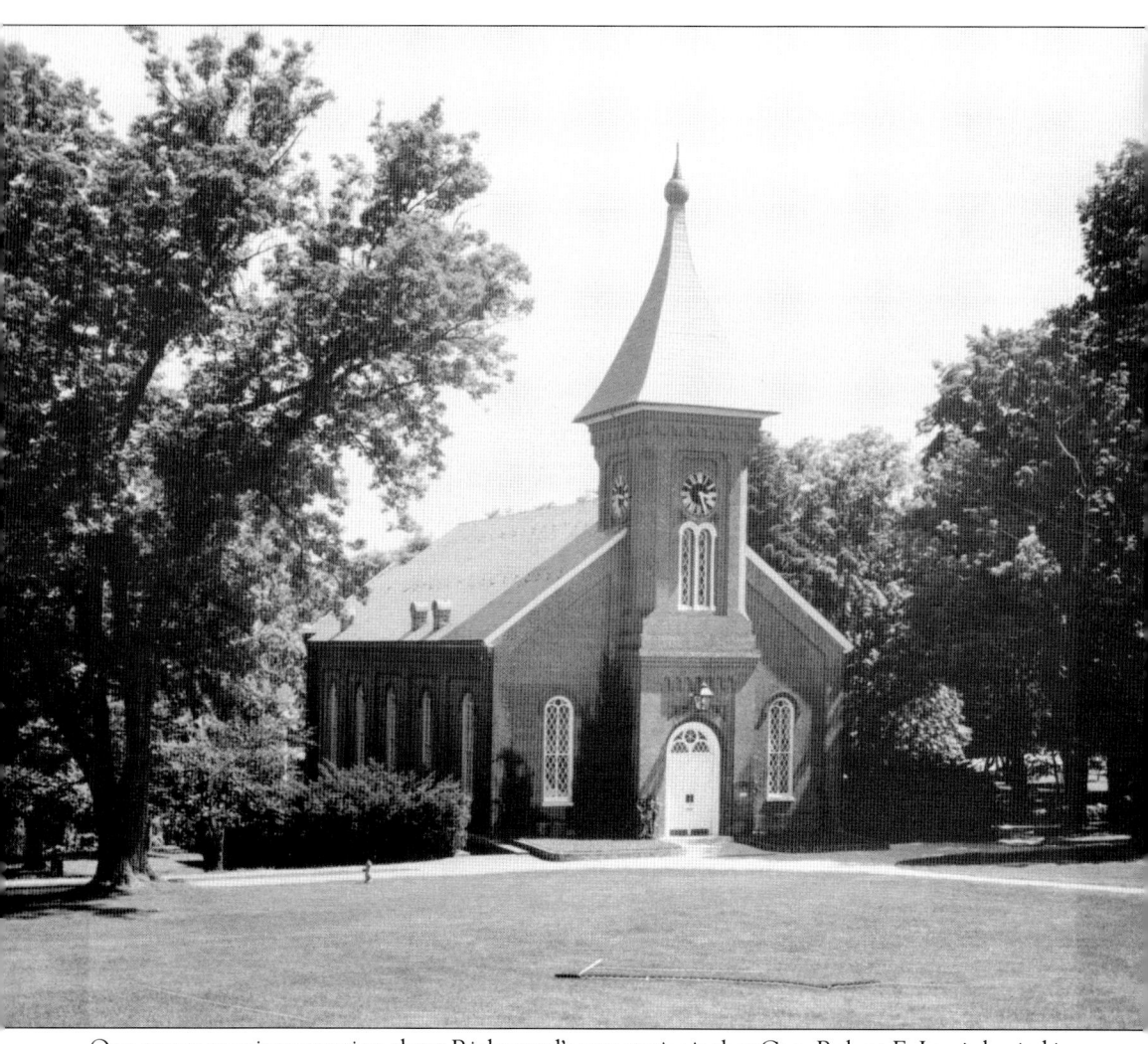

One common misconception about Richmond's cemeteries is that Gen. Robert E. Lee is buried in one of them, with Hollywood Cemetery being the most popular contender. He is in fact buried at the Lee Chapel at Washington & Lee University in Lexington, Virginia. Lee was buried beneath the chapel after he died on October 12, 1872. The chapel boasts, however, a few Richmond connections, such as the sculpture of Lee by Edward Valentine. Lee's family was buried in the crypt added to the chapel in 1883. (Courtesy of the Library of Congress.)

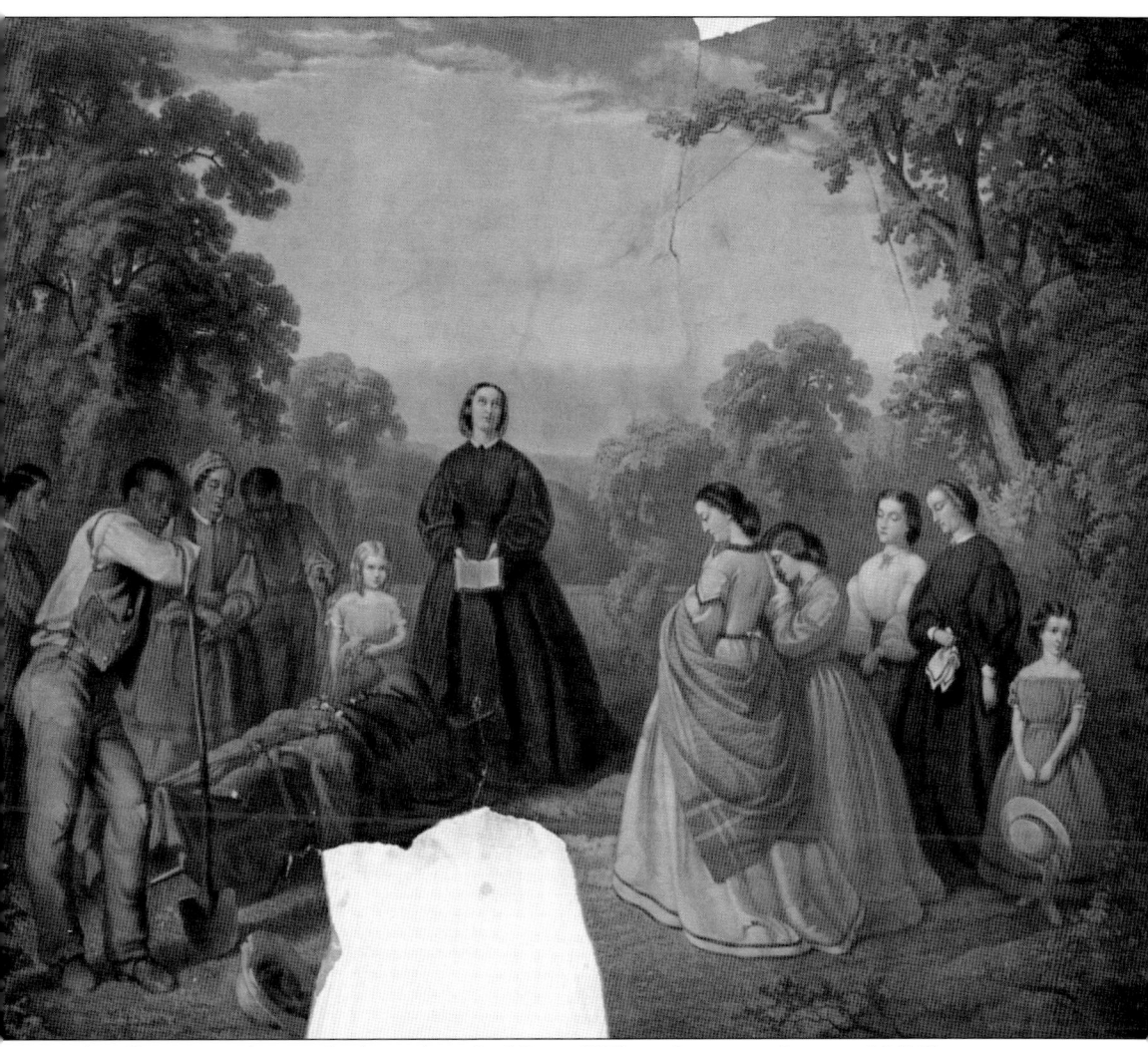

This illustration depicts the hasty burial of Capt. William Latané at Summer Hill Plantation in Hanover County outside of Richmond. His impromptu burial was representative of many Civil War burials prior to the creation of national ceremonies. Legend has it that Latané's family minister was stopped by Union soldiers, so a couple of Latané's female relatives were left to conduct the service. Children and slaves bore witness. No gravestone marks Latané's final resting place. (Courtesy of the Library of Congress.)

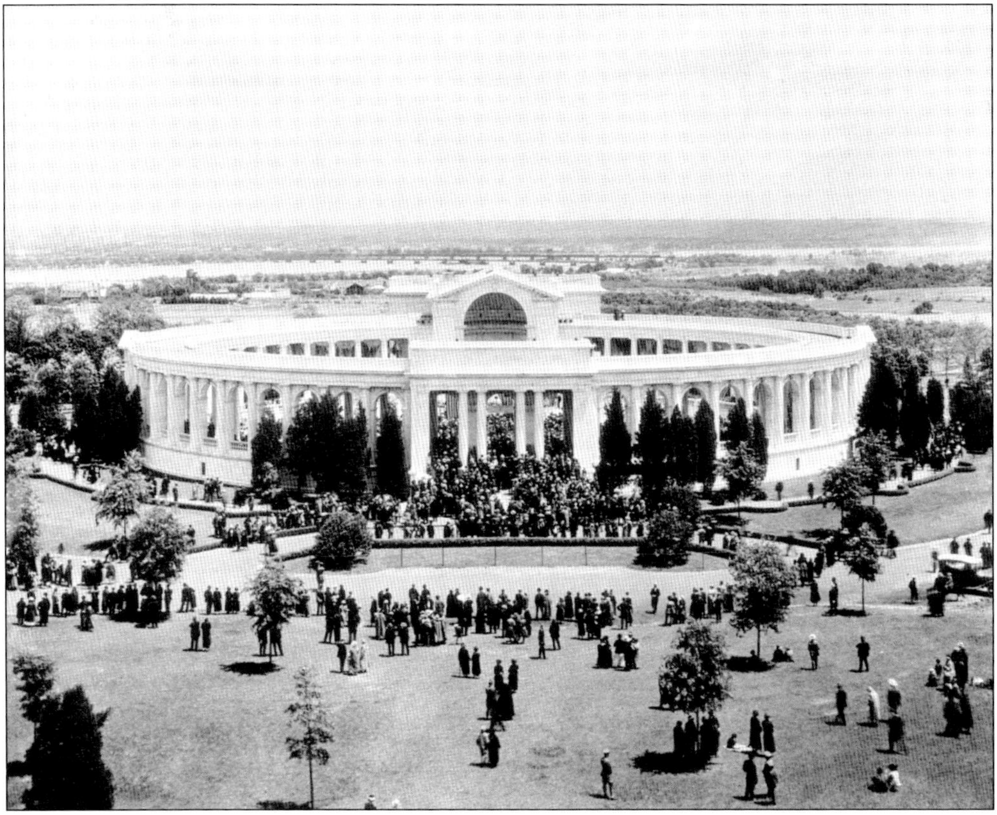

Arlington National Cemetery, located just outside Washington, DC, in Arlington, Virginia, about 90 miles north of Richmond, is the most famous national cemetery. It contains the graves of mostly Union soldiers. Arlington lays claim to more than 300,000 veterans in gravesites that span more than 600 acres. Shown here is the cemetery's amphitheater. (Courtesy of the Library of Congress.)

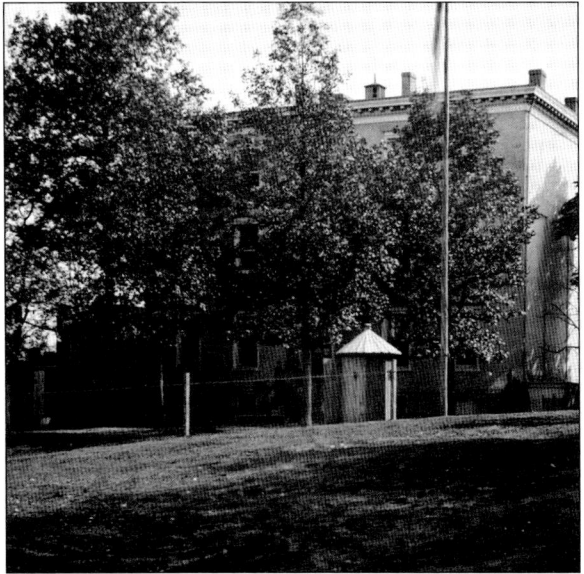

In preparation for the 150th anniversary of the Civil War, several organizations created an itinerary of all of the Civil War–era national cemeteries in the country. Among these organizations were the National Park Service's Education Services and Federal Preservation Institute and the Department of Veterans Affairs Historic Preservation Office and National Cemetery Administration History Program. In the Richmond area alone, these cemeteries include Cold Harbor Fort Harrison, Glendale, Richmond, and Seven Pines. An administrative building at Seven Pines is pictured here. (Courtesy of the Library of Congress.)

Five

SHOCKOE HILL AND HEBREW CEMETERIES

Shockoe Hill Cemetery is another of the most popular cemeteries in Richmond. The final resting place of John Marshall, the fourth chief justice of the United States, the cemetery is located in the heart of Richmond, just minutes from the John Marshall House, at Hospital Street between Second and Fourth Streets. Opened in 1822, Shockoe Hill is the second-oldest municipal cemetery in Richmond.

Many of Richmond's most famous and renowned scholars, politicians, and soldiers are buried in Shockoe Hill. Among the notables are pastor John D. Blair, Rev. John Buchanan, John Wickham, James Gibbon, William Foushee, Gov. William H. Cabell, Civil War spy Elizabeth Van Lew, Revolutionary War hero Peter Francisco, John M. Patton, lawyer and politician Benjamin W. Leigh, and Mississippi senator and federal judge Powhatan Ellis.

Shockoe Hill Cemetery is filled with much of Richmond's history, buried six feet underground. Visitors to the cemetery will notice its dedication to the soldiers who fought in the Revolutionary War and those who fought in the Civil War. There are about 661 soldiers buried in Shockoe Hill who fought in the Civil War, including members of the Confederate army, prisoners of war, and Union soldiers who were wounded on Virginia ground.

Among those laid to rest at Shockoe Hill are some of the loves of Edgar Allan Poe's life. His foster mother, Frances K. Allan, is buried here, along with his childhood best friend, Robert Craig Stanard. Poe's greatest love, Sarah Elmira Royster Shelton, is also buried here. She is among the women who may have inspired his writing of "The Raven" and "Annabel Lee." Shelton became engaged to Poe at the very young age of 15. Another of Poe's inspirations, Jane Stanard, is also buried in Shockoe Hill. She is the mother of Poe's childhood best friend, and she inspired the nurturing poem "To Helen."

The City of Richmond owns and maintains Shockoe Hill. The Friends of Shockoe Hill help to raise funds for the cemetery and to keep it preserved. Meanwhile, the Hebrew Cemetery across the street from Shockoe Hill Cemetery is maintained by Congregation Beth Ahabah. It is one of the biggest Jewish cemeteries in the South.

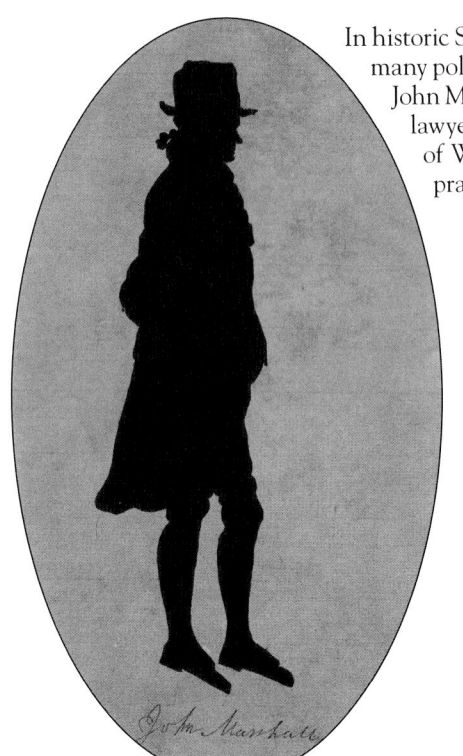

In historic Shockoe Hill Cemetery, visitors will find the graves of many politicians and their families. One of the most famous is John Marshall, the fourth US Supreme Court chief justice. A lawyer from Virginia, Marshall studied law at the College of William and Mary and was very successful with his practice. (Courtesy of the Library of Congress.)

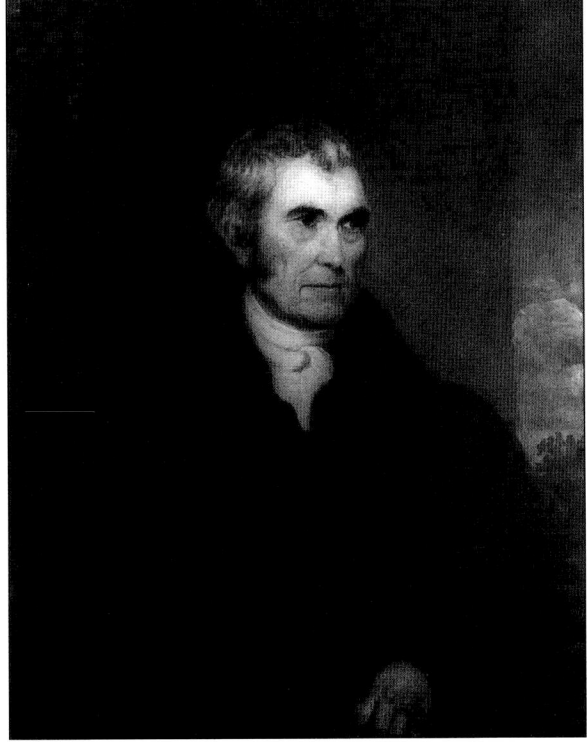

Marshall was a very brave man, fighting as a captain in the Revolutionary War, and he was also very intelligent. He studied not only law, but the works of Horace, Shakespeare, and Milton. His gravesite is in the Marshall family plot, where he is laid to rest next to his beloved, Mary Willis Ambler Marshall. (Courtesy of the Library of Congress.)

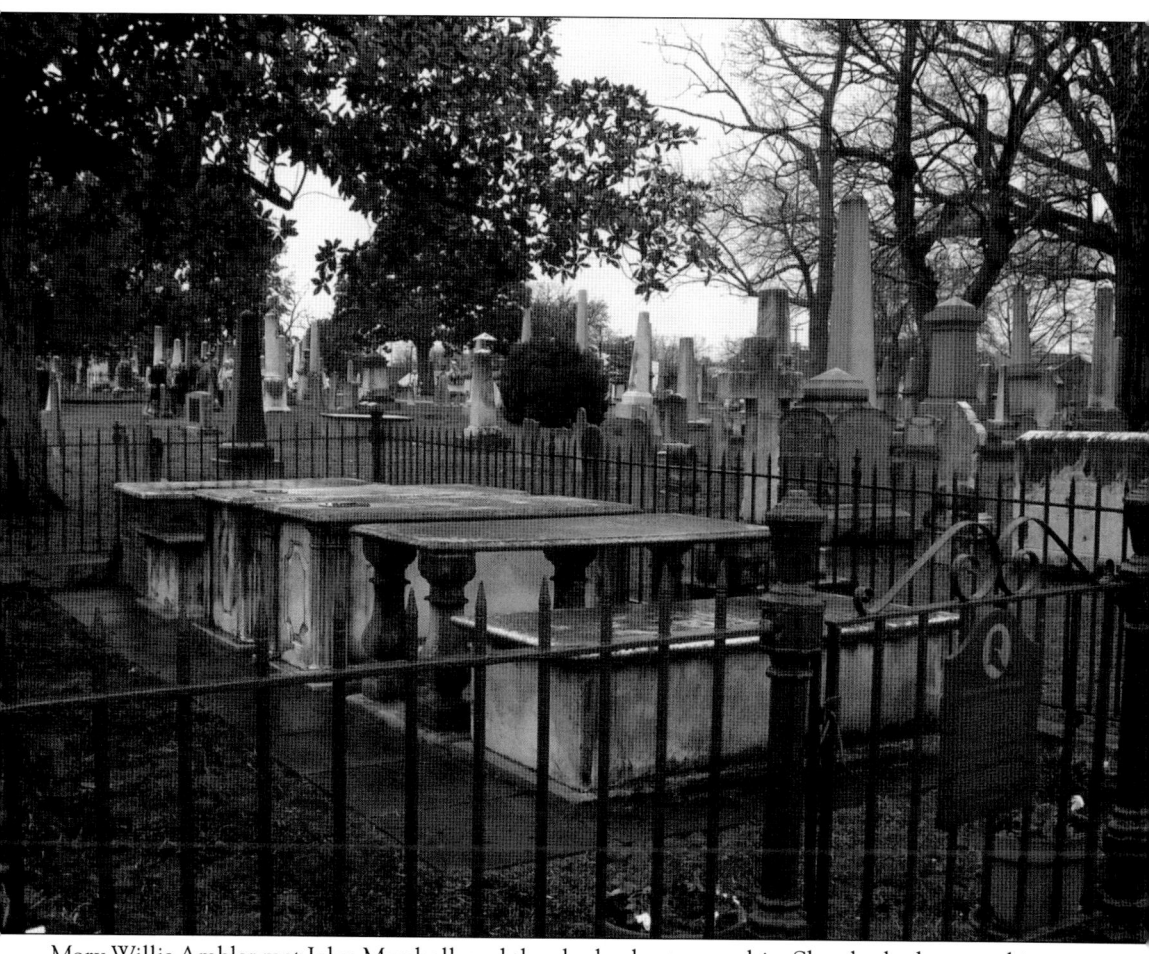

Mary Willis Ambler met John Marshall, and they had a short courtship. She also had a courtship with Thomas Jefferson that lasted only a short time. Mary and John married in 1783, and he was known to call her "my dearest Polly." He was crushed by her death in 1831. They are buried next to each other in Richmond's second-largest municipal cemetery. (Courtesy of the Library of Congress.)

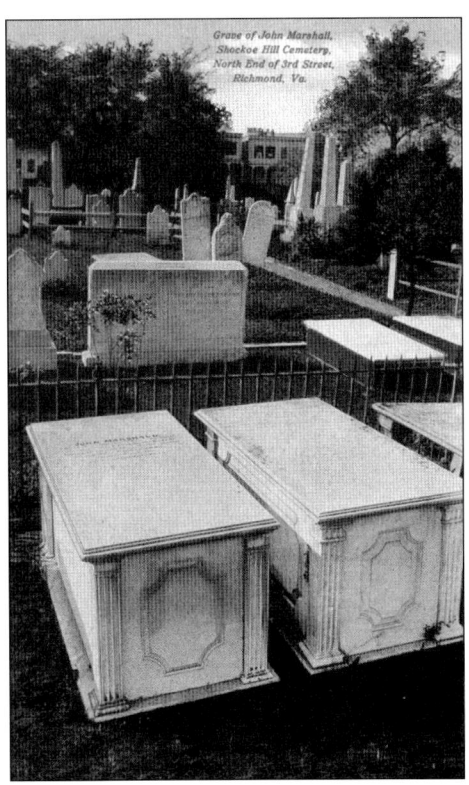

When John Marshall's wife, Mary, died, he was quoted as saying that he had lost the "solace of his life." They are said to have fallen in love quickly after only a very short courtship. Some say it was love at first sight. They had a total of ten children, four of whom died before adulthood. John, who died in July 1835, wished to be buried with his love. (Courtesy of the Library of Congress.)

Located on East Marshall Street, the Marshalls resided in this house from 1790 until John's death in 1835, when he was buried alongside Mary in Shockoe Hill. He was known for being a great politician and serving in many different branches of the US government. He was also considered one of the leading members of Richmond society. (Courtesy of the Library of Congress.)

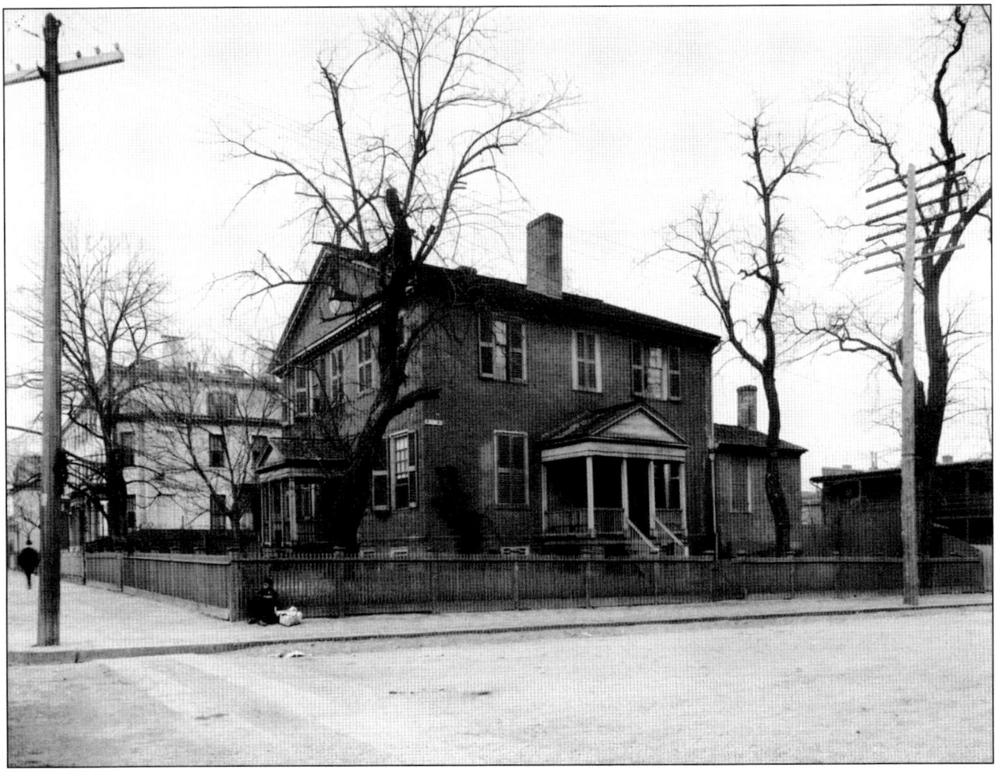

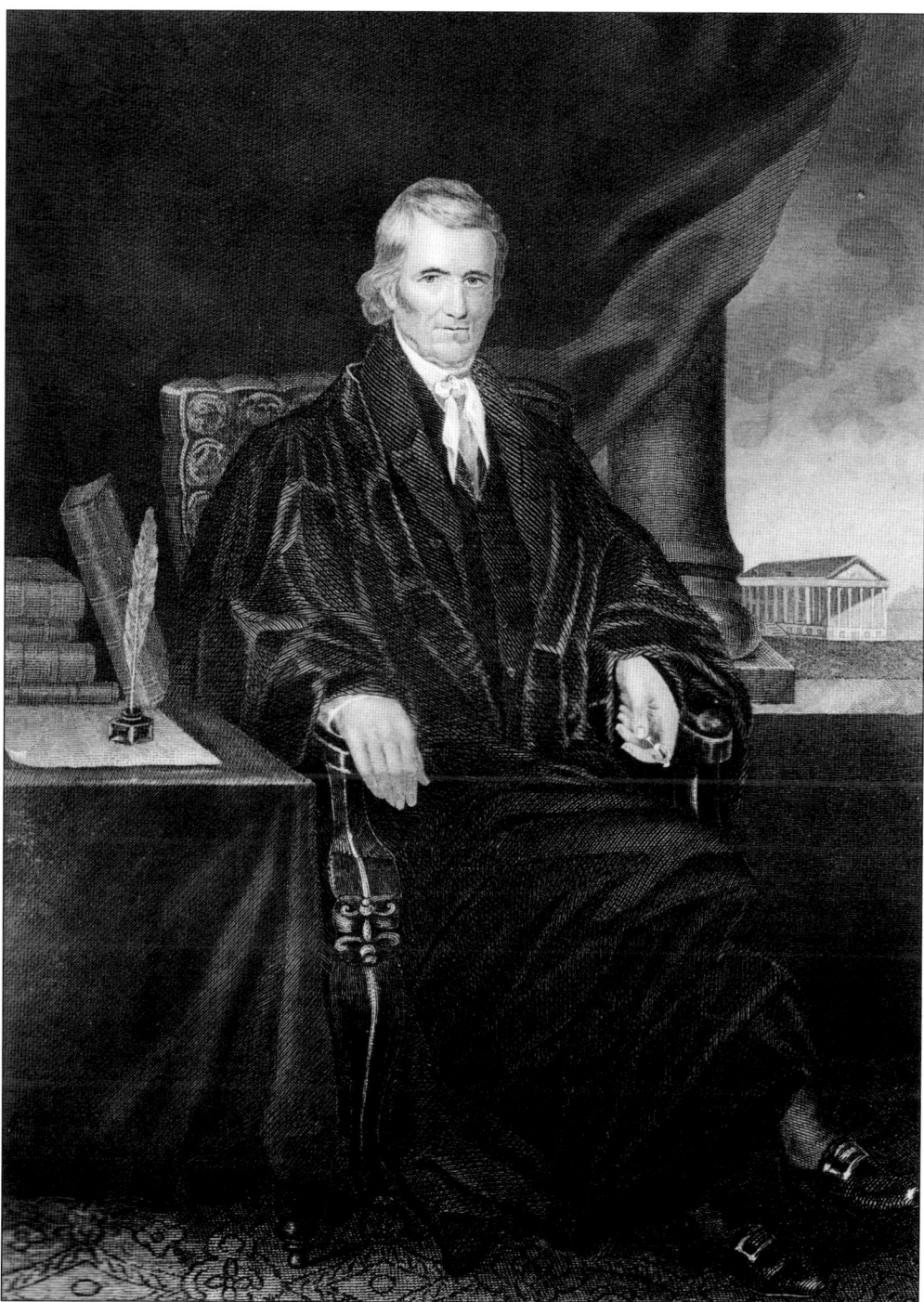

Not only was John Marshall known to be a grand host, he was also a kind man. He showed that he could be a great leader while serving as a Supreme Court justice. He made some decisions that were not quite popular, but always stood by his findings. Visitors to Shockoe Hill Cemetery can see how great he loved, by seeing how close he is buried to his beloved wife, Mary. (Courtesy of the Library of Congress.)

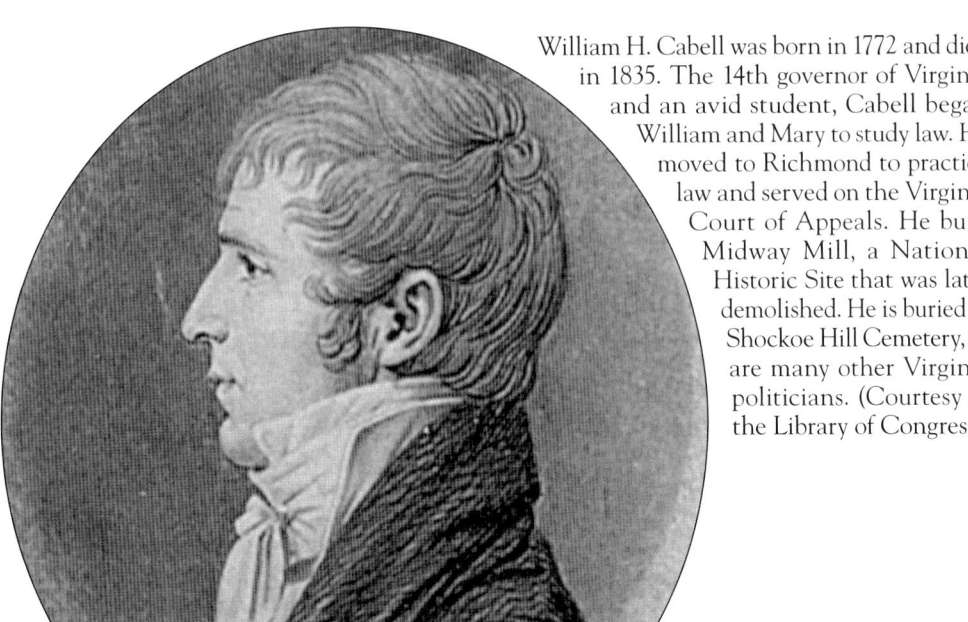

William H. Cabell was born in 1772 and died in 1835. The 14th governor of Virginia and an avid student, Cabell began William and Mary to study law. He moved to Richmond to practice law and served on the Virginia Court of Appeals. He built Midway Mill, a National Historic Site that was later demolished. He is buried at Shockoe Hill Cemetery, as are many other Virginia politicians. (Courtesy of the Library of Congress.)

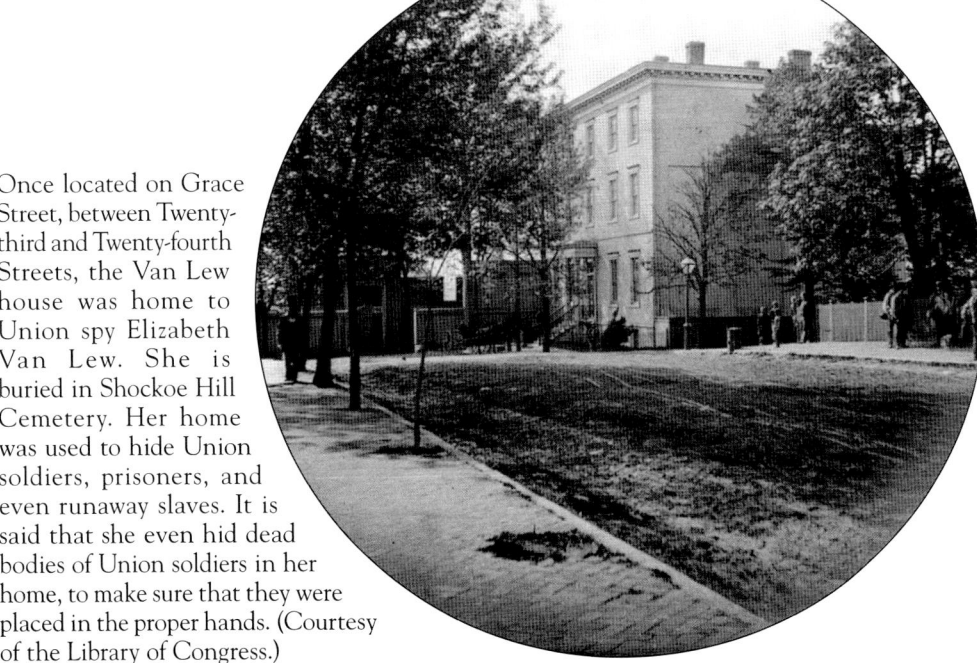

Once located on Grace Street, between Twenty-third and Twenty-fourth Streets, the Van Lew house was home to Union spy Elizabeth Van Lew. She is buried in Shockoe Hill Cemetery. Her home was used to hide Union soldiers, prisoners, and even runaway slaves. It is said that she even hid dead bodies of Union soldiers in her home, to make sure that they were placed in the proper hands. (Courtesy of the Library of Congress.)

After the Civil War, Ulysses S. Grant made Elizabeth Van Lew the postmistress of Richmond. This position angered many of the city's citizens, and Van Lew was eventually despised throughout Richmond. She spent most of her fortune trying to help out the Union army, so when she died, she died nearly penniless. She is buried under a large rock donated by her "Boston friends." (Courtesy of the Library of Congress.)

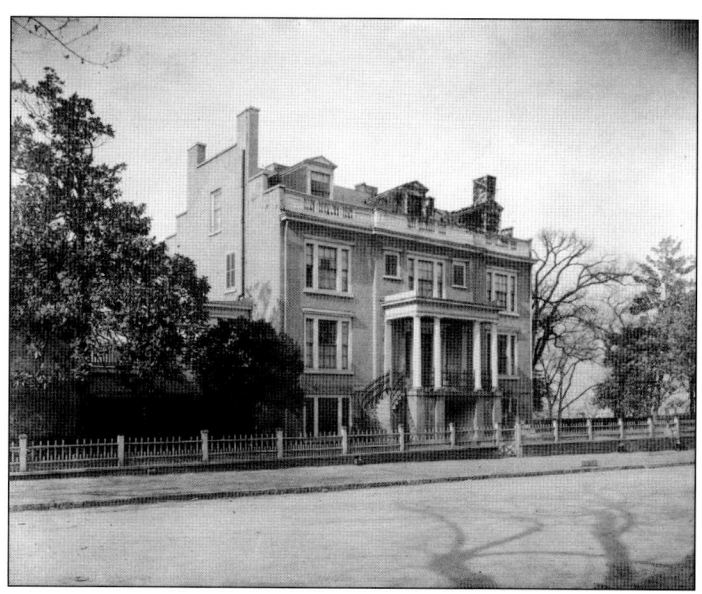

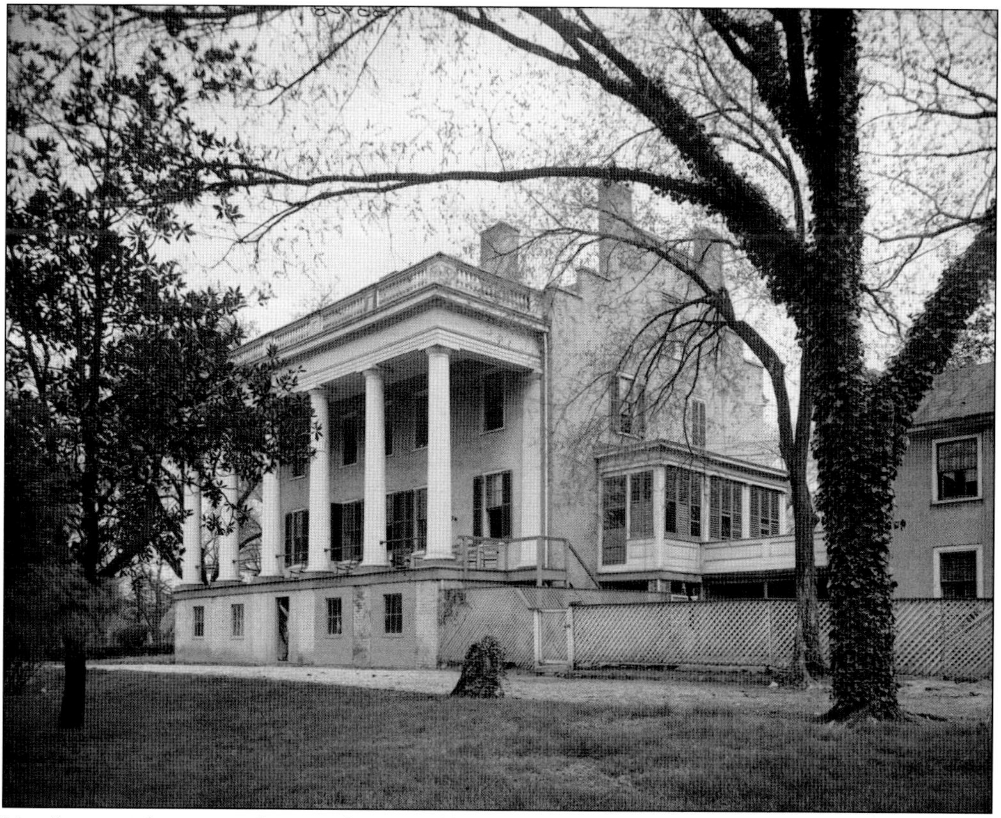

Van Lew was known early on to be a troublemaker. Her parents sent her to a Quaker school in Philadelphia, where she learned about the evils of slavery. She came back to Richmond with this new attitude. With her inheritance, she bought slaves so that she could give them a good life. She died a fighter and is one of the most famous persons buried in Shockoe Hill. (Courtesy of the Library of Congress.)

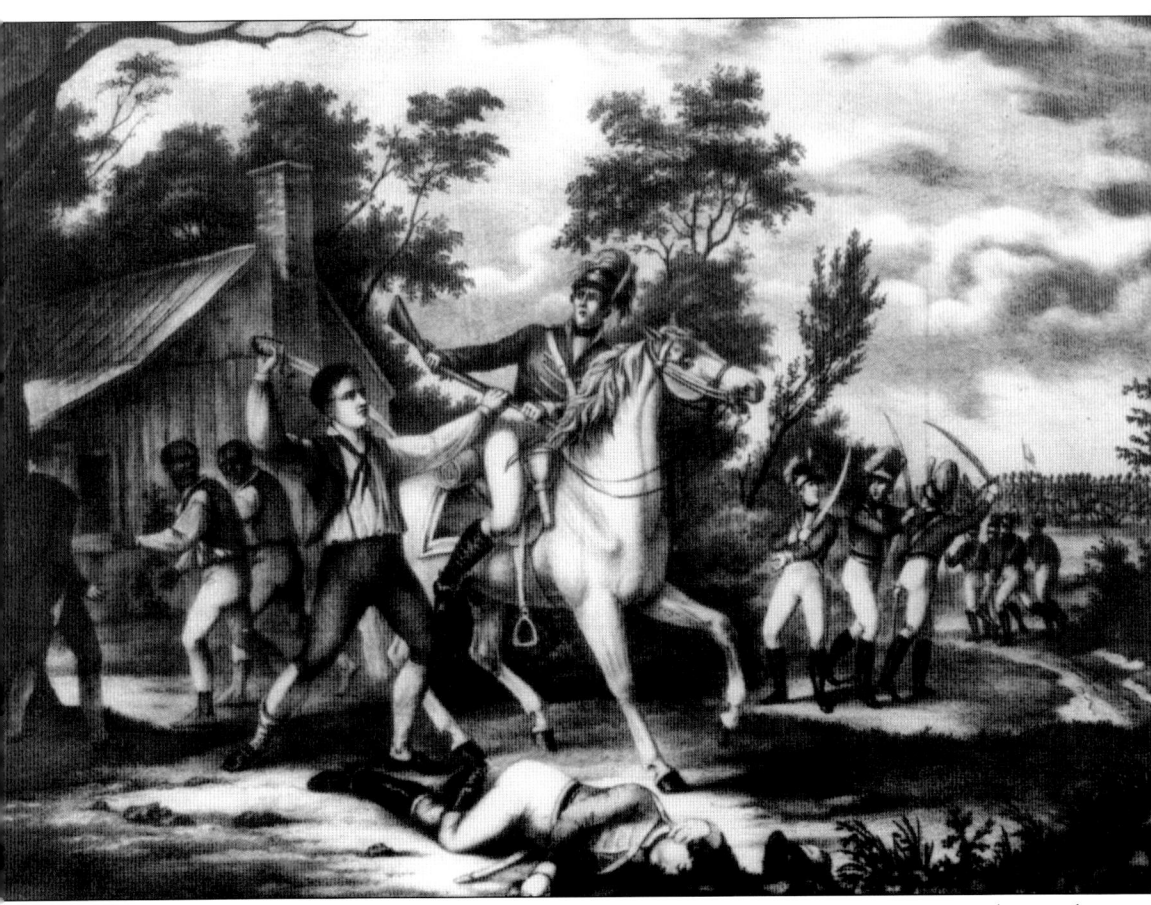

Revolutionary War hero Peter Francisco is buried in Shockoe Hill Cemetery. He was known by many different nicknames, including "Virginia Giant," "Virginia Hercules," and "The Giant of the Revolution." He joined the 10th Virginia Regiment at the young age of 16. Francisco spent a few years as Virginia's sergeant at arms. (Courtesy of the Library of Congress.)

Born in 1790, Powhatan Ellis began his political career by studying law at William and Mary. Like other politicians buried in Shockoe Hill, he was quite successful. He served in the US Senate in 1832 and was appointed by Andrew Jackson to be the chargé d'affaires of the United States to Mexico. He moved to Richmond later in his life and died there in 1863. (Right, courtesy of the Trout Gallery; below, courtesy of the Library of Congress.)

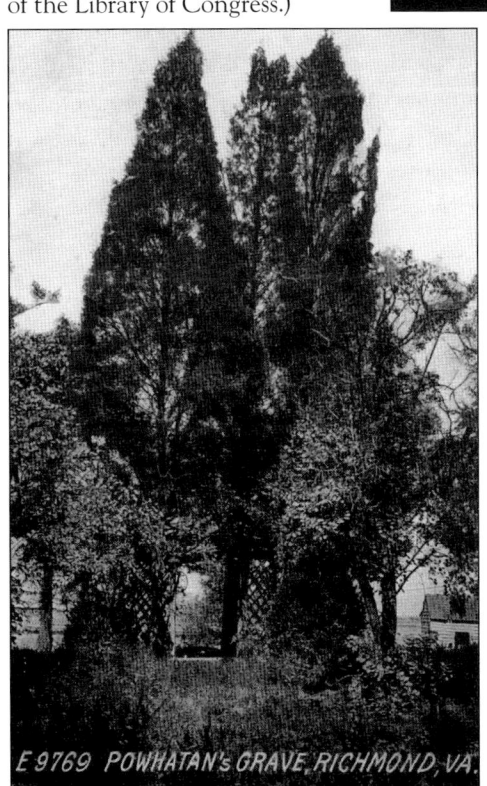

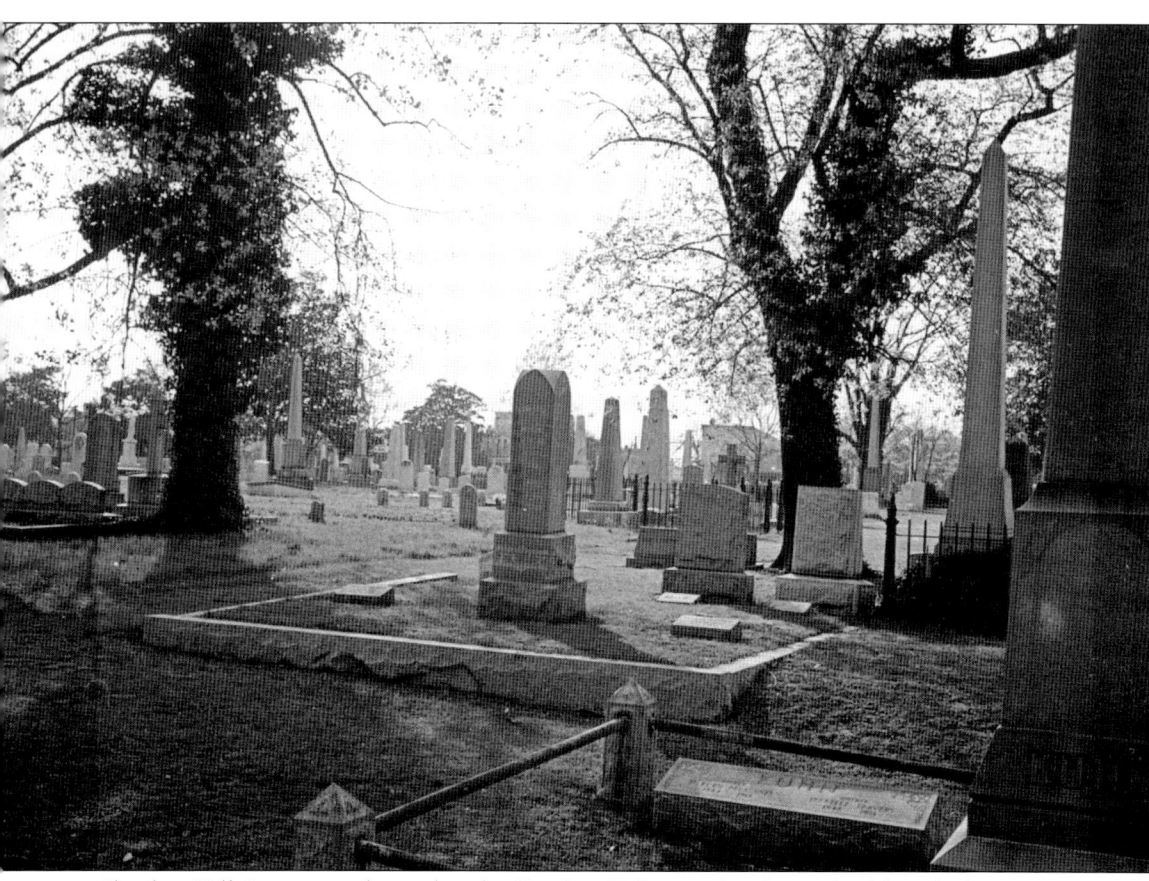

Shockoe Hill Cemetery is located in the Shockoe Hill area of Richmond. Although the cemetery was established in 1820, the first burial did not take place until 1822. It was the first municipal cemetery owned by the City of Richmond. Located on about 13 acres of land, it is listed in both the Virginia Landmarks Register and the National Register of Historic Places. (Courtesy of the Library of Virginia.)

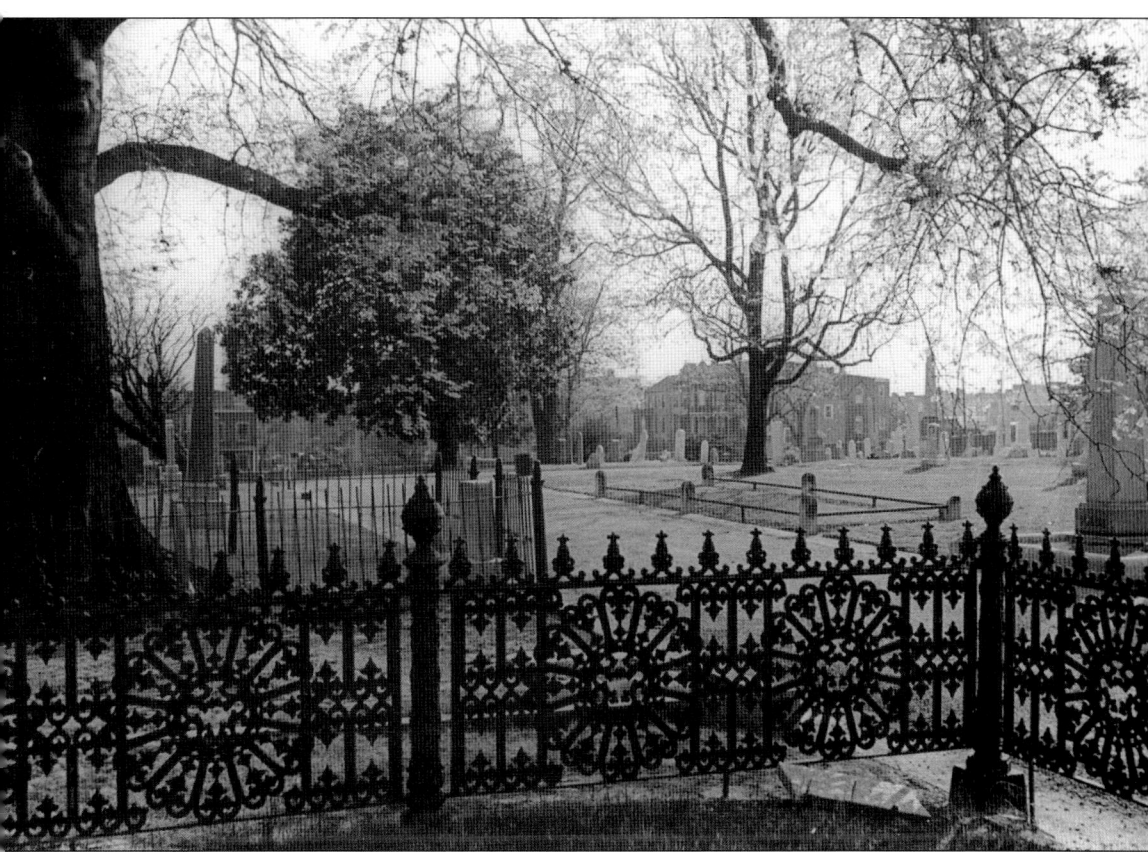

There were about 500 Union soldiers buried outside of Shockoe Hill Cemetery from 1861 to 1863. Their remains were later moved to Richmond National Cemetery. Markers in Shockoe Hill pay respect to those who fought in the Civil War. One of the markers was installed by the Daughters of the Confederacy in 1938. (Courtesy of the Library of Congress.)

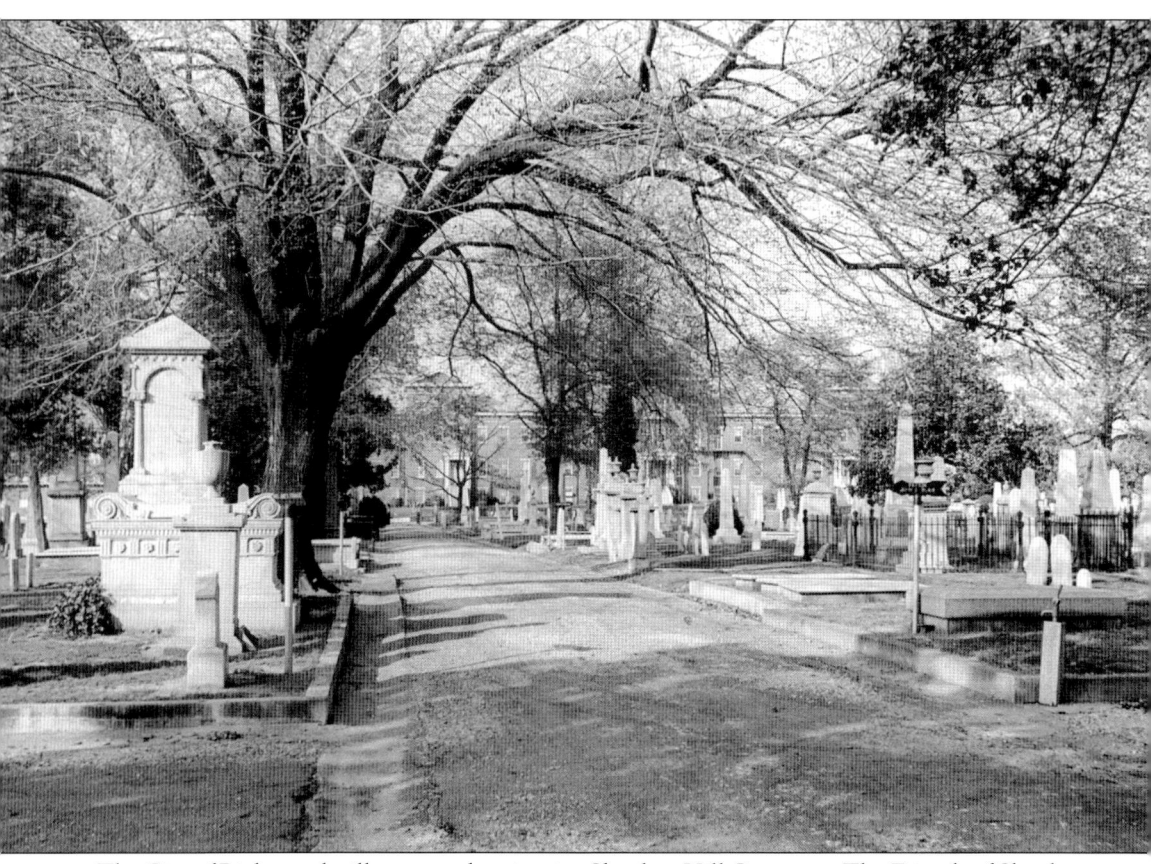
The City of Richmond still owns and maintains Shockoe Hill Cemetery. The Friends of Shockoe Hill, a group of volunteers, help out with maintaining the grounds and the graves. The group was formed in Richmond in 2006, and it acts as a steward to the cemetery. (Courtesy of the Library of Congress.)

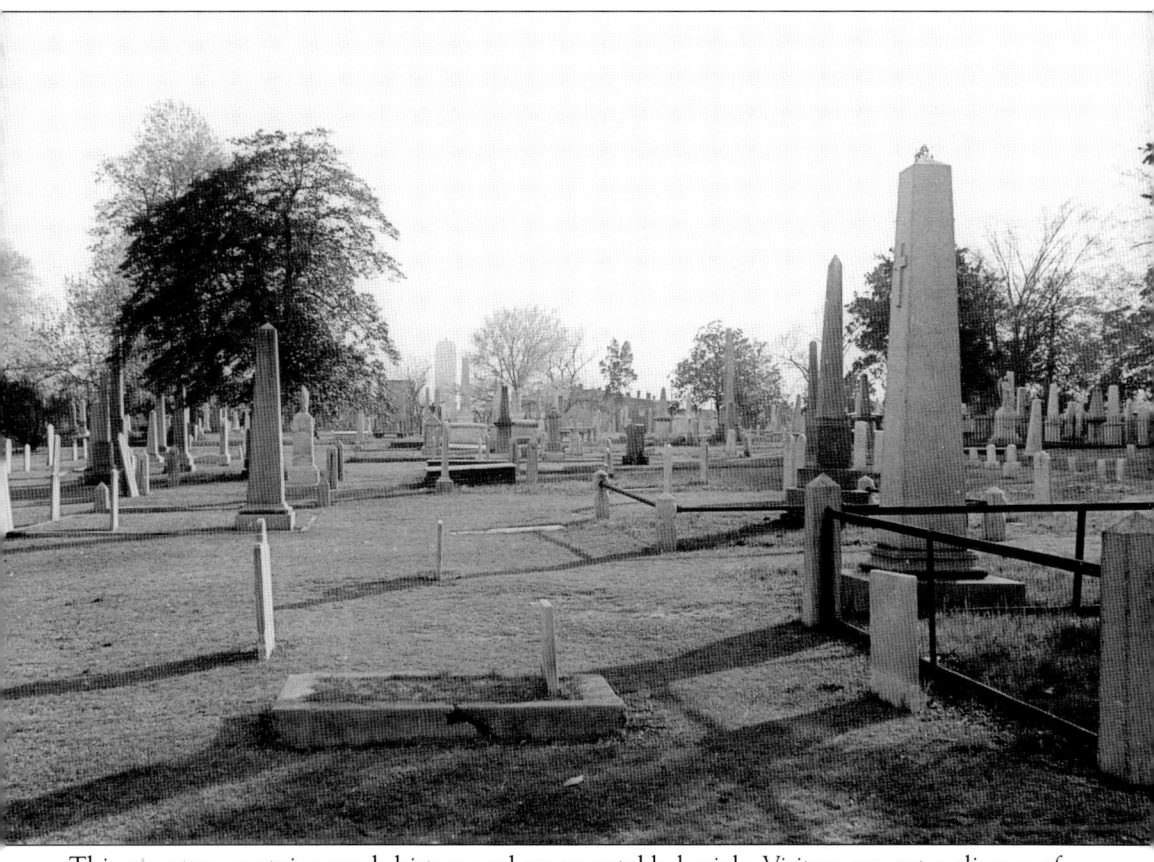

This cemetery contains much history and many notable burials. Visitors can get a glimpse of Richmond's vast history by looking at the aging tombstones of interesting figures, including a Union spy, a governor of Virginia, dozens of soldiers, senators, and even judges. Shockoe Hill Cemetery is located directly across the street from the Hebrew Cemetery. (Courtesy of the Library of Congress.)

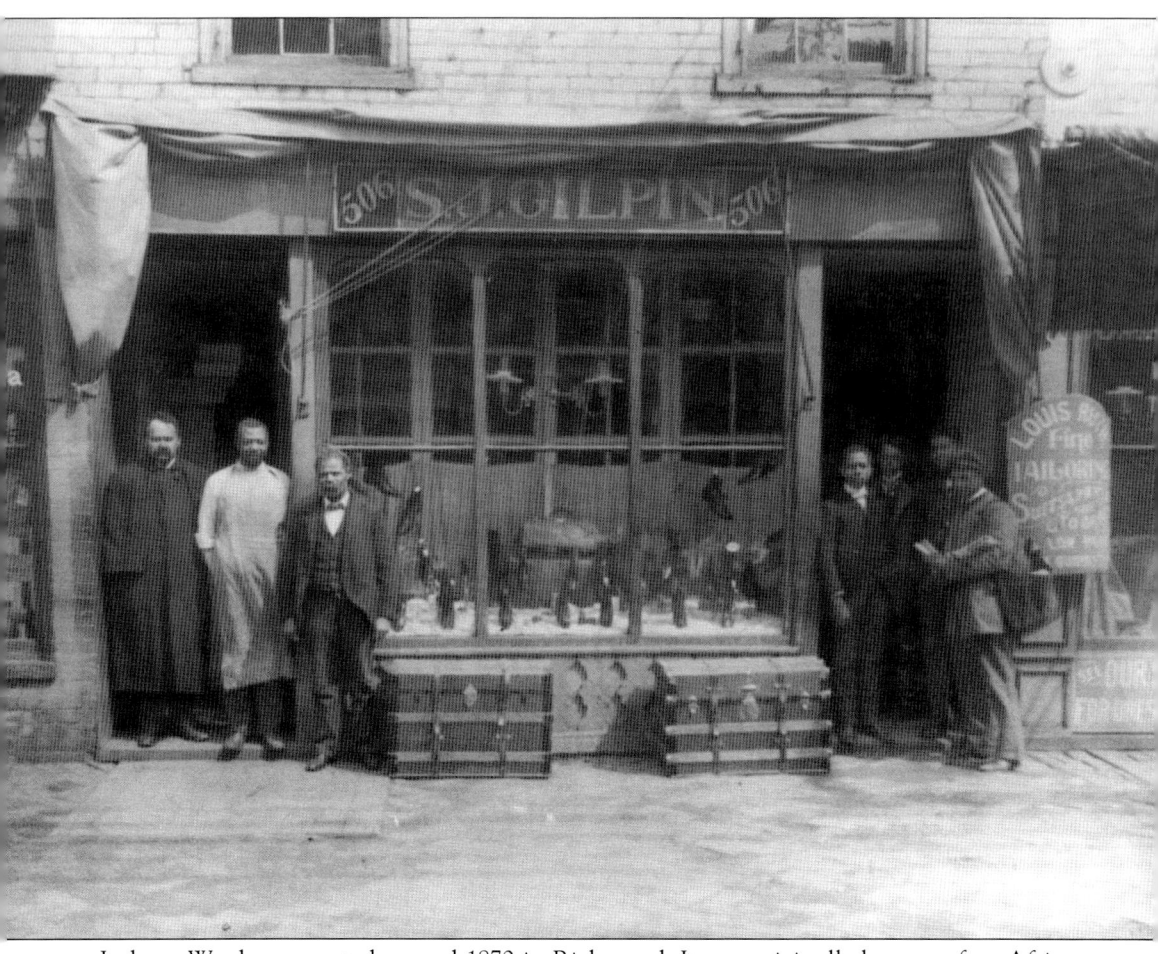

Jackson Ward was created around 1870 in Richmond. It was originally home to free African Americans as well as Italian, Irish, and German immigrants. It soon became the hub of business for African Americans and was sometimes called the "black Wall Street." The Gilpin shoe store is seen here. Gilpin Court, a predominately black neighborhood, is located next to Shockoe Hill Cemetery and is near the Hebrew Cemetery as well. (Courtesy of the Library of Congress.)

Only 13 years old when she married Edgar Allan Poe, Virginia Clemm was the writer's first cousin. She is considered one of the possible inspirations for many of his works, such as "Annabel Lee," "The Raven," and "Ligeria." Clemm fell ill and died at the young age of 25. It has been said by some that she is buried at Shockoe Hill, but most historians have her burial in Maryland. (Courtesy of the Library of Congress.)

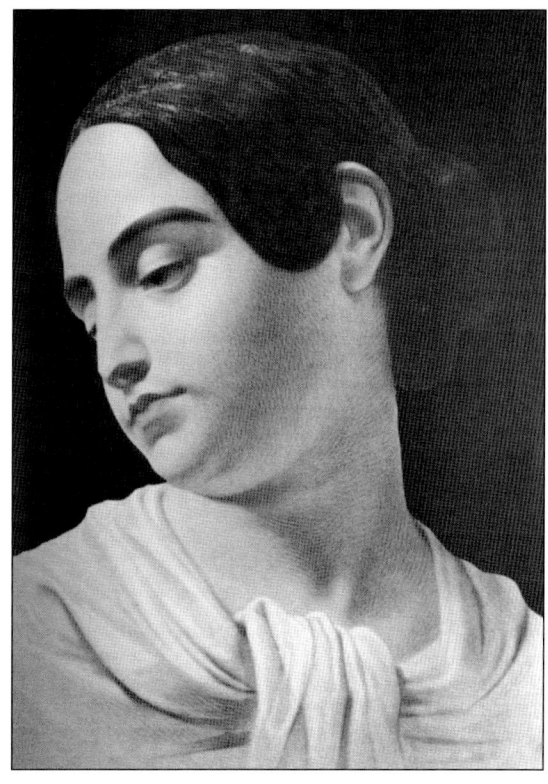

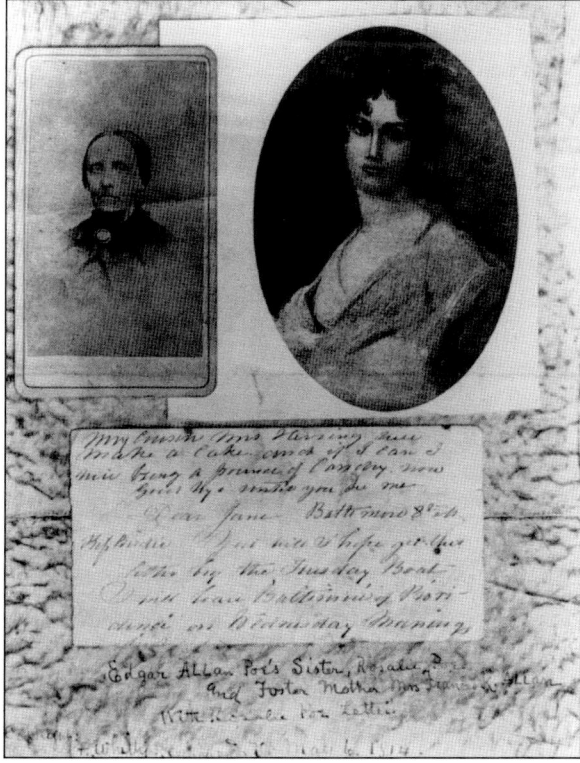

Frances K. Allan, the adopted mother of Edgar Allan Poe, is pictured at left. Also shown is Rosalie Poe, Edgar's sister. Rosalie is a mystery in the Poe family. There are no records of her father. Allan is buried in Shockoe Hill Cemetery, along with Edgar's boyhood friend Robert Stanard. (Courtesy of the Library of Congress.)

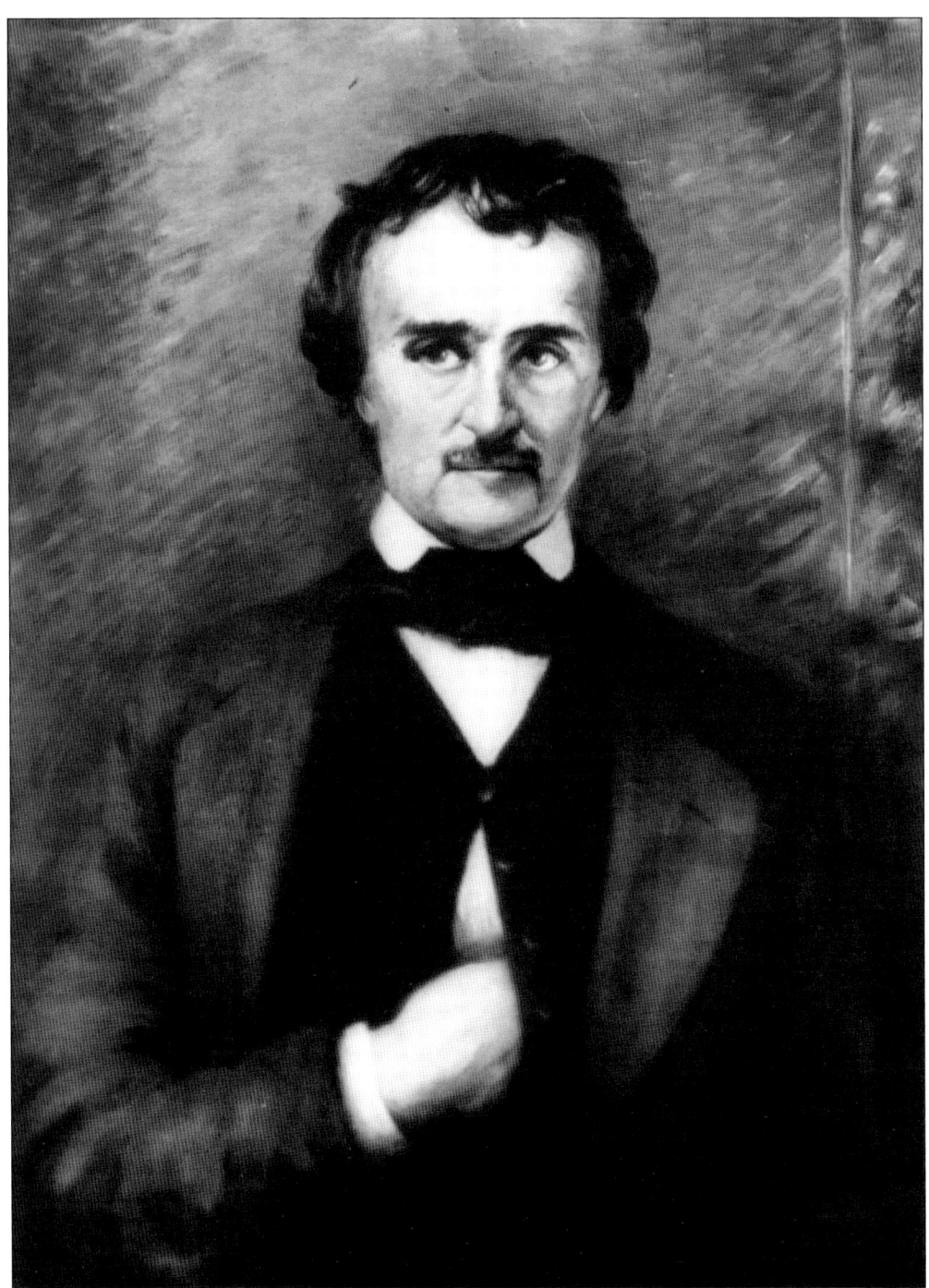
Edgar Allan Poe always called himself a Virginian. He grew up in Richmond and set upon his career as a writer while in the city. Poe's biological parents were both actors. His mother is buried in St. John's graveyard. It is said that one of Poe's favorite places in Richmond was Shockoe Hill Cemetery. This is fitting enough, as his adopted mother, Frances K. Allan, is buried there. (Courtesy of the Library of Congress.)

Edgar Allan Poe's associations with Baltimore, Maryland, have been mythologized to the point of propaganda. Though the nomadic writer briefly lived and eventually died in Baltimore, Poe spent more years of his life in Richmond than he did in any other city. However, at the time of his death, and for many years afterwards, Richmond rejected Poe as a social outcast and a writer of lowbrow popular stories. As such, Poe was buried at Westminster Hall in Baltimore (his grave is pictured). Today, some Richmonders believe that Poe should be reinterred in Richmond. (Courtesy of the Library of Congress.)

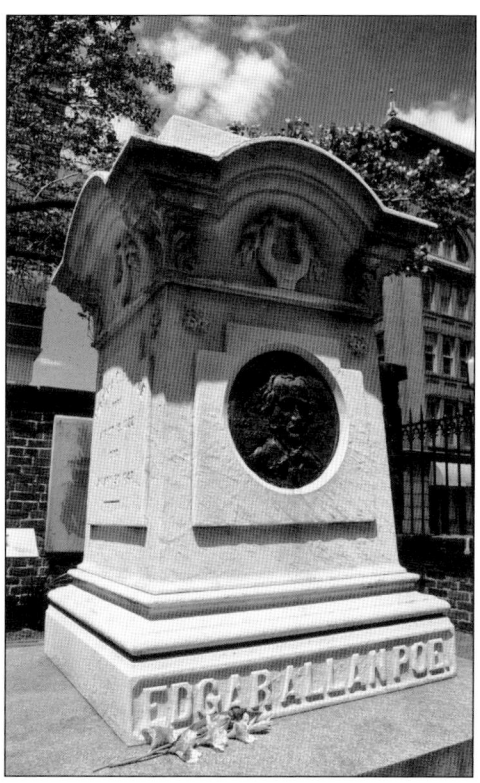

The Edgar Allan Poe Museum on Richmond's East Main Street dedicates itself to telling the story of Poe's life in Virginia. Poe never lived in the Old Stone House, which serves as the main entrance to the museum complex, and none of his relatives are buried on the property. Yet, because of the museum's symbol as Poe's self-proclaimed "Virginian" identity, it is one of the proposed spots for his reinterment. (Courtesy of the Library of Congress.)

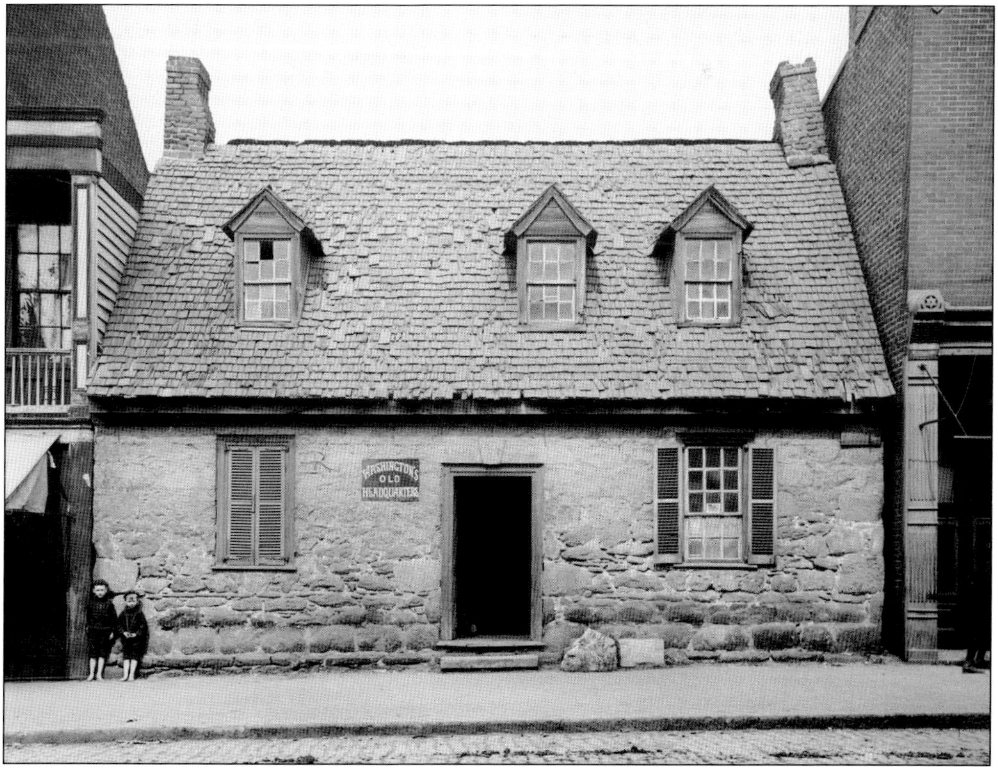

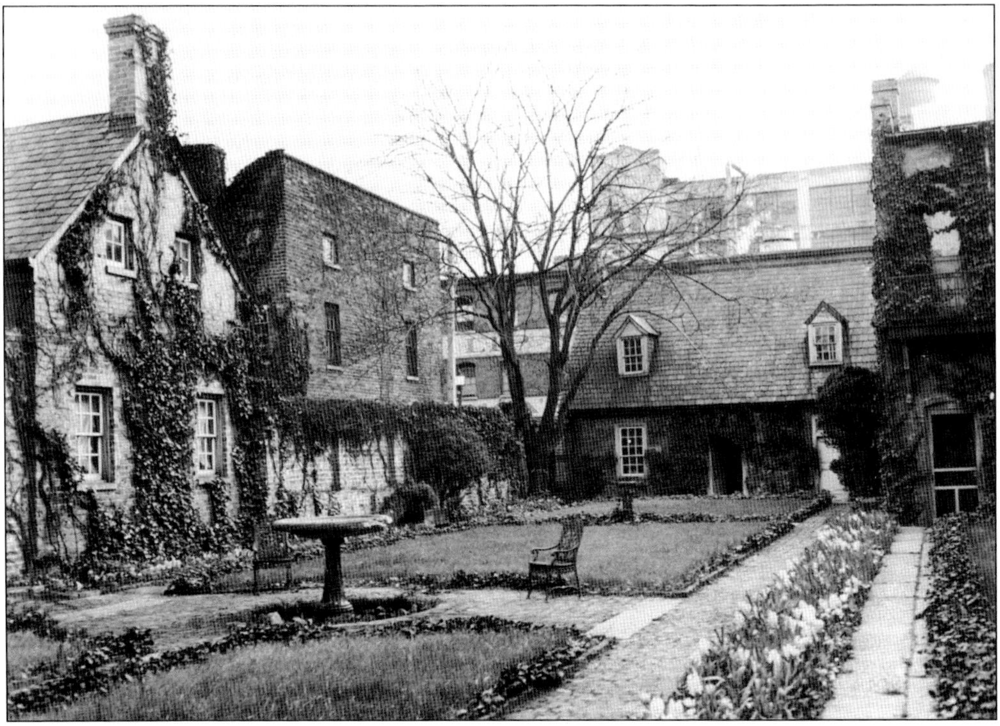

Richmond's Poe Museum contains a shrine to the Virginia-raised writer in an area known as the Enchanted Garden. The Poe Shrine includes a bust of the writer that Edmun Quinn created in 1908. The shrine's architectural design evokes the feeling of a mausoleum. (Courtesy of the Library of Congress.)

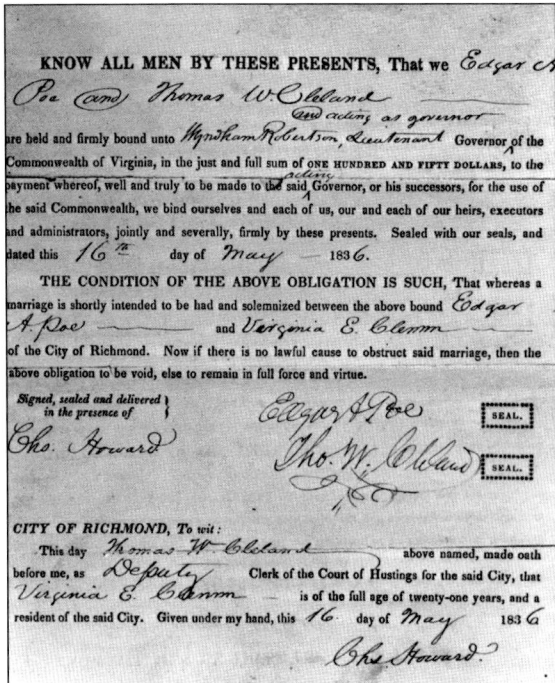

Few details are known about Edgar Allan Poe's wedding to his cousin, Virginia Clemm. One thing, however, is certain: It took place in Richmond, Virginia. The wedding certificate is shown here. Little more than a decade after their wedding, Clemm died of tuberculosis. She was buried in a vault owned by the Poes' landlords at Fordham Cottage in the Bronx, New York. The landlords, the Valentines, were a prestigious Richmond family. Clemm's remains were later transferred to Baltimore so she could rest with her husband. (Courtesy of the Library of Congress.)

Poe's foster mother, Frances Allan, died young, just as Poe's biological mother had. Frances died of tuberculosis before her husband, tobacco merchant John Allan. She is buried beside her husband, along with his second wife, whom Poe publicly disliked and disapproved of. As with many of the other women in his life, Poe put Frances on a pedestal, especially following her death. (Courtesy of the Edgar Allan Poe Museum.)

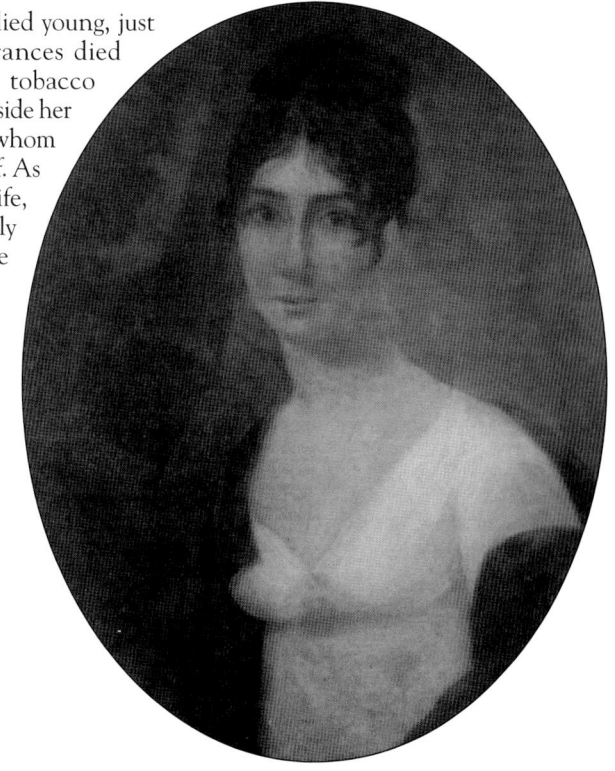

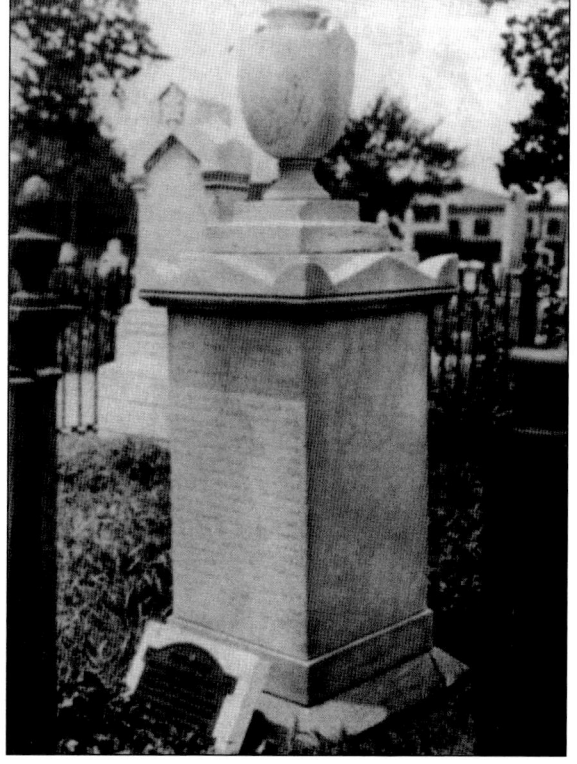

This is the monument of Jane Stith Craig Stanard, Poe's alleged "Helen." Her marker reads: "To the Memory of Jane Stith Stanard, Daughter of John Craig, late of the city of Richmond and the beloved wife of Robert Stanard. This monument is dedicated by the conjugal affection which retaining a fondly cherished recollection of the graces of mind and person by which it was inspired of the purity and tenderness of heart." (Courtesy of the Edgar Allan Poe Museum.)

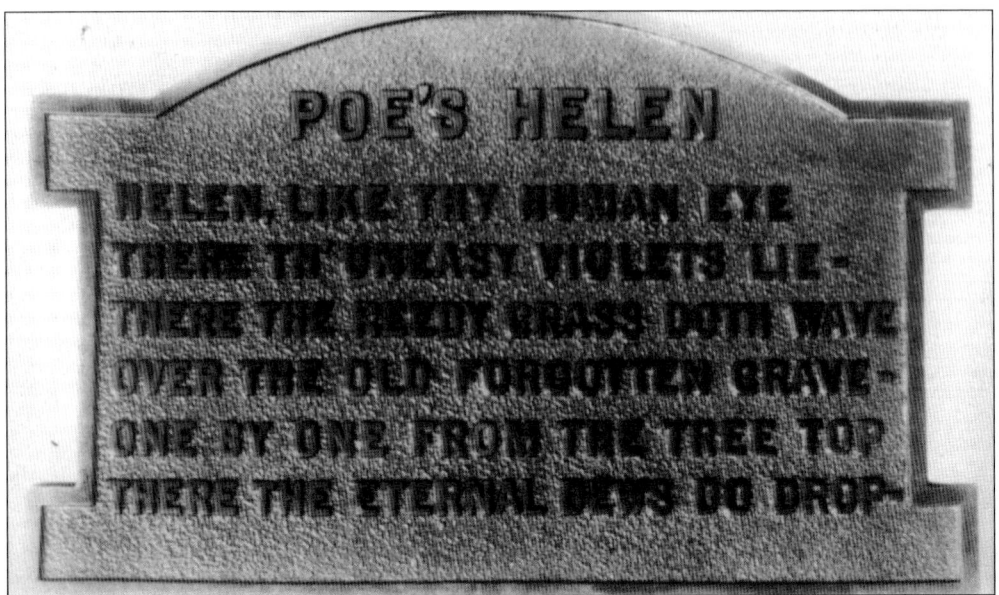

This plaque is located by the grave of Jane Stanard in Shockoe Hill Cemetery. Jane, the mother of Poe's childhood best friend, was the writer's inspiration for his poem "To Helen." The plaque—which was put in place by Poe Museum founder James Whitty—misquotes the poem, but does give unique insight into Poe's life. As a rampant storyteller, Poe often exaggerated and embellished the details of his life, making it difficult for biographers to track down the truth. In this case, Jane is only Poe's speculated Helen. (Courtesy of the Edgar Allan Poe Museum.)

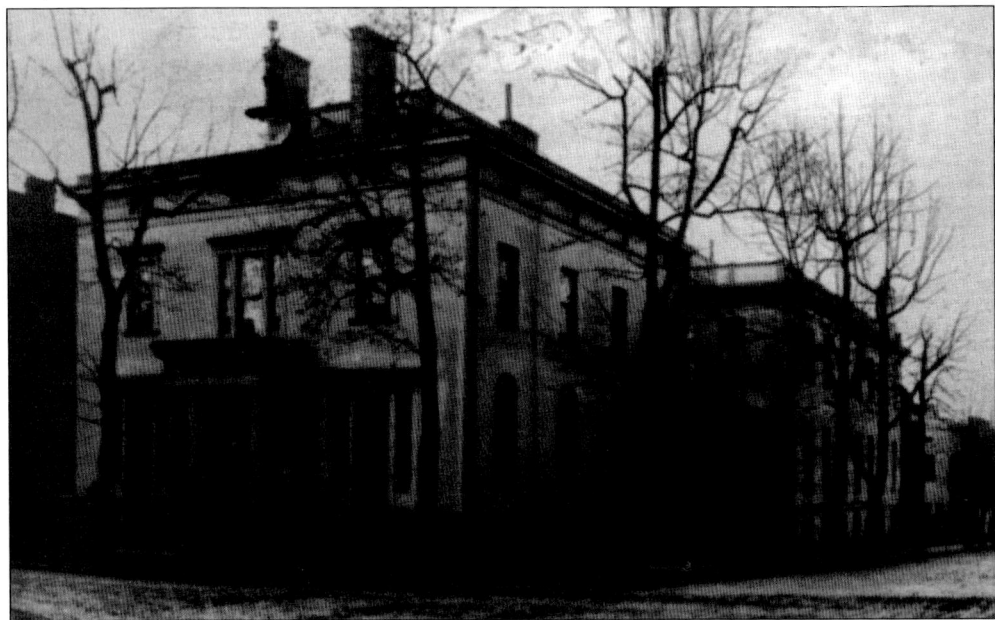

This is the home of Edgar Allan Poe's childhood sweetheart and fiancé, Elmira Royster Shelton, in Richmond's Church Hill neighborhood. The two were engaged twice—once in their youth, before Poe went off to attend the University of Virginia, and again shortly before Poe's mysterious death in Baltimore. Shelton, like many of Poe's other friends and acquaintances, is buried in Shockoe Hill Cemetery with a table-like tombstone. (Courtesy of the Edgar Allan Poe Museum.)

Robert Standard was Poe's best friend as a child. At various times during Poe's childhood, his classmates ostracized him because of his status as an orphan and the child of actors. Perhaps because of this, Poe was reportedly fiercely close to the friends he did have. Having spent much time with Robert's mother, Jane, he became infatuated with her. When Jane died (supposedly of some form of hysteria), Poe and Robert held vigil at her grave in Shockoe Hill. (Courtesy of the Edgar Allan Poe Museum.)

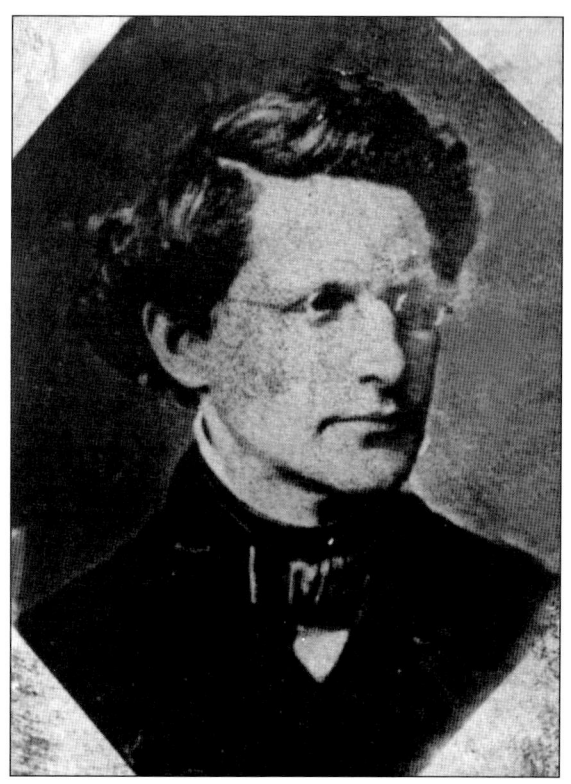

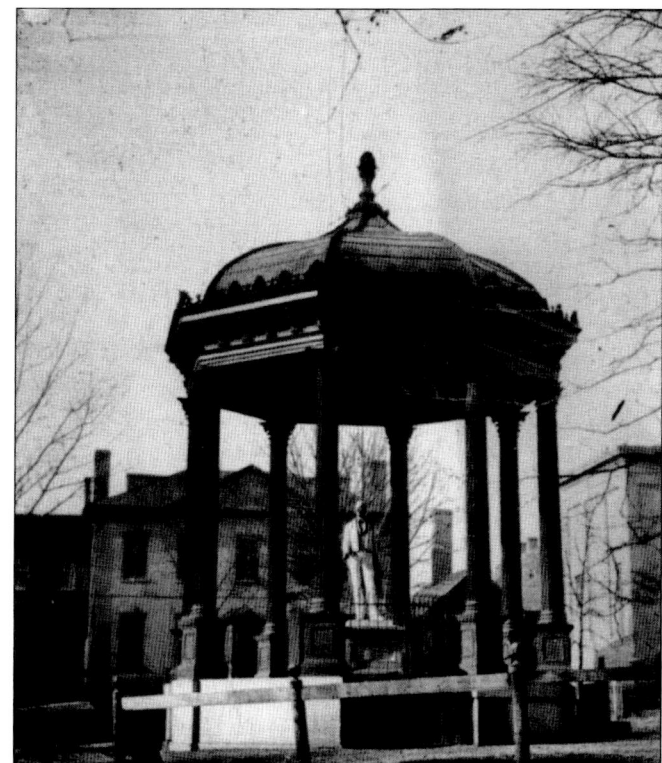

Visible behind the Henry Clay gazebo and statue on Capitol Square is the home of Jane Stanard. She is emblematic of the well-to-do Richmonders buried at Shockoe Hill. The cemetery is older than Hollywood Cemetery by about a quarter of a century. (Courtesy of the Edgar Allan Poe Museum.)

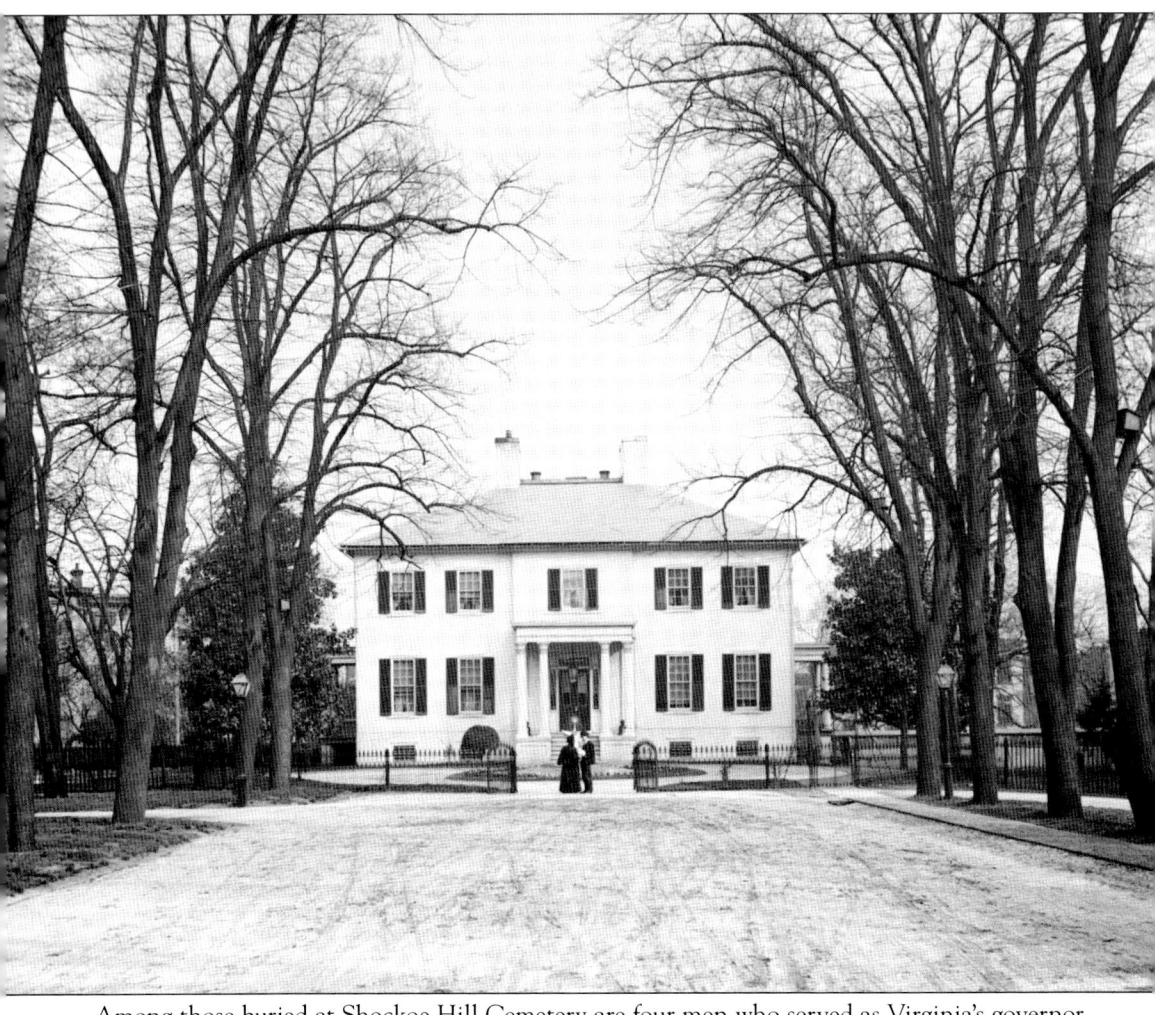

Among those buried at Shockoe Hill Cemetery are four men who served as Virginia's governor or provisional governor. These men include William H. Cabell, John Mercer Patton, John Rutherfoord, and John Munford Gregory. In addition, many state employees are buried there. (Courtesy of the Library of Congress.)

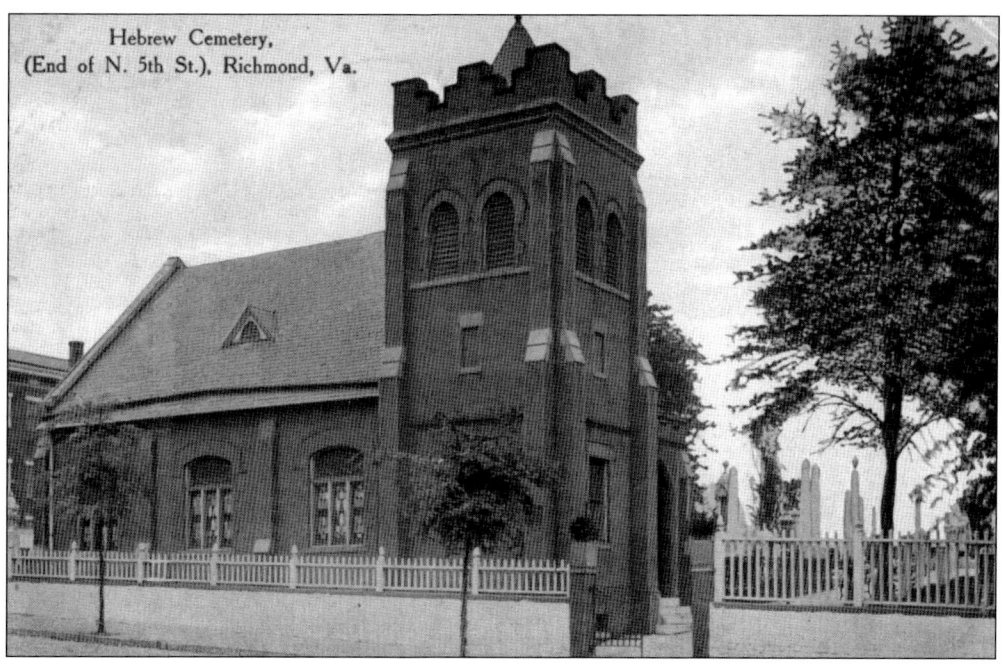

The Hebrew Cemetery, dating to 1816, is one of the oldest Hebrew cemeteries in the United States. One of the most notable burials here is Josephine Cohen Joel, the founder of the Richmond Art Company. The cemetery contains a Confederate soldiers section, which has 30 graves for those who died in or near Richmond. This is the only Jewish military cemetery located outside of Israel. These postcards depict the entrance at Hospital and North Fifth Streets (above) and the Hebrew Confederate Soldiers Cemetery (below). (Both, courtesy of the Library of Congress.)

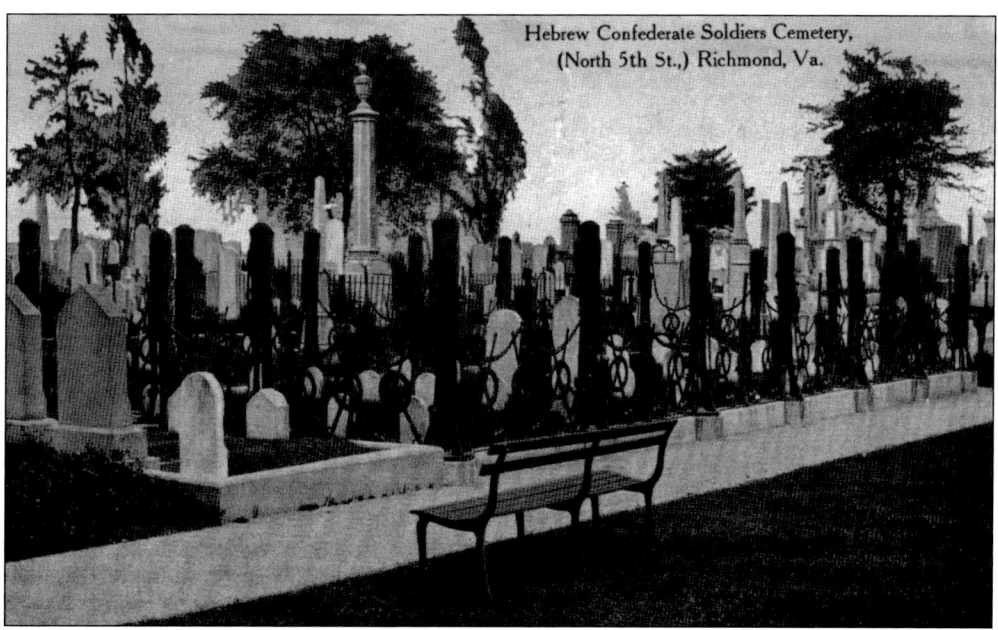

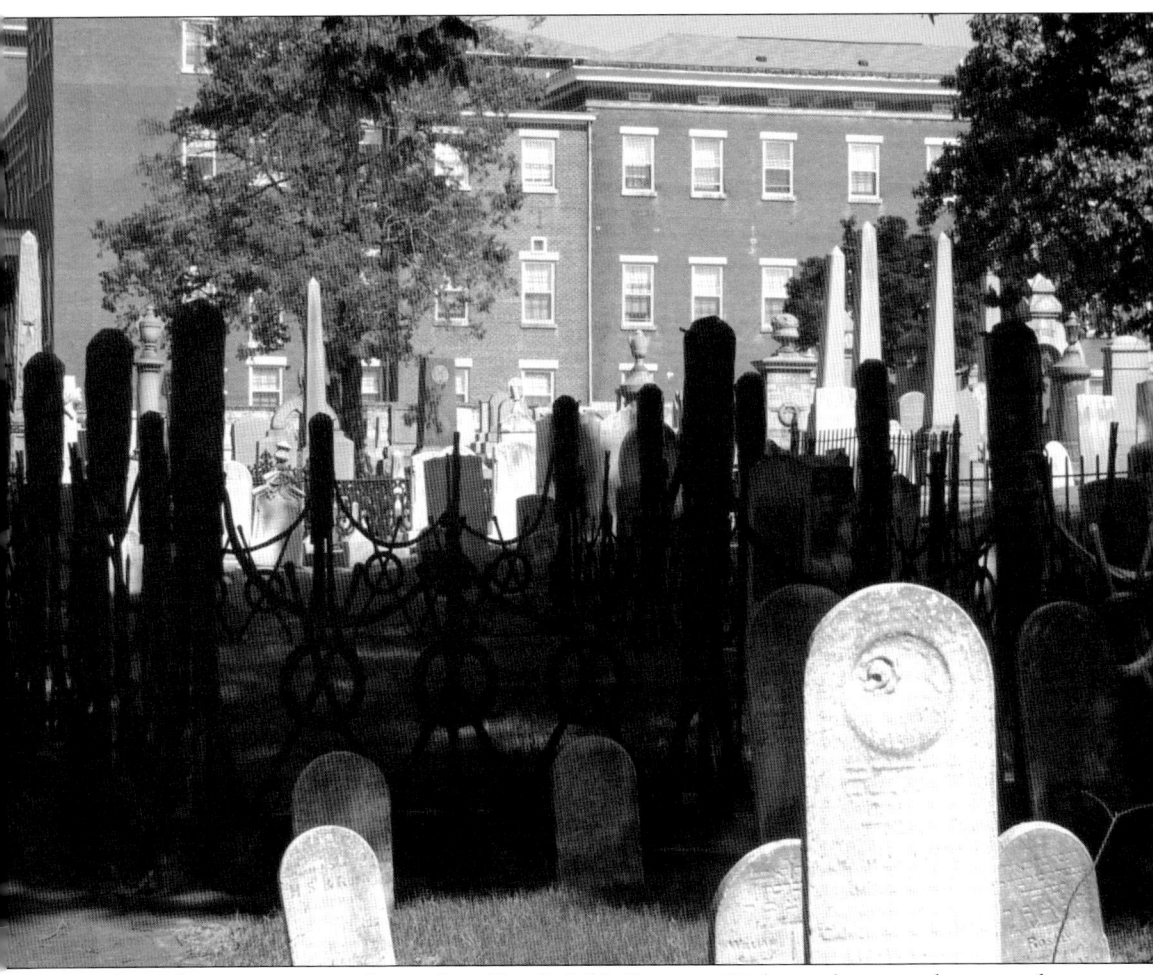

The Hebrew Cemetery is located on North Fifth Street in Richmond, across the street from Shockoe Hill Cemetery. Its roots extend all the way to 1791. It includes a restored Confederate Soldiers section. This was the first Jewish cemetery in Virginia, and it is still maintained by Congregation Beth Ahabah today. (Courtesy of VCU Special Collections.)

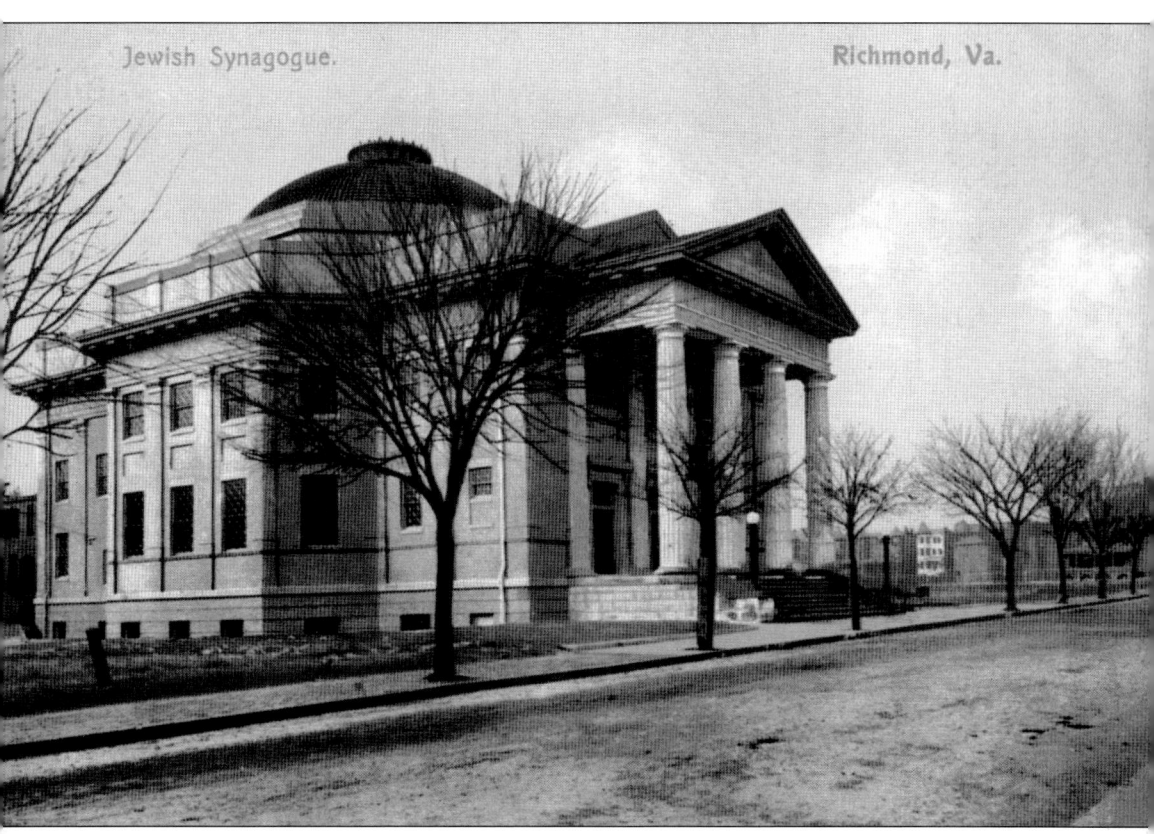

Beth Ahabah is located at Ryland and Franklin Streets. The building, the central portion of which is a perfect octagon, is one of the most beautiful in the South. This congregation founded the first Jewish school in Richmond in 1846. The synagogue has 29 stained-glass windows and is known for its grand beauty. The window on the building's eastern wall depicts Mount Sinai and is signed by Louis Comfort Tiffany. (Courtesy of the Library of Congress.)

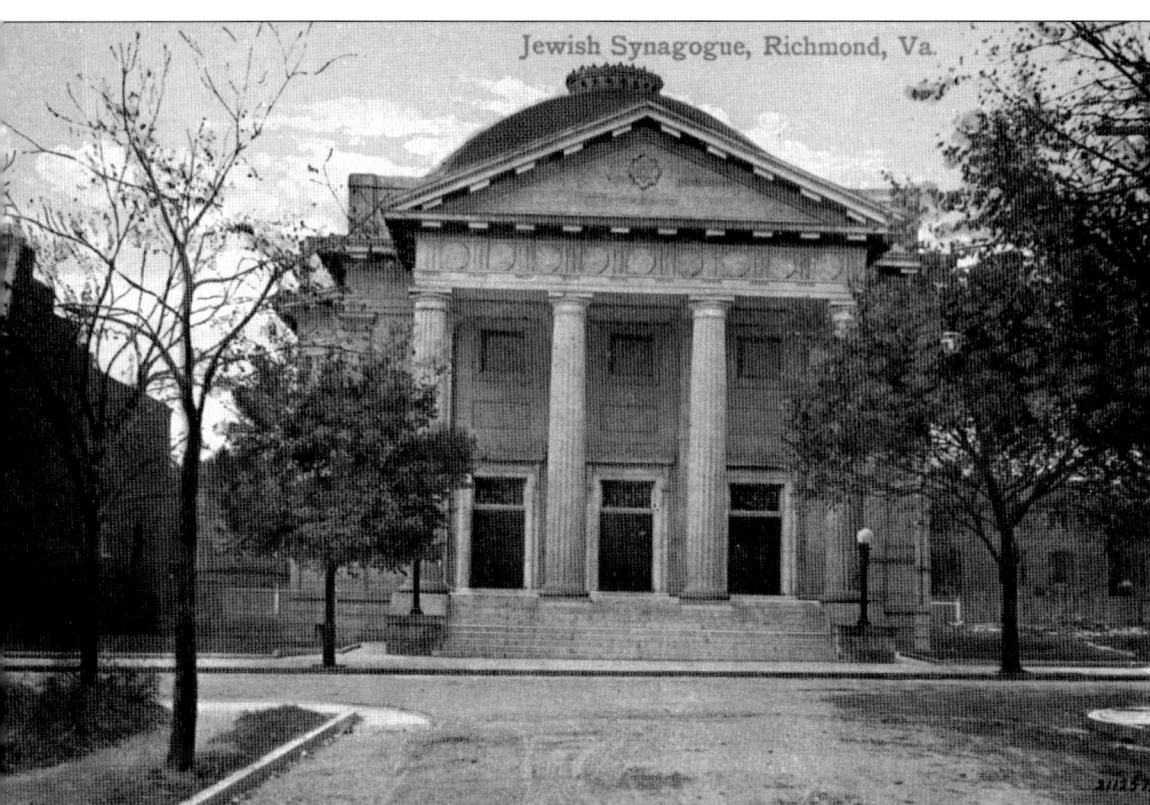

Congregation Beth Ahabah is one of the oldest synagogues in the United States. Founded in 1789 by Spanish and Portuguese Jews, its name means "house of love." In 1846, the congregation built its first Jewish school in Richmond. Beth Ahabah helps to maintain the Hebrew Cemetery and the Cemetery for Hebrew Confederate Soldiers. The congregation is also home of the Beth Ahabah Museum and Archives. The museum, established in 1977, focuses on the history and culture of Richmond's Jewish community and the Southern Jewish experience. There are three galleries in the museum that feature changing exhibits. The synagogue is in charge of maintaining the Hebrew Cemetery grounds. (Courtesy of the Library of Congress.)

Six

THE BURIAL GROUND FOR NEGROES

Because of their historically lower-class status and as a result of unmarked graves, it is impossible to know of every place where Richmond's African American slaves were buried. However, several slave burial grounds have been identified in the city, including one in Shockoe Bottom, one of Richmond's oldest sections. Flanked by Main Street Station on one side and North Fourteenth Street on the other, the burial grounds lie between East Broad and East Main Streets. This area is known as the Burial Ground for Negroes.

In recent years, this ground has received a fair amount of media attention after Virginia Commonwealth University (VCU) paved over the alleged graveyard boundaries and put up a parking lot. A professor of African American studies, Shawn O. Utsey, wrote and directed a documentary about the controversy, entitled *Meet Me in the Bottom* (2010). To this day, the area remains a parking lot.

The Burial Ground for Negroes has been the resting place for Richmond's enslaved and free blacks for generations, serving as an active gravesite from 1786 to 1819. It is said to be the burial site of Gabriel Prosser, a literate enslaved blacksmith who led a slave rebellion in 1800. Shockoe Bottom was long known as the city's slave district, which laid claim to at least 40 different auction houses, six slave jails, and many service businesses that relied on slave labor. In the 1810s, the City of Richmond opened a new cemetery for blacks on Shockoe Hill (an area to the northwest of Shockoe Bottom) in response to petitions from black residents.

Local activists from groups such as the Defenders for Freedom, Justice and Equality fought to have the parking lot removed and the burial ground recognized. In collaboration with Mayor Dwight Jones and representatives of the Richmond Slave Trail Commission, Gov. Bob McDonnell bought the property from VCU using state funds, making it the property of the City of Richmond in 2011. The same property that was saved in 2011 is now being considered for the new 7,200-seat baseball stadium of the Flying Squirrels, the AA farm team of the San Francisco Giants.

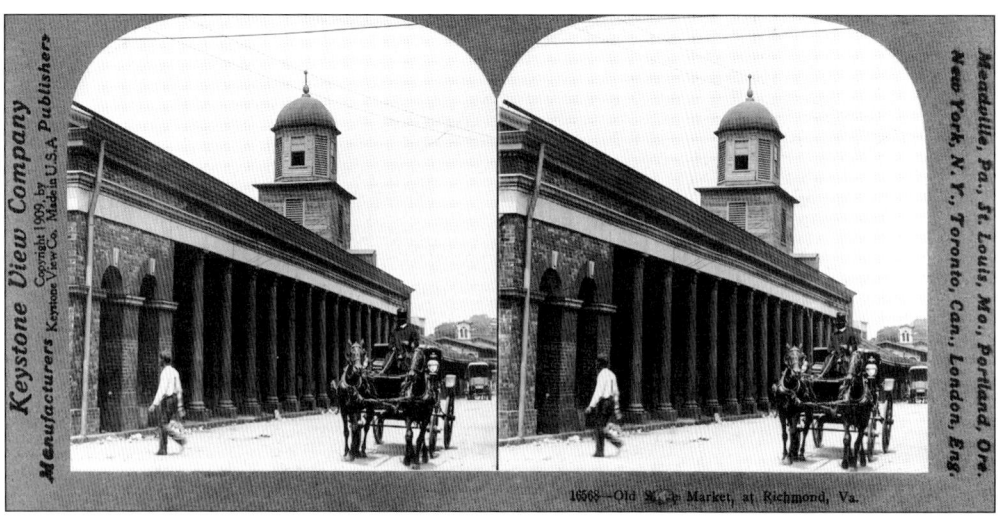

The Seventeenth Street Market has served as one of Richmond's main marketplaces since nearly the founding of the city. At one time, it was a place where not only animals and produce were sold, but humans as well. African slaves were regularly sold in the square, close to Lumpkin's Jail and the so-called Burial Ground for Negroes. Today, the area remains a location of Richmond's darker history. (Both, courtesy of the Library of Congress.)

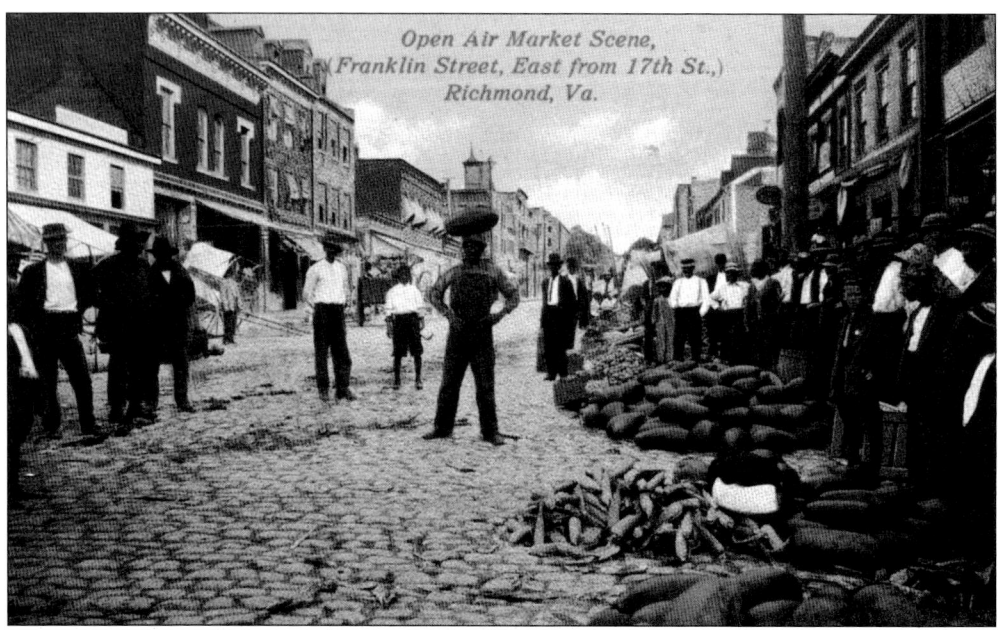

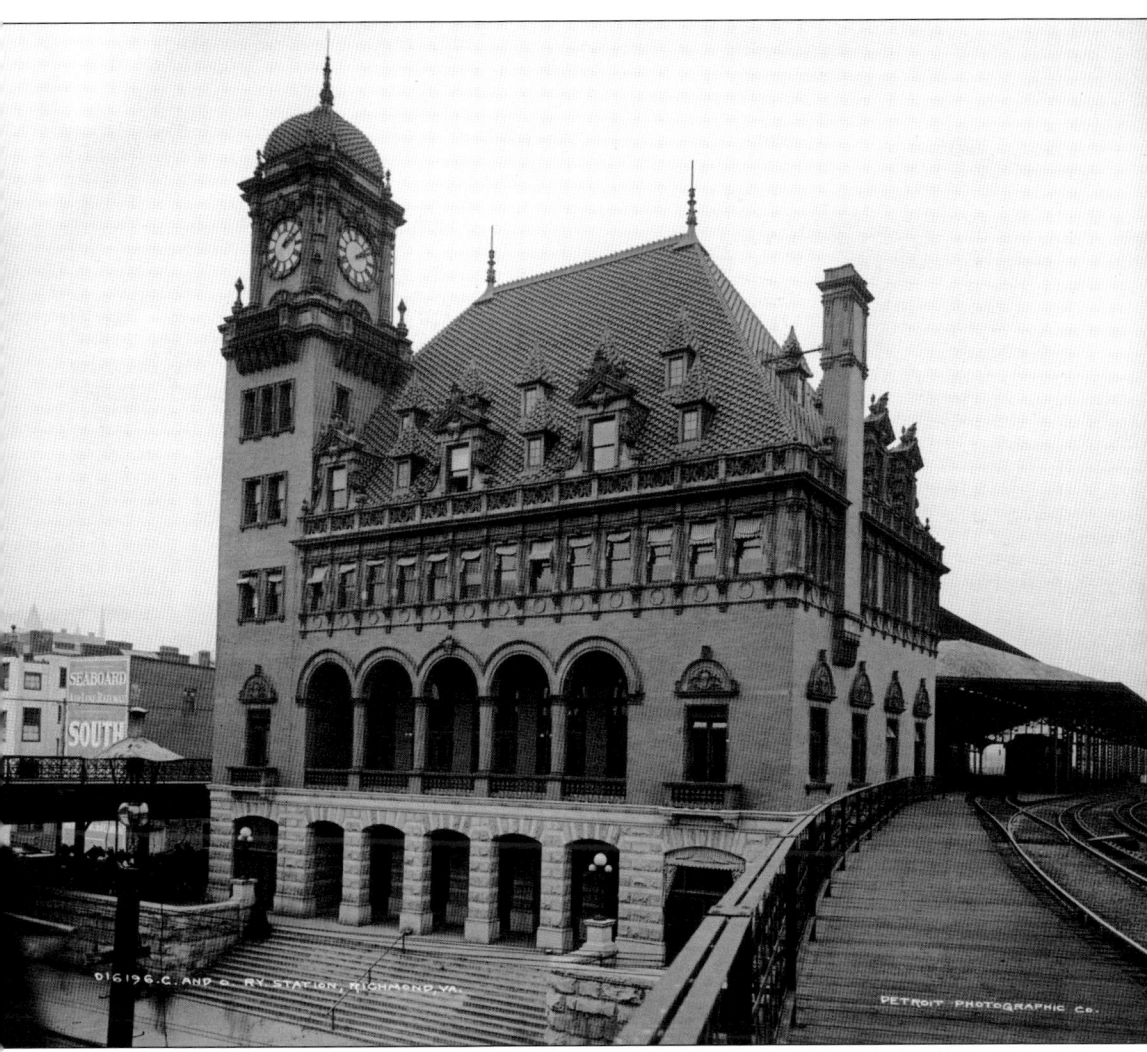

Main Street Station, downtown Richmond's train station, physically and symbolically separates the Seventeenth Street Market from the Burial Ground for Negroes. It was opened in 1901, about 100 years after the Burial Ground for Negroes stopped accepting new interments. Today, Main Street Station obscures the Main Street view of where the burial ground is believed to be located. (Courtesy of the Library of Congress.)

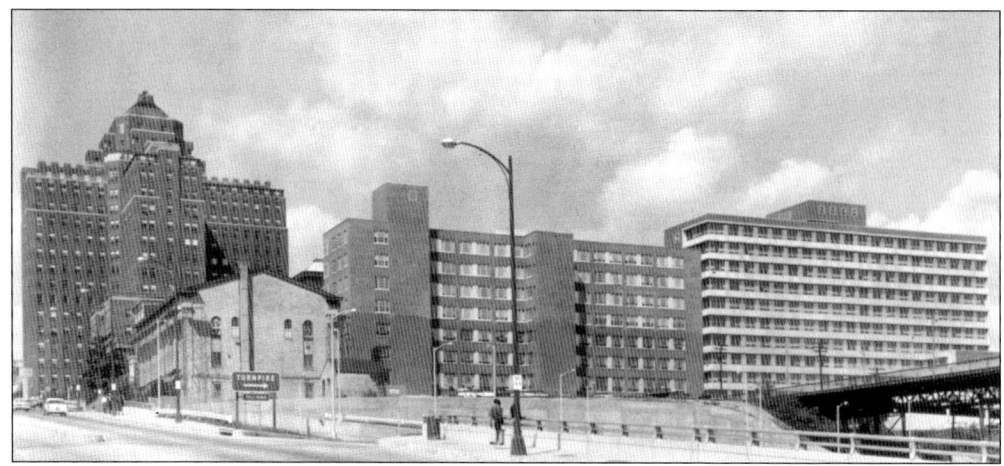

Up the hill from where the Burial Ground for Negroes is believed to be stands the Medial College for Negroes. For years, the school was rumored to hire gravediggers to unearth newly buried black bodies for anatomy classes. This rumor was confirmed in Dr. Shawn Utsey's award-winning documentary film *Until the Well Runs Dry*. (Courtesy of the Library of Congress.)

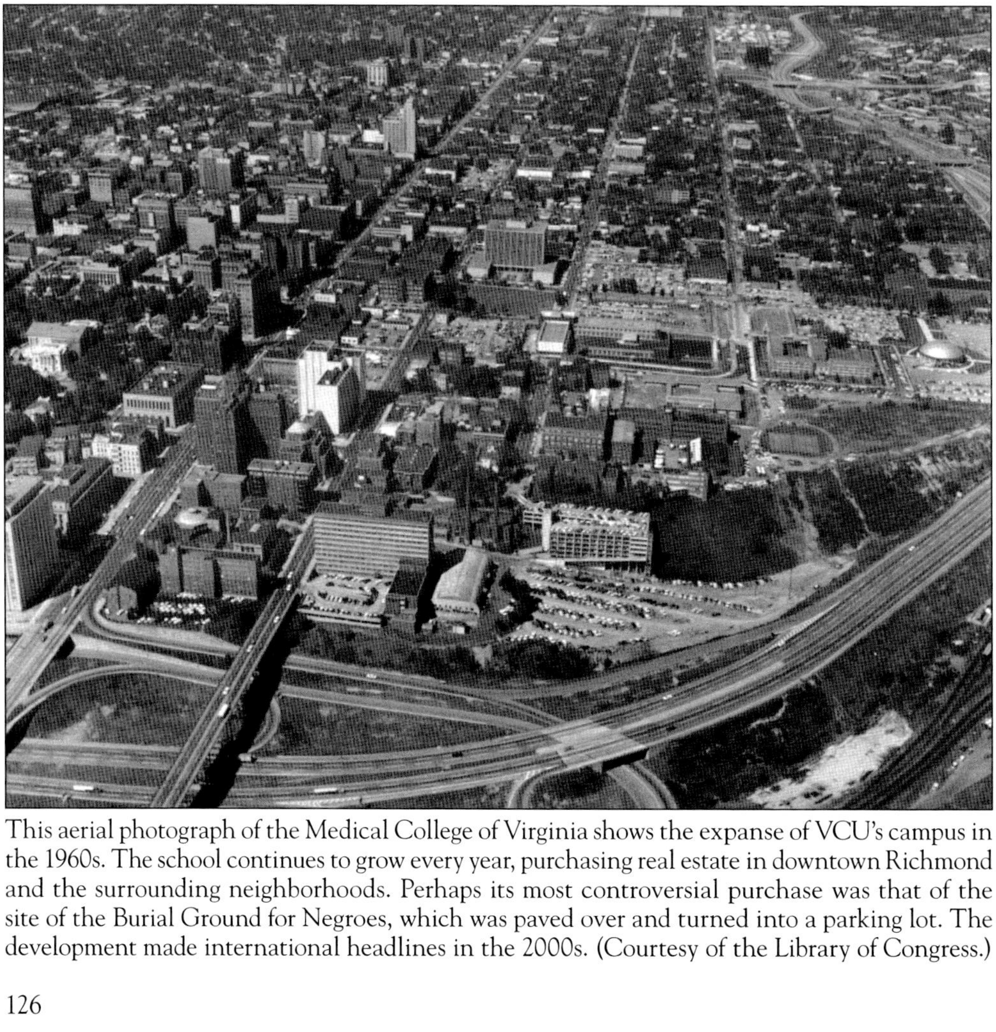

This aerial photograph of the Medical College of Virginia shows the expanse of VCU's campus in the 1960s. The school continues to grow every year, purchasing real estate in downtown Richmond and the surrounding neighborhoods. Perhaps its most controversial purchase was that of the site of the Burial Ground for Negroes, which was paved over and turned into a parking lot. The development made international headlines in the 2000s. (Courtesy of the Library of Congress.)

BIBLIOGRAPHY

Bowen-Sherman, Judith. *The Burying Ground at Old St. John's Church: A Concise History with Fifty Family Profiles and a Parish Burial Register.* Richmond, VA: St. John's Episcopal Church, 2011.
Case, Keshia A., and Christopher P. Semtner. *Edgar Allan Poe in Richmond.* Charleston, SC: Arcadia Publishing, 2009.
Crumley, Marguerite, and John G. Zehmer. *Church Hill: The St. John's Church Historic District.* Richmond, VA: The Council of Historic Richmond Foundation, 1991.
Davis, Veronica A. *Here I Lay My Burdens Down: A History of the Black Cemeteries of Richmond, Virginia.* Richmond, VA: The Dietz Press, 2003.
Hughes, Mark. *Confederate Cemeteries, Volume 2.* Berwyn Heights, MD: Heritage Books, 2009.
Potterfield, T. Tyler. *Nonesuch Place: A History of the Richmond Landscape.* Charleston, SC: The History Press, 2009.
Richardson, Selden. *Built by Blacks: African American Architecture and Neighborhoods in Richmond.* Charleston, SC: The History Press, 2008.
Rudd, Alice Boehmer. *Shockoe Hill Cemetery.* Richmond, VA: Self-published, January 1960.
Upton, Dell. *Holy Things and Profane: Anglican Parish Churches in Colonial Virginia.* Boston: MIT Press, 1986.

Discover Thousands of Local History Books
Featuring Millions of Vintage Images

Arcadia Publishing, the leading local history publisher in the United States, is committed to making history accessible and meaningful through publishing books that celebrate and preserve the heritage of America's people and places.

Find more books like this at
www.arcadiapublishing.com

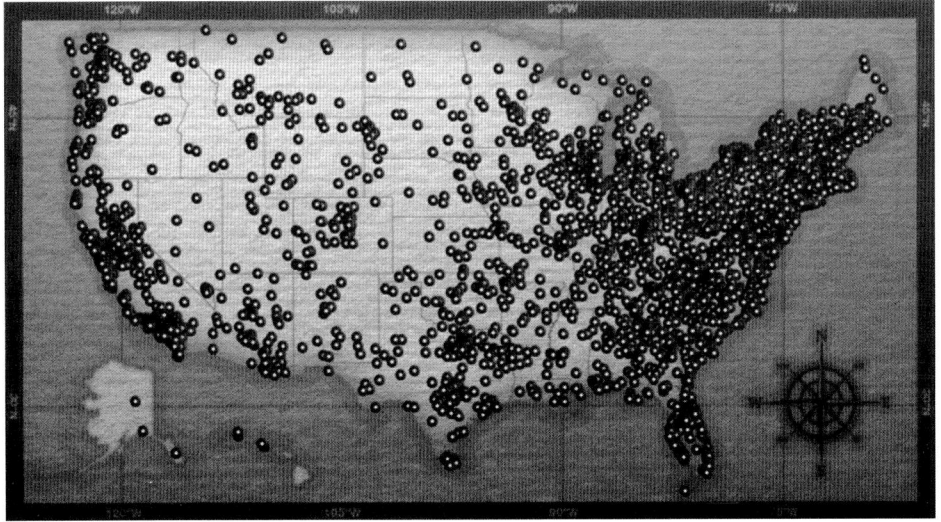

Search for your hometown history, your old stomping grounds, and even your favorite sports team.

Consistent with our mission to preserve history on a local level, this book was printed in South Carolina on American-made paper and manufactured entirely in the United States. Products carrying the accredited Forest Stewardship Council (FSC) label are printed on 100 percent FSC-certified paper.

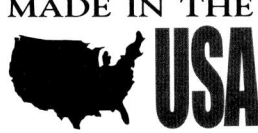